EFFECTIVE EARLY EDUCATION

STUDIES IN EDUCATION AND CULTURE
VOLUME 11
GARLAND REFERENCE LIBRARY OF SOCIAL SCIENCE
VOLUME 1120

Studies in Education and Culture

David M. Fetterman, *Series Editor*

Effective Early Education

Cross-Cultural Perspectives

Edited by
Lotty Eldering and Paul P.M. Leseman

Falmer Press
A member of the Taylor & Francis Group
New York and London
1999

Published in 1999 by
Falmer Press
A Member of the Taylor & Francis Group
19 Union Square West
New York, NY 10003

10   9   8   7   6   5   4   3   2   1

Library of Congress Cataloging-in-Publication Data

Effective early education : cross-cultural perspectives / edited by Lotty Eldering
    and Paul P. M. Leseman.
        p.   cm. — (Garland reference library of social science ; v. 1120.
    Studies in education and culture ; v. 11
        Includes biliographical references and index.
        ISBN 0–8153–2444–8 (alk. paper)
        1. Early childhood education Cross-cultural studies.   2. Socially handi-
    capped children — Education (Early childhood) Cross-cultural studies.   I.
    Eldering Lotty, 1939- . II. Leseman, Paul. III. Series: Garland reference
    library of social science ; v. 1120. IV. Series: Garland reference library of
    social science. Studies in education and culture ; vol. 11.
    LB1139.23
    372.21—dc21   99-16472
                                                                      CIP

Printed on acid-free, 250-year-life paper
Manufactured in the United States of America

Contents

Series Editor's Preface

This series of scholarly texts, monographs, and reference works is designed to illuminate and expand our understanding of education. The educational activity each volume examines may be formal or informal. It may function in an exotic and distant culture or right here in our own backyard. In each book, education is at once a reflection and a creator of culture.

One of the most important motifs sounding through the series is the authors' efforts to shed light on educational systems from the insider's viewpoint. The various works are typically grounded in a phenomenological conceptual framework. However, they will vary in their manifestation of this common bond. Some authors explicitly adopt anthropological methods and a cultural interpretation of events and circumstances observed in the field. Others adopt a more generic qualitative approach—mixing methods and methodologies. A few adhere to a traditional phenomenological philosophical orientation.

These books are windows into other lives and other cultures. As we view another culture, we see ourselves more clearly. As we view ourselves, we make the familiar strange and see our own distorted images all the more clearly. We hope this immersion and self-reflection will enhance compassion and understanding at home and abroad. An expression of a common human spirit, this series celebrates our diversity.

David M. Fetterman
Stanford University and
Sierra Nevada College

Acknowledgments

This book is the product of a long and continuous collaboration, which started for most of the authors at a conference organized and funded by the Netherlands National Unesco Commission, Unesco Paris, and the Bernard van Leer Foundation in The Hague in 1993.

We wish to thank Marijke Hamel of Leiden University for her administrative support in organizing the manuscript, and Joy Burrough-Boenisch for advising the second-language authors. Leiden University and the University of Amsterdam gave us the opportunity to invest research time in this project.

EFFECTIVE EARLY EDUCATION

Enhancing Educational Opportunities for Young Children

Lotty Eldering and *Paul P. M. Leseman*

This book examines child development and early educational intervention strategies from a cross-cultural perspective. In an attempt to answer the core question of how educational opportunities and literacy acquisition for young disadvantaged children all over the world can be enhanced, it brings together recent theoretical insights, the results of empirical research, and experiences with well-evaluated early educational intervention programs. Its purpose is to critically examine current strategies of early education and literacy for disadvantaged children and to offer building blocks for constructing culture-sensitive approaches.

At the World Conference on Education for All in Jomtien, Thailand, in 1990, the international community, including virtually all of the world's governments, made a commitment to increase significantly the educational opportunities for over 100 million children who have no access to literacy and basic education. High-quality education is a major concern to developing and industrialized countries alike. Even in the latter countries, where school systems are accessible and schooling is compulsory up to adulthood, education fails to equip about a quarter of students to be literate and numerate for everyday life (for a discussion of findings, see Calamai, 1987; Kirsch & Jungeblut, 1986; MacGinitie & MacGinitie, 1986; Ortiz, 1989). It is the disadvantaged children who are most likely to drop out of school prematurely or end their school careers with lower qualifications.

THE FIRST GENERATION OF EDUCATIONAL
INTERVENTION PROGRAMS

Early educational interventions on a large scale started in the United States more than 30 years ago. The 1960s were imbued with a spirit of political change. Young men and women—the teachers, researchers, policymakers, and politicians of the near future—railed against the establishment. The famous war on poverty in the United States initiated under the Johnson administration was imitated by many other countries. There was a strong faith in socially engineering society. In developmental and educational psychology there was a parallel pedagogic optimism, which provided a scientific basis for the social movement (Hunt, 1961). This optimism was rooted in converging lines of theorizing in neo-behaviorism and neuropsychology that stressed the importance of rich stimulus environments in periods critical for intellectual development. There was also a new, exciting conception of intelligence. Although Piaget never intended his genetic epistemology to be a developmental theory, let alone a psychological theory, many saw it as the foundation for a new theory of intelligence surpassing the traditional approaches based on individual differences and psychometric assessment that had a strong scent of nativism and hereditarianism (Ginsburg, 1972). With only a few months of preparation, the project Head Start was introduced in over 3,000 communities in the United States in 1965, involving more than 150,000 children at risk of educational failure.

The high expectations accompanying Head Start and similar programs inevitably led to disappointment. The Westinghouse evaluation in 1969 showed that Head Start's one-year program had only modest short-term effects that had largely disappeared within two years after the intervention. A more thorough meta-analysis of the various Head Start projects until 1982 by McKey et al. (1985) came to similar conclusions.

The disappointing results of Head Start led to a revival of the nature-nurture debate with Jensen's (1969) article in the Harvard Educational Review entitled "How much can we boost IQ and scholastic achievement?" The bottom line of Jensen's argument is well-known. Since 80 percent of the variance in intellectual abilities in a given population is attributable to genetic variance and probably less than 10 percent is attributable to environment (Scarr & Kidd, 1983; Scarr, 1992), very little potential impact remains for compensatory educational programs. This would, in Jensen's view, explain Head Start's failure to meet expectations. Other authors, however, notably Urie Bronfenbrenner, a member of the Head Start planning committee in 1965, concluded that the intervention strategy of Head Start was not sufficiently tailored to the ecological context of child development; that is to say, the home environment and the wider social and cultural context, including the school (Bronfenbrenner, 1975; see also Zigler, Styfco, & Gilman, 1993). Bronfenbrenner's early plea for context-sensitive intervention programs is at the heart of the present book.

The lessons learned from the first generation intervention programs led to recommendations for two changes in basic intervention strategy. The first recommendation was to increase the intensity and duration of programs. An example is the program Success for All by Slavin and Madden and their colleagues, which is extensively discussed and evaluated in this book. The second recommendation entailed shifting the focus to include the parents, the families, the communities, and socioeconomic circumstances as targets of an intervention. Examples of programs in which children, parents, family, and community are addressed in a comprehensive approach are the Turkish Early Enrichment Program, the Dutch HIPPY program, and the ICDS program in India, all of which are discussed in this book. Family support programs, including empowerment strategies and parent basic education, complementing child-focused educational interventions in a strict sense, are currently seen as the catalysts for change (Weiss & Kagen, 1989; Yoshikawa, 1994). However, the evidence on effectiveness is still mixed, a fact which calls for a further analysis, which is taken up in this book (cf., White, Taylor, & Moss, 1992).

DEVELOPMENTS IN PSYCHOLOGY AND ANTHROPOLOGY

Recent developments in psychology and anthropology pertinent to the issue of child development and early education show two trends. Whereas, still in 1981, Schwartz remarked that anthropology has ignored children in culture while developmental psychology has ignored culture in children (p. 4), both disciplines are currently converging, opening new avenues for research and leading to important new insights for the general aim of enhancing educational opportunities for disadvantaged children. Developmental and educational psychology are paying increasing attention to the social and cultural context of child rearing, child development, and learning. The recent theorizing on cognitive development, emergent literacy, and numeracy in family and school settings has been profoundly influenced by anthropological and ethnographic research. The key to the chemistry of the different research programs is Vygotsky's sociohistorical psychology, which has opened psychology to anthropological approaches for studying the social and cultural context. Within anthropology, educational anthropology has evolved as a subdiscipline focusing on educational processes at school, particularly those involving ethnic minority students (Anthropology and Education Quarterly; Fetterman, 1984; Spindler, 1982; Spindler & Spindler, 1987; Trueba, 1989). A second field of research in anthropology integrating psychological perspectives is psychological or cognitive anthropology (see, e.g., Schwartz, White, & Lutz, 1992). Moreover, cultural anthropologists are nowadays paying more attention to intracultural variation at subgroup and individual level (cf., Borofsky, 1994).

Psychology is seeing the unmistakable rise of the behavioral genetics paradigm accompanied by a further expansion of nativist or hereditarian explanations over more domains of human development and behavior (for instance, see Plomin, DeFries, & Fulker, 1988; Rowe, 1994). Riding on the wave of behavioral genetics, Herrnstein and Murray (1994) published the "The bell curve," in which they give short shrift to educational priority policy and affirmative/positive action, and reinforcing Jensen's early critique of educational intervention programs. Although Herrnstein and Murray's analysis is not convincing, and at times is demonstrably mistaken (Bronfenbrenner, McClelland, Wethington, Moen, & Ceci, 1996), it has set a certain tone.

The evidence from behavioral genetics seems quite strong and, at first glance, not in favor of early intervention to enhance educational opportunities for the disadvantaged. However, a major problem is the acontextual, content-free approach to psychological traits and their behavioral instantiations. This issue has recently been examined by Bronfenbrenner and Ceci (1994) in their article "Nature and Nurture Reconceptualized," in which they develop an elementary model of the interaction of genes and environments departing from Bronfenbrenner's socioecological theory. They argue that genetic potential as such is void, a disposition, a code existing in DNA proteins. It literally needs flesh and bones and, as far as psychological traits are concerned, symbolic content and behavioral instantiations in actual sociocultural contexts to come into real existence. This points to the fact that actualization of genetic potential does not take place in a cultural vacuum but necessarily involves appropriation and construction of specific knowledge, skills, and attitudes which may differ fundamentally between contexts, cultures, and historical eras in terms of content and phenotypical appearance.

THE CONCEPT AND IMPACT OF CULTURE

The present book deals with processes of early education in different cultural contexts. Although relevant for analyzing human development, the concept of culture is complex, much debated, and often defined very differently. A distinction can be made here between a broad, more inclusive concept of culture and a narrower one. The broad concept of culture, for instance, includes all phenomena that are not natural or biological, that is to say, are not logically reduceable to the laws of physics and biology. It refers to the intergenerationally transmitted sociohistorical forms of economy, social organization, family life, religion, language, tools, and other products of human agency and creativity that reflect functional adaptation to physical circumstances and biological constraints. The other concept of culture refers to a set of shared ideas, values, and meanings that are manifested and communicated in everyday discourse and social practices. Related to this notion of culture are the concepts of cultural capital (Bourdieu, 1986), lifestyle (Kohn & Schooler, 1983), value system (Hofstede, 1980), and the cognitive-anthropological concept of cultural models (Quinn & Holland, 1987).

The authors in this book relate to both concepts of culture and have different views on the impact of culture on child development (cf., Poortinga and Richter with Harkness & Super, all this volume). The research findings presented have been obtained in different countries, involving different social and cultural groups. One recurring issue in several chapters is the transferability of educational programs, or even more fundamentally, of basic intervention strategies and educational goals, from one cultural context to the other. In addition, much attention is paid to the influence of cultural factors in a narrower sense, such as the impact of parental beliefs, lifestyles, and patterns of literacy use on child-rearing practices, developmental outcomes, and school learning. Another recurring issue is the necessary scope of early educational programs and the sensitivity to cultural "content" that is required when designing and implementing educational programs.

PROSPECTS

In the 1990s the young child was reinstated at the top of the agenda, and in addition to the commitment to education for all, concern grew about the disintegration of the family; the economic pressure on parents; rising school dropout rates; the increase in teenage pregnancies, violence, juvenile delinquency and drug abuse; and the relative ineffectiveness of measures *after* problems have become manifest in late childhood and adolescence. As a consequence, the focus has been redirected to early childhood as a pedagogically critical phase. In developing countries, awareness has grown that investment in human capital, (i.e., in healthy biological and psychological development), and in literacy and schooling of all youngsters is the key to empowering nations to take control of their own destiny. The prerequisites for this include high-quality programs that can be transferred to different sociocultural contexts, and insight into effective early intervention strategies.

ABOUT THIS BOOK

The contributions from experts from various disciplines and different parts of the world have been divided into three parts. In Part One, the role of context and culture in children's development and its implications for early intervention programs are discussed from a theoretical perspective. Part Two, in contrast, presents empirical findings about the relationship between the social, economic, and cultural context, and development, particularly language development and literacy. Part Three approaches the field of study from the perspective of intervention practice, presenting four large-scale early intervention programs currently running in different parts of the world.

In Part One, dealing with the role of culture and context in children's development and learning, Poortinga presents three orientations on the relationship between culture and human behavior. After discussing the strong and weak points of cultural relativism, psychological universalism, and behavioral universalism or absolutism, he opts for psychological universalism, a moderate form of universalism, acknowledging the primacy of universal psychological functions and viewing cultural variation as an empirical issue. In the final part of his chapter, Poortinga addresses the question of the extent to which transfer of intervention programs across cultural boundaries is meaningful, concluding that intervention programs should be indigenized at the level of presentation and content.

Serpell identifies the major theoretical constructs of developmental psychology that have practical relevance for the design of early intervention programs. He divides the field broadly into theories that treat context as a form of external stimulation and those that treat context as an incorporating system. Conceptualizing the context of development as an incorporating system of social activity and cultural meanings, which, according to Serpell, reflects a cumulative progression of insights, implies that educational curricula must take the everyday practices and technologies of the child's eco-cultural niche into account. In his view the co-construction of goals in terms of a system of shared meanings provides an optimal entry point for the design of programs to ameliorate human development. Early intervention programs in the real world, however, tend to deviate from the precise implications of the theoretical models. Serpell explores the lines of reasoning behind such deviations, using the intervention programs presented in Part Three as illustrations.

Harkness and Super's theoretical framework of the "developmental niche" is a concrete example of a theory that views development as an incorporating system of social activity and cultural meanings. They point out how the concept of culture has been used in the social sciences to signify a wide range of different things. Although the various ideas of culture seem in some ways opposed to each other, these ideas share the concept of systematicity, which makes culture a necessary although complex construct for analyzing human development in context. Harkness and Super conceptualize the developmental niche in terms of three major subsystems operating together as a larger system and interacting with other features of the culture. They assign a leading role to parental ethnotheories, which are the cultural models held by parents regarding children, families, and themselves as parents, instantiated in customs and practices of care. From this perspective, it follows that any program that aims to change parental behavior—or the behavior of children—must take parents' ideas into account.

Jacob and Phipps focus on the development of the concept of context within the field of culture and cognition, and its implications for teaching practice. The earliest work in this field did not explicitly address context, but focused on comparing cultural groups or observable traits within cultures. By providing a more integrated framework for understanding context, the cultural-historical school has stimulated researchers to elaborate aspects of context at micro, meso, and macrolevels as well as the concept of context itself. Drawing on research on ethnic minorities in the United States, Australia, and South Africa, Jacob and Phipps illustrate the contribution that the increased understanding of the relationships between context and cognition can make to instructional practices for young children.

Can interventions permanently change intelligence? Van de Vijver approaches this question by distinguishing two types of theories of intelligence: the "lumpers" and the "splitters." Theories of the first type consider intelligence as a general capacity for acquiring knowledge, whereas theories of the second type view intelligence as composed of many separate mental abilities that operate more or less independently. Van de Vijver opts for a componential view of intelligence and discusses the modifiability of its various components. He concludes that although pragmatic knowledge is easily modifiable, intervention programs should focus on metacognitive knowledge because of its broader effects.

The chapters in Part One substantiate the importance of culture in child development and learning. Culture is taken as an incorporating meaning system, that is to say, as a system with contents, tools, and skills that are appropriated in social interaction. Theoretical building blocks are provided covering insights from the psychology of intelligence to the cultural anthropology of belief systems.

Part Two presents empirical evidence on the impact of the sociocultural and economic context on young children's development. The basic premise of Snow's chapter is that literacy development and school success are promoted most effectively during the preschool period by paying attention to the development of oral language skills. The model of literacy development presented by Snow pays particular attention to the role of such skills. The Home-School Study of language and literacy conducted among low-income families in the United States showed that during book-reading, engagement in talk that goes beyond the immediate demands of the text and exposure to extended discourse and rare vocabulary items predicted successful literacy. She concludes her chapter with some implications for the design of preschool classrooms and family intervention programs.

Leseman critically examines the potential of the home environment in preparing young children for literacy and schooling in a multicultural society. He identifies three issues that need further consideration in order to strengthen the theoretical basis of context-sensitive early educational intervention programs. The first issue concerns the effective ingredients of home literacy. On the basis of a study conducted in the Netherlands in a socioeconomically varied and multiethnic sample, he concludes that home literacy, and informal home education in a broader sense, is multifaceted, including opportunities for interactions, quality of communication and instruction, and quality of affective experience. The second issue is about the importance of home literacy relative to other kinds of cognitive apprenticeships, such as joint play and problem-solving. The evidence indicates that there are probably multiple routes of preparation for school literacy, not exclusively connected to literacy in a narrow sense. The final issue refers to the contextuality of literacy and informal education at home. Research findings suggest that socioeconomic and cultural factors strongly determine the characteristics of educational processes at home. Implications for early educational intervention programs are discussed.

It has been mentioned that Leseman hypothesizes that interactions in the home vary with the family's sociocultural background. Richter extends this theory, arguing that stimulation itself is dependent on a more basic parental affective availability. She further emphasizes the hidden potential of poor parents in developing countries; in this case, in South Africa. This potential, however, has been obscured by scientists by deliberately ignoring individual differences in people's adaptation to poverty and hardship and an unconscious blindness to the psychological substance of poor people. Reviewing available research in South Africa, Richter confirms her hypothesis that mothers vary individually in coping with economic hardship, particularly with regard to the provision of nurturing and instructive experiences of young children. Most South African mothers seem to cope with the hardship of their lives, but for some women the burden is too great and leads to psychological distress and emotional detachment. Richter pleads for intervention to be directed primarily at caregivers, strengthening family ties and promoting paternal commitment.

The final chapter of this part deals with literacy and schooling in a multilingual society—an important topic in many countries of the world. Verhoeven discusses the appropriateness and effectiveness of literacy programs for immigrant and ethnic minority children speaking a nonmajority language at home. He points out that the acquisition of literacy in a second language requires a certain level of oral proficiency in that language. Many children of immigrants, however, are dominant in their home language when they enter kindergarten. He further questions whether these children can attain a native proficiency in their home language when immersed in a dominant second-language environment. Policymakers in both North America and Europe tend to view home-language instruction as a temporary facility, whereas in Verhoeven's view, first-language proficiency should be seen as an independent goal.

The common strand running through the chapters in the second part of the book is the notion that families' and communities' own cultural belief systems and practices concerning child rearing, education, and language should be respected, and, in the case of intervention, be seen as starting points instead of shortcomings. A second common strand is that educational interventions should focus on improving the quality of proximal processes at home as well at school, in order to obtain lasting effects.

Part Three deals with the intervention practice. Four intervention programs are presented which have been evaluated and are currently being implemented at a large scale, and which also represent different approaches and different socioeconomic and cultural contexts in the world. Although these programs may be considered as examples of good intervention practice, they are presented here primarily in order to help identify issues important in practice and evaluation.

Kağıtçıbaşı begins her chapter by delineating the prerequisites for effective early enrichment that need to be considered when examining and designing programs to enhance children's opportunities. She describes the Turkish Early Enrichment Project conducted in low-income areas of Istanbul as a case study of how culture-sensitive early education can empower parents and children. The intervention program focuses on the training of mothers, and has two components: the mothers are trained to do cognitive enriching activities with their children (HIPPY), and they participate in a mother enrichment program consisting of group discussions on relevant child-rearing topics. Kağıtçıbaşı attributes the program's short and long-term effects on children and mothers primarily to the mother-enrichment component.

Eldering and Vedder discuss how the Home Intervention Program for Preschool Youngsters (HIPPY), developed in Israel, has been adapted culturally and organizationally to immigrant families in the Netherlands. They pay much attention to aspects of implementation, particularly the dropout rate, the intensity of participation, and the involvement of the families. One relevant characteristic of HIPPY is that the mothers are trained by paraprofessionals: somewhat better educated mothers from the target group itself. HIPPY is an interesting case for researchers as well as policymakers and practitioners, because this program has been transferred to many different countries and cultural groups around the world. It merits further study, because of the differences in its outcomes.

The third program presented is the Integrated Child Development Services (ICDS), a package of services aiming at the total development of young children in India. In addition to regular medical checkups, supplementary nutrition and growth monitoring, the program includes preschool education. Muralidharan and Kaul point out how, since its launch in 1975, ICDS has been universalized in the country and currently encompasses more than 290,000 centers. The evaluation and impact studies conducted in this period reflect the shift in focus from the enrollment of the target groups (primarily scheduled casts and tribal groups) and the health and nutrition component of the scheme, to the quality of the preschool component and its effect on children.

In contrast with the programs presented previously, Success for All (SFA) is an example of a program in the United States with a more narrow focus, aiming to improve reading performance. Success for All is run exclusively in pre-school settings and carried out by professionals. Slavin and Madden describe the elements characteristic of Success for All: the reading program, one-to-one tutoring, and periodic assessments of students' progress. Success for All is increasingly used in large schools with many children who enter school speaking little or no English (most are Spanish dominant). The results of evaluations from all schools and all years involved show that the program significantly increases the children's reading performance and reduces the need for special education services.

CONCLUDING CONSIDERATIONS

There is an incomplete match between theory and intervention practice. This may be due to institutional constraints and demands for accountability heavily influencing educational programming and evaluation (Eldering, 1990/1991; Serpell, this volume), but it certainly also concerns the feasibility and practicability of theoretical insights. Various authors in this volume have pointed out that in order to be effective, educational interventions need to be geared to the particular needs of the children and families. Rather than implementing a preconceived ideal program, it would be more effective to appropriate a programmatic concept through a gradual learning process approach, involving parents and communities in planning and designing educational intervention programs. These theoretical principles raise questions about the negotiability of program goals when there are cultural differences between parents and program makers, and also about qualifications that program staff should have. Before recommending these principles from the ivory tower of theoreticians, their practicability needs to be studied.

REFERENCES

Anthropology and Education Quarterly. Arlington, VA: American Anthropological Association.

Borofsky, R. (Ed.). (1994). *Assessing cultural anthropology.* New York: McGraw-Hill, Inc.

Bourdieu, P. (1986). *Distinction. A social critique of the judgement of taste.* London: Routledge & Kegan Paul.

Bronfenbrenner, U. (1975). Is early intervention effective? A report on longitudinal evaluation of preschool programs. In M. Guttentag & E. L. Struening (Eds.), *Handbook of evaluation research* (Vol. 2, pp. 519–603). London: Sage.

Bronfenbrenner, U., & Ceci, S. J. (1994). Nature-nurture reconceptualized in developmental perspective: A bioecological model. *Psychological Review, 101,* 568–586.

Bronfenbrenner, U., McClelland, P., Wethington, E., Moen, P., & Ceci S. J. (1996). *The state of Americans.* New York: The Free Press.

Calamai, P. (1987). *Broken words. Why five million Canadians are illiterate.* Toronto: Literacy Southam Newspaper Group.

Eldering, L. (1990/1991). Intervention programmes for preschoolers from immigrant families. In N. Bleichrodt & P. Drenth (Eds.), *Contemporary issues in cross-cultural psychology* (pp. 50–63). Selected papers from a regional conference of the International Association for Cross-Cultural Psychology. Amsterdam/Lisse: Swets & Zeitlinger.

Fetterman D. M. (Ed.). (1984). *Ethnography in educational evaluation.* Beverley Hills/London: Sage.

Ginsburg, H. P. (1972). *The myth of the deprived child: poor children's intellect and education.* Englewood Cliffs, NJ: Prentice Hall.

Herrnstein, R. J., & Murray, C. (1994). *The bell curve: Intelligence and class structure in American life*. New York: Free Press.

Hofstede, G. H. (1980). *Culture's consequences: International differences in work-related values*. London: Sage.

Hunt, J. McV. (1961). *Intelligence and experience*. New York: Roland Press.

Jensen, A. R. (1969). How much can we boost IQ and scholastic achievement? *Harvard Educational Review, 39*, 1–123.

Kirsch, I. S., & Jungeblut, A. (1986). *Literacy: Profiles of America's young adults. Final report*. Princeton, NJ: National Assessment of Educational Progress.

Kohn, M. L., & Schooler, C. (1983). *Work and personality: An inquiry into the impact of social stratification*. Norwood, NJ: Ablex.

MacGinitie, W. H., & MacGinitie, R. K. (1986). Teaching students not to read. In S. de Castell, A. Luke, & K. Egan (Eds.), *Literacy, society, and schooling* (pp. 256–269). Cambridge: Cambridge University Press.

McKey, H. R., Condelli, L., Ganson, H., Barrett, B., McConkey, C., & Plantz, M. (1985). *The impact of Head Start on children, families, and communities*. Washington, DC: DHHS publication.

Ortiz, V. (1989). Language background and literacy among hispanic young adults. *Social Problems, 36*(2), 149–164.

Plomin, R., DeFries, J. C., & Fulker, D. W. (1988). *Nature and nurture during infancy and early childhood*. Cambridge: Cambridge University Press.

Quinn, N., & Holland, D. (1987). Culture and cognition. In D. Holland & N. Quinn (Eds.), *Cultural models in language and thought* (pp. 3–42). Cambridge: Cambridge University Press.

Rowe, D. C. (1994). *The limits of family influence: Genes, experience, and behavior*. New York: The Guilford Press.

Scarr, S. (1992). Developmental theories for the 1990s: Development and individual differences. *Child Development, 63*, 1–19.

Scarr, S., & Kidd, K. K. (1983). Developmental behavior genetics. In P. H. Mussen, M. M. Haith, & J. J. Campos (Eds.), *Handbook of child psychology (Vol. 2): Infancy and developmental psychobiology.* (pp. 345–433) New York: Wiley.

Schwartz, T. (1981). The acquisition of culture. *Ethos, 9*(1), 4–17.

Schwartz, T., White, G. M., & Lutz, C. A. (Eds.). (1992). *New directions in psychological anthropology*. Cambridge: Cambridge University Press.

Spindler, G. (Ed.). (1982). *Doing the ethnography of schooling: Educational anthropology in action*. New York: Holt, Rinehart & Winston.

Spindler, G., & Spindler, L. (Eds.). (1987). *Interpretive ethnography of education, at home and abroad*. New Jersey/London: Erlbaum.

Trueba, H. T. (1989). *Raising silent voices: Educating linguistic minorities for the 21st century.* Cambridge: Newbury House Publishers.

Weiss, B., & Kagen, S. L. (1989). Family support programs: Catalysts for change. *American Journal of Orthopsychiatry, 59*(1), 20–31.

White, K. R., Taylor, M. J., & Moss, V. D. (1992). Does research support claims about the benefits of involving parents in early intervention programs? *Review of Educational Research, 62,* 91–125.

Yoshikawa, H. (1994). Prevention as cumulative protection: Effects of early family support and education on chronic delinquency and its risks. *Psychological Bulletin, 115*(1), 28–54.

Zigler, E., Styfco, S. J., & Gilman, E. (1993). The national Head Start program for disadvantaged preschoolers. In E. Zigler & S. J. Styfco (Eds.), *Head Start beyond: A national plan for extended childhood intervention* (pp. 1–42). New Haven, CT: Yale University Press.

PART 1

Culture, Context, and Development: Theoretical Issues

Culture-Behavior Relationships
Ype H. Poortinga

The world of a child is complex. Barker and Wright (1951) followed a 7-year-old boy in a small midwestern American community for one day, from the time he woke up until the time he went to sleep. They found that their subject participated in hundreds of different activities over a range of settings with scores of objects and with dozens of persons. Getting around in one's world is a baffling achievement, which requires a variety of social skills and a whole arsenal of factual knowledge.

The impact of what is popularly called "culture" on the skills and knowledge of the 7-year-old is evident. Although there seems to be no systematic study in any other society matching that of Barker and Wright, this is obvious after a brief reflection on the life of a child in a hunting-gathering society like that of the Biaka Pygmies, or in an agricultural society like that of the neighboring Bangandu (cf., van de Koppel, 1983). The skills and items of knowledge required by these societies in many respects will not even remotely look like those in the American midwest. This point is emphasized to avoid the impression that the cultural context of development would be seen here as unimportant. The thesis of this chapter is that culture is very important, but perhaps in a different way than is often believed—and that this has certain consequences for the construction and cross-cultural transfer of intervention programs.

In psychology, as elsewhere in the behavioral and social sciences, there is a wide range of opinions on the nature of the relationship between culture and human behavior. Berry, Poortinga, Segall, and Dasen (1992) make a distinction between three orientations; namely, cultural relativism, psychological universalism, and behavioral universalism or absolutism. These can serve also to classify the main perspectives on the relationship between environmental influences (including the natural as well as the sociocultural context) and developmental outcomes. These three orientations are outlined in the following section and some of the strong and weak points of each are mentioned. In the third section, a problem is raised that is common to all three approaches, namely, the level of inclusiveness or generality at which culture-behavior relationships should be conceptualized. Implications of the various conceptual perspectives for early intervention programs are discussed in the fourth section. Some conclusions are drawn in the final section.

THREE APPROACHES TO BEHAVIOR-CULTURE RELATIONSHIPS

Cultural Relativism

Primacy of cultural context in the analysis of culture-behavior relationships is the main characteristic of cultural relativism. It is emphasized that behavior can be understood only in the context of the culture in which it occurs. Culture and behavior are seen as essentially inseparable, and the focus is on the meaning that is attached to behavioral actions in a given cultural population. The essence of psychological functioning is defined in terms of meaning. According to Shweder (1990), culture and behavior are co-constructing each other. Some authors in this tradition even object to the notion of a "psychic unity of mankind" (cf., Miller, 1997). One of the implications of relativism is the rejection for non-Western societies of the current methods and theories of psychology, because they do not fit the local psychic reality. Although predominantly an anthropological orientation, relativistic notions are also popular among psychologists.

There are both stronger and more moderate forms of cultural relativism. Authors in the early culture-and-personality school had outspoken ideas about the role of culture as the dominant force in shaping adult personality through socialization in early childhood. There was little modesty in the analyses of Benedict (1934), who labeled whole populations with clinical terms, like "Dionysian" (seeking excess in sensory and motor activities) or "paranoid." Equally inclined to overgeneralization was Mead (e.g., 1928), whose ideas about the malleability of human nature have not stood up to empirical scrutiny in any way. Later authors in the culture-and-personality school, like Whiting, were less outspoken. However, the idea based in psychoanalytic theory that there are systematic relationships between the ways children are socialized and their adult personalities was maintained (Whiting, 1974).

Nowadays strong forms of cultural relativism are found in writings with a historical-psychological orientation; for example, Kessen (1979) speaks about the child as a cultural construction, questioning the validity of most basic principles of contemporary developmental psychology. Also some forms of life-span development are strongly contextual. For example, Valsiner (e.g., Valsiner & Lawrence, 1997) emphasizes individual life trajectories in a cultural context as essential to psychological understanding.

The primacy of the social context in ontogenetic development has been a major concern in the sociocultural theories that go back to Vygotsky (1978). He saw the development of so-called higher mental functions as a sociohistorical process. In individual development functions like inductive and deductive reasoning become manifest at the social level as *inter*psychological phenomena before they can occur within the individual person as *intra*psychological categories (Vygotsky, 1978). The social nature of these mental functions is inspired by the Marxist philosophy of dialectical materialism, in which the human being is seen as determined by material conditions but intervenes in these conditions through a dialectical process (cf., Peeters, 1996).

A moderate form of relativism is implied by the notion of the "developmental niche" as described by Super and Harkness (1986, 1997; Harkness & Super, this volume). Although reminiscent of the biological notion of the ecological niche (i.e., the way of life of a species in interaction with an ecological environment), the three ingredients of the developmental niche, namely, (1) the physical and social setting of the child, (2) culturally regulated customs of child care and child rearing, and (3) parental ethnotheories about children, point to the cultural structuring of child development. An interactional approach in which biological maturation is mentioned explicitly next to cultural context has been formulated by Cole (1992a, 1992b; M. Cole & S. R. Cole, 1993). It can be argued that Cole adheres to cultural relativism, because he considers culture in the sense of historically rooted features of the environment as a constituent factor of behavior separate from universal aspects of the environment.

Finally, various movements can be mentioned to indigenize psychology in Third World countries. The major characteristic is a critical attitude toward Western psychology that tends to address issues largely irrelevant to nonindustrialized societies, and in a more general sense tends to be acultural and ahistorical. The development of a local psychology for the Philippines with own concepts and methods based on the ideas and insights of local informants has been propagated by Enriquez (1990) and his colleagues. More common is research that pays attention to selected local concepts and local social problems. Although indigenous psychologies lean toward cultural relativism, many researchers consider indigenization as an intermediate step toward universal but culture-informed theories (Kim & Berry, 1993; Sinha, 1997).

Behavioral Universalism

The main characteristic of this second approach to culture-behavior relationships is the primacy of behavior as observed. Absolutism, or behavioral universalism, presumes that behavior from all cultural contexts cannot only be interpreted in terms of common theoretical concepts, but that also, with minor exceptions, the same methods should be valid in all cultural populations. The clearest examples of an absolutist orientation are found in the analysis of cross-cultural differences, or even racial differences, in complex cognitive concepts like intelligence (e.g., Jensen, 1980) and personality dimensions (e.g., H.J. Eysenck & S.B.G. Eysenck, 1983), when cross-cultural comparisons are made in terms of test score levels. In such comparisons the culture-embeddedness of assessment instruments, and thus the possibility of cultural bias in scores, is largely ignored.

Strong empirical evidence supporting cross-cultural invariance in an absolutist sense is found in ethological research. For example, in each society of the wide range that has been investigated, Eibl-Eibesfeldt (1989) has documented on film the presence of behavior patterns such as the kiss (as a sign of affection to children) and the display of coyness. Such similarities can only be explained in terms of genetic predispositions. Examples of universal patterns of development have been identified in studies of early mother-child interactions (e.g., Bornstein, 1991; Keller, Schölmerich, & Eibl-Eibesfeldt, 1988; H. Papousek & M. Papousek, 1991) in which not only young babies but also parents showed very similar behavior patterns cross-culturally. For example, their manner of speech in the interaction of parents with young infants, conveniently called "motherese," is found to be characterized by cross-culturally invariant features. There is not much controversy about these findings as such, but the question is how far they can be generalized. According to Eibl-Eibesfeldt, the evidence demonstrates that there is a universal grammar of human social behavior. The biological function of psychological development is the preparation of the young members of the species for their role in reproduction; development is essentially complete when adulthood has been reached. The differential effects of culture on behavior are often seen as no more than a ripple on the surface (Lumsden & Wilson, 1981).

Maturational theories do not always reduce the role of the ecological and social environment to a position of secondary importance. In recent theorizing within the context of evolutionary psychology, it is considered that developmental tasks have to be mastered in interaction with specific environments (Keller, 1997). One example of a sociobiological study stressing the role of proximate variables like family context and childhood experiences has been reported by Belsky, Steinberg, and Draper (1991). In their view, low and inadequate resources in the family are accompanied by low parental investment and rejection of the child. This leads to the development of low attachment quality. The emotional state that results from this in turn leads to an early onset of puberty and to sexual activity with unstable pair bonding and early parenthood. This completes a cycle that will repeat itself in the next generation.

Psychological Universalism

This third perspective is portrayed by Berry et al. (1992) as a position between the two poles of cultural and biological orientation. The main axiom is the primacy of universal psychological functions, that is, all basic psychological traits and processes can be found everywhere. At the same time, the manifestations of these invariant processes can differ substantially across cultures. Inasmuch as psychological concepts and theories are formulated in a particular time and cultural location, they are likely to be biased and in need of revision on the basis of information from a broader range of cultures. This holds also for psychological measurement instruments, because these cannot be constructed without the use of behavioral manifestations that are understandable within a given cultural context. For this reason, comparative studies are seen as methodologically difficult and the interpretation of observed differences in behavior repertoire as problematic. Instruments are likely to be culturally inappropriate or biased, and it may even be necessary to use quite different operationalizations across cultures to capture the same trait or process.

A universalistic approach to development is found in much of the research based on the theory of Piaget. According to Piaget, there are stages in the cognitive development that can be defined in terms of characteristic operations. The stages unfold in a fixed order; each new stage results from the interaction between organism and environment. Educational and environmental factors are acknowledged as sources of differences, but Piaget (e.g., 1966) did not expect major differences in the ages at which children in different societies would acquire each of the stages. Therefore, it can be argued that his theory borders on an absolutist perspective (Segall et al., 1990). Empirical research shows large differences in the age level at which children in various societies can solve certain types of problems. The question remains controversial whether the stage of formal operations (the stage of abstract thinking, e.g., solving syllogistic problems) as described by Piaget, is reached in all societies. The large cross-cultural differences in cognitive operations, or at least in the readiness with which they are applied, has led to a shift in emphasis; in so-called neo-Piagetian research a new integration is sought of the structurally invariant framework and context (Demetriou & Efklides, 1987).

Strengths and Weaknesses

A strong point of behavioral absolutism is the emphasis on cross-cultural similarity in the antecedents of human behavior, whether these are sought in biological predispositions or in shared human ecological and social conditions. This forms a basis for the explanation of the evident cross-cultural similarities in cognitive and social behavior. A weak point of behavioral absolutism, at least in the eyes of those with another orientation, is the interpretation at face value of observed cultural differences. For example, test scores tend to be interpreted independent of the cultural background of the subjects who obtained them. As a rule, subjects from societies with low formal schooling and from minority groups do less well on all tests of cognitive abilities and other maximum performance tests than do subjects with more exposure to the cultural context of the test authors. In this way, an absolutist orientation becomes easily associated with "deficit" notions, such as a "culture of poverty" (cf., Howard & Scott, 1981).

The strong and weak points of cultural relativism are quite the opposite of those mentioned for absolutism. Relativists will not easily fall into the trap of an insufficient recognition of the influence of cultural context. The focus on social context and subjective reality as experienced by members of a society has given impetus to the study of parental ethnotheories and of differences in the expectations and demands that children have to meet. The age at which children are given responsibilities and are assigned economically relevant tasks differs greatly, especially between agricultural and industrialized societies (cf., Schliemann, Carraher, & Ceci, 1997; Segall et al., 1990). However, obvious similarities in behavior patterns are given scant attention by relativists. If mentioned at all, such similarities are taken to point to the equality of social conditions (or perhaps to cultural diffusion), rather than to universal psychological processes.

The major strength of psychological universalism is that the extent of cultural variation is an empirical issue. For example, it has been found that social perceptions of the characteristics of men and women are widely shared across societies (Williams & Best, 1982), and that there is a universal tendency to rate one's own group more favorably than other groups (Brewer & Campbell, 1976). But there is also evidence that even the susceptibility to simple visual illusions is influenced by the ecological environment (Segall, Campbell, & Herskovits, 1966) and that the desire for more children differs according to the economic needs of parents (Kağıtçıbaşı, 1982). As a middle-of-the-road position, moderate universalism is less open to criticism than the more extreme positions of relativism and absolutism, and it can incorporate empirical evidence from both these perspectives. Perhaps the most problematic aspect of universalism is that it offers (as yet) little theoretical rationale for the specification of cultural variation and psychological invariance.

Berry et al. (1992) implicitly question whether a precise specification of culture-behavior relationships is theoretically possible. In their opinion, the commonly found notion that there exists a close relationship (one-to-one correspondence) between cultural factors and behavior patterns may be incorrect. Human behavior has a high degree of plasticity. This implies that a choice can be made between alternative courses of action. Potentially, individuals have a large set of alternative actions at their disposal in almost any situation, but the range of responses actually observed is far more limited. Apparently, there are constraints that limit the set of alternatives available to a person, including cultural constraints, such as norms, beliefs, and conventions. However, some of these constraints can be quite arbitrary in terms of psychological functions, and thus escape systematic explanation. This arbitrariness imposes limits on the precision of explanation and prediction for individuals within a culture, but even more so when one seeks to explain differences in behavior between cultural populations (Poortinga, 1992).

The distinction between relativist and universalist orientations has methodological as well as theoretical implications. Universalistic traditions value the principle that researchers should protect their inferences and interpretations against plausible alternatives. Experimental designs, systematic observation, and psychometric instruments potentially lead to objective evidence, in the sense that other observers can critically scrutinize findings and even replicate studies. The fact that these methods are western discoveries does not make them a priori suspect for use in non-Western societies. Relativistic research, which often is qualitative or interpretive, is less hemmed in by methodological canons; there is more reliance on methods that are dependent on the person of the researcher. On the one hand, this enlarges the scope for research; on the other hand, it makes the validity of interpretations a more problematic issue. Post hoc interpretation of casual observations and reports based on the understanding of a single action in cultural context without a possibility of independent validation are more respectable in the eyes of relativists than in the eyes of universalists.

LEVELS OF INCLUSIVENESS

In the previous section, differences between three perspectives on culture-behavior relationships have been emphasized. There are also common problems. One of these concerns is the level of inclusiveness or generality at which cross-cultural differences can be interpreted most fruitfully (cf., Pettigrew & Van de Vijver, 1991). With respect to cognition, for example, explanations of cross-cultural differences can be found at many levels of comprehensiveness, ranging from "general intelligence" via "stages," "styles," and "abilities" to highly specific "skills." In general, the literature on the relationship between culture and behavior reflects a tendency toward interpretations at a high level of inclusiveness encompassing wide ranges of behavioral phenomena. Against this common trend, a modular approach to culture has been advocated by Cole (cf., Laboratory of Comparative Human Cognition, 1983) from a relativistic perspective. Also in more universalist writings, there are arguments to warning for overgeneralization (Poortinga, 1997).

Generalization to Traits and Abilities

One popular idea is that the thought processes of literate peoples differ in essential ways from those of nonliterates. Segall et al. (1990) have labeled such notions as "great divide theories," and have listed a variety of conceptions that all amount to a general superiority of Western thinking. One of the authors in their list is Luria (e.g., 1971). In a famous study conducted in the thirties, he found that illiterate Siberian farmers did not seem capable of solving simple syllogistic problems. A little schooling had a strong impact on their performance. In line with Vygotskian thinking, Luria saw this as evidence of the priority of sociocultural development, and drew far-reaching conclusions on the presence and absence of "higher mental functions," such as inductive and deductive reasoning, in cultural populations. In later studies it was shown that not a faculty for logical thinking, but rather the acceptance of a logical (as opposed to an empirical) mode of the syllogistic problem by the subjects is the most important determinant of their answers (Scribner, 1979). A persuasive study on the limited effects of reading and writing *per se* on modes of thinking has been conducted by Scribner and Cole (1981) among the Vai. They demonstrated that local forms of literacy, in the Vai script or in Arabic, had very limited effects on the performance for a range of cognitive tests. In contrast, literacy based on Western-style education had a strong impact. This points to cultural mediation of complex cognitive processes at the level of skills and metacognitions (when to use which algorithm), rather than at a more comprehensive level. In other words, the mere fact of being literate or illiterate appears to have few consequences for cognitive functioning in nonwriting and nonreading situations.

Not only in cognition, but also in the sphere of social behavior, there is evidence favoring limited generalizability. Specific to a class of situations are so-called conventions, that is, generally accepted, often implicit notions about what is appropriate in social interactions or within a field of activity. It is characteristic of many cross-cultural differences in conventions that they have no systematic relationship with any broader psychological variable. A clear case are traffic rules. The British and Europeans living on the continent differ very consistently in keeping to the left side or the right side of the road. At the same time, the generalizability of this pattern to other aspects of behavior is extremely limited, if not entirely absent. Moreover, the convention is readily reversible, even after years of practice, as demonstrated by drivers who cross the Channel. Of course, conventions generally are less precisely demarcated both in terms of how to behave and in terms of the class of situations in which the behavior is prescribed or expected. Girndt (1995) has given examples of conventions about factual beliefs, approaches to problem-solving, and even conventional arguments to justify conventions. She proposes a major distinction between task conventions (related to "facts" and procedures) and communication conventions (i.e., rules about how to act). Going back to the study by Barker and Wright (1951) mentioned in the introduction, the question can be raised how much of the extensive range of activities in the life of the 7-year-old from a cross-cultural perspective is best interpreted in terms of specific skills and conventions.

A related query is to what extent cross-cultural differences can be explained as a direct consequence of prevailing external conditions, and to what extent it is necessary to postulate internal dispositions. It is almost axiomatic in the literature that differences in behavior repertoire are manifestations of differences in internalized values, norms, beliefs, attitudes, or meanings. The idea of culture-as-a-system that is so prevalent in culture research assumes coherence between various aspects of behavior. In the culture-and-personality school, internalization through socialization of the economic mode of existence was developed into an important dogma (e.g., Kardiner & Linton, 1945; Levine, 1973). In more recent times there has been a shift from personality to value dimensions. Well-known is the large-scale study among national subsidiaries of IBM on the basis of which Hofstede (1980) postulated four value dimensions. It may be noted that two of Hofstede's dimensions are based on only three items each, which by itself suggests a danger of overgeneralization. More important, the dimension that has become most famous, individualism-collectivism, showed a strong correlation ($r = .82$) with economic wealth (GNP per capita). This correlation is so high that it suggests a very close relationship between behavior repertoire and available resources.

In many instances a parsimonious explanation is possible by postulating a direct link between the actions of persons and the external circumstances they are living in. Research on locus of control provides an example in the sphere of personality research. A distinction is made between external control (when success in life is seen as due to chance or powers outside oneself), and internal control (when success is attributed to one's own abilities and skills). Both within and across societies it has been repeatedly found that results correspond with the actual control that people can exert on their own lives; the less educated, minority groups, and samples from countries with a low GNP tend toward low internal control (Dyal, 1984). An example from social psychology is a study on intergroup norm violation in India and the Netherlands (DeRidder & Tripathi, 1992). In each of these two countries there were two group contrasts; in India, Muslims versus Hindus and workers versus managers, in the Netherlands, Turkish migrants versus autochthonous Dutch and also workers versus managers. Subjects were asked for the expected reaction of members of their own group to various norm violations by someone of the other group, as well as for the expected reaction of the outgroup to a norm violation by someone of the subject's own group. Four context variables were included in the design of this study to explain differences in expected reactions between groups, namely, (1) the perceived power of a group, (2) the social position of a group, (3) the attitudes toward the other group, and (4) own-group identity. It emerged that the two external variables (1 and 2) explained much more of the differences in reactions than the internal variables (3 and 4). From these examples it appears that a simple learning paradigm, postulating a causal connection between current environmental conditions and a person's reactions, can provide a parsimonious account of many cross-cultural differences.

Generalization on the Course of Development

The issues raised here are also pertinent for cross-cultural differences in individual development. When critically examined, the cross-cultural evidence for effects of socialization practices on major modes of cognitive and social development may be less extensive than often thought. The most famous cross-cultural study of social development, the *Children in Six Cultures Project* (Whiting & Whiting, 1975), showed impressive commonalities. For example, toward the mother children in all the six societies displayed more dependent behavior, toward slightly younger children more dominance, and toward infants more nurturance, suggesting panhuman predispositions. This and other evidence from cultural anthropology has been reviewed by R. H. Munroe and R. L. Munroe (1996; R. L. Munroe & R. H. Munroe, 1997). Unfortunately, very little research exists in which the limits of the effects of prevailing cultural conditions on developmental outcomes are investigated explicitly.

To be added to this is the uncertainty about the long-term consequences of early childhood patterns of caretaking that by Western standards point to severe stimulus deprivation. Kagan and Klein (1983) have studied a village in Guatemala where during the first year of their lives children are mainly left inside a small, windowless hut. These children were apathetic. The 11 to 13-year-old children in the same village could not observe any ill effects of this treatment. It may be noted in passing that an American psychologist, Rebelsky (1967), writing in the 1960s criticized Dutch mothers for leaving their children alone for long hours, either inside the house in a crib, or outside the house in a carriage or enclosure. In this case as well, no ill effects have been traced, and Rebelsky and Daniel (1976, p. 292) later argued that the human organism "can undergo various kinds of deprivation without significant loss and with the possibility of 'catching up' later."

Although this is difficult to document, one gains the impression that evidence favoring the continuity assumption tends to come from studies in which a section of the children in a population are exposed to a disadvantageous environment for most of their youth, not only during the early years of life. It may be noted explicitly that such evidence is compatible with the wealth of studies on the poor school performance of children from minority groups and groups with low socioeconomic status (e.g., Leseman, 1989; Eldering & Vedder and Slavin & Madden, this volume). Many negative conditions, economic as well as social, are likely to operate for such long periods that they are a permanent feature of the environment of a child for its lifetime. Thus, children growing up in difficult circumstances tend to face an array of conditions disruptive to their development. According to this view, the accumulation of specific antecedents across a range of situations and over a long timespan is a key factor. In addition, the difficulties a child has to face may also accumulate if the tasks have a hierarchical order. This seems to be the case in the school, where later elements in the curriculum presume familiarity with previous elements.

IMPLICATIONS FOR EARLY INTERVENTION PROGRAMS

The point of view that one holds on cross-cultural differences has implications for the use of intervention programs. Even the main goal of organizations like UNESCO, which is to achieve literacy for everyone independent of cultural background and expectations for future adult life, reflects an educational philosophy that does not hold true for all times and societies (Serpell, 1993; Serpell & Hatano, 1997). Differences of opinion tend to focus on a more culture-specific definition of intervention programs (e.g., Woodhead, 1996) and a more global outlook on the educational needs of children in non-Western societies (e.g., Kağıtçıbaşı, 1996). This is not the place to discuss the moral and social assumptions underlying contemporary intervention strategies. It will be taken for granted that cross-culturally common educational objectives, especially those related to literacy, are worthwhile.

Levels of Transfer

Many of the consequences that follow from the three perspectives outlined in the second section above can be clustered around the debate as to what extent transfer of intervention programs across cultural boundaries is meaningful, and to what extent each cultural population requires separate programs developed for its specific circumstances. Transfer is possible to the extent that there is cross-cultural invariance. In the literature on the transfer of psychometric tests various levels of invariance have been distinguished (Van de Vijver & Poortinga, 1982; Poortinga & van der Flier, 1988), which, with some modification, also apply to intervention.

The first level is invariance of psychological functions. If the cross-cultural identity of psychological functioning is in doubt, there is no basis for any transfer. If in each cultural context performances, such as reading and writing skills, are developed in a psychologically distinctive manner, the construction of intervention programs has to be culture-specific. The evidence reviewed in this chapter and presented in other chapters of this volume (e.g., Eldering & Vedder, this volume) is rather incompatible with an extremely relativistic viewpoint and further discussion about possible variation at this first level does not seem fruitful.

The second level of invariance is that of psychological constructs and theories. Are current Western theories and concepts universally valid, or are they culturally specific, like the parental ethnotheories that have emerged from descriptive studies in various non-Western societies? If we consider the brief history of intervention programs, it is obvious that there have been major changes in the course of a few decades. For example, in the late 1960s there were serious plans to introduce Western play materials on a large scale in African societies to stimulate creativity and the development of cognitive abilities. Today such an approach, which did not at all consider the wider social and eco-cultural environment, is unlikely to be found. From the position of cultural relativism, it may be questioned whether seeking a universal definition of psychological concepts should even be attempted. From the position of moderate universalism, this is an objective that can be pursued meaningfully, and one that seems to fit in well with the trend toward common educational goals—at least in literacy education. Of course, transfer is impossible to the extent that the initial position of children or the educational objectives in different societies are not the same, but these are extrinsic reasons that should be recognized by educationists and which should not be confused with cross-cultural differences in psychological functioning.

The third level of invariance has to do with the presentation of intervention programs. Procedures for administration, including instructions for effective communication, ways to engage children in active participation, style of presentation, etc., are described in manuals that come with good programs. The question is, to what extent can the same procedures be used for culturally different groups, and to what extent do procedures have to be adapted to local circumstances and practices? For example, although more effective and less effective teaching styles have been identified in Western educational research, this does not rule out the fact that members of some non-Western group may be more familiar and at ease with a style that is considered less effective in Western groups (e.g., Philips, 1972). As a rule, adaptation of program procedures on the basis of information of local experts would seem to be indicated.

The fourth and final level of invariance is that of program content. At this level, the uncontrolled transfer of programs would be quite inappropriate. Interventions have to link up with the experiential world of the child (i.e., the level of manifestations distinguished by universalists). In view of the differences between children in, for example, Western urban and non-Western rural societies, an indigenous approach to intervention programs is not only desirable at this level, but appears to be absolutely necessary.

In summary, there are various considerations that plead for transfer, namely, invariance of educational objectives (e.g., reading and writing), invariance of cognitive and linguistic processes, and relevance of theoretical formulations in other cultural contexts than the one in which they were developed. Limitations to transfer are imposed by differences in specific educational objectives and socialization practices, differences in cultural conventions, and differences in skills and knowledge at the start of the intervention.

The Rationale for Effectiveness

Some further implications relate to the poor theoretical basis of many intervention programs. Authors generally seem to be confident that they know what is good for children, but on closer inspection the psychological mechanisms through which programs, especially the broader ones, are operating, remain fuzzy and unclear. The absence of the name of Piaget, still the main developmental theorist, from the name index of an important recent book by Myers (1992) is a telling illustration of this.

From a universalist perspective, the absence of explicitly formulated theory has at least two negative consequences for the implementation of intervention programs. In the first place, it is far easier to evaluate the validity of a program if testable hypotheses can be derived from theoretical claims about effectiveness. Effect studies of intervention programs tend to depend heavily on variables that have been identified post hoc (cf., Eldering & Choenni-Gobardhan, 1990/1991); the dangers of such validation are well-known. In the second place, vague knowledge is not very helpful when reconstruction or adaptation of a program is needed for a different society than the one it was developed for originally.

However, both relativistic views and moderate forms of universalism that emphasize the danger of overgeneralization make it questionable as to whether program makers construct good theories about intervention (cf., Serpell, this volume). If one looks at the historical development of intervention programs for children in disadvantageous conditions, there has been a major shift from focused short interventions, usually meant to improve performance on cognitive school tasks, to programs that start much earlier in life and address a wide range of topics (cf., Kağıtçıbaşı, Muralidharan & Kaul, and Richter, this volume). It follows from the empirical evidence presented in this chapter that this should be a worthwhile development. Programs focused on specific skills, or some limited domain of behavior, can also be successful, when they are started later in life. The plasticity of behavior guarantees success, provided that there are no sociocultural constraints (e.g., negative attitudes) that are barriers to effectiveness. But if an intervention program is to have a broader and more lasting impact, it would have to influence a sufficient part of the behavior repertoire for a sufficient part of the developmental course. If the behavior repertoire of a person is seen as the outcome of a large array of interactions with the cultural environment, then the best one can do is to represent as much as possible of the desirable repertoire in the program. Thus, the variety of conventions, skills, and factual knowledge that a child has to own for proper functioning makes it likely that only long-term programs with a high intensity of intervention are likely to lead to noticeable changes, effective over a longer period of time, in the behavior repertoire (Kağıtçıbaşı, 1996). If this argument has any merits, the differential validity of programs, to a large extent, should be a function of the time and energy invested in each child.

CONCLUSION

The arguments in this chapter tend toward a moderate form of universalism. This provides a pragmatically sound basis for looking at intervention programs. For the purpose of educational interventions, it can safely be assumed that learning principles are the same everywhere. Thus, the transfer of intervention principles which have proven to be effective in one cultural context to another society should be a meaningful enterprise.

The repertoire of actions expected from children varies greatly between societies such as urbanized industrialized countries and traditional agricultural communities. It is worth questioning to what extent different manifestations of behavior can be understood in terms of the same psychological processes, and to what extent cross-cultural differences in the repertoire of actions can be seen as a reflection of differences in circumstances and conventions. Postulates of culture-specific internalized dispositions acquired during the process of socialization may place a wrong emphasis on cultural factors. However, with a reduction of cultural context too strong to separate variables, one may loose sight of interdependencies and coherence in the cultural context in which behavior is embedded.

In any case, the many differences that exist in educational goals and educational climates, and in culture-specific skills and knowledge of children when they enter a program, make it necessary to adapt procedures and contents of programs to local circumstances.

A corollary of moderate forms of both relativism and universalism with regard to cross-cultural differences is that intervention programs with general objectives, such as success at school, can only be expected to have a lasting impact, if they address a significant part of the many aspects that make up the total repertoire of an individual's activities. The theoretical question of how culture is organized, whether as a complete and in itself unique system, or as a large set of conventions, determines the scope for transfer of existing intervention programs, but has little bearing on the intensity of intervention that is needed for long-term success.

REFERENCES

Barker, R. G., & Wright, L. S. (1951). *One boy's day: A specimen record of behavior.* New York: Harper & Brothers.

Belsky, J., Steinberg, L., & Draper, P. (1991). Childhood experience, interpersonal development, and reproductive strategy: An evolutionary theory of socialization. *Child Development, 62,* 647–670.

Benedict, R. (1934). *Patterns of culture.* New York: Mentor.

Berry, J. W., Poortinga, Y. H., Segall, M. H., & Dasen, P. R. (1992). *Cross-cultural psychology: Research and applications.* Cambridge: Cambridge University Press.

Bornstein, M. H. (Ed.). (1991). *Cultural appoaches to parenting.* Hillsdale, NJ: Erlbaum.

Brewer, M., & Campbell, D. T. (1976). *Ethnocentrism and intergroup attitudes: East African evidence.* London: Sage.

Cole, M. (1992a). Culture in development. In M. H. Bornstein & M. Lamb (Eds.), *Developmental psychology: An advanced textbook* (3rd ed., pp. 731–789). Hillsdale, NJ: Erlbaum.

Cole, M. (1992b). Context, modularity, and the cultural constitution of development. In L. T. Winegar & J. Valsiner (Eds.), *Children's development within social context* (Vol. 2, pp. 5–31). Hillsdale, NJ: Erlbaum.

Cole, M., & Cole, S. R. (1993). *The development of children* (2nd ed.). New York: Freeman.

Demetriou, A., & Efklides, A. (1987). Experiential structuralism and neo-Piagetian theories: Toward an integrated model. *International Journal of Psychology, 22,* 679–728.

DeRidder, R., & Tripathi, R. C. (Eds.). (1992). *Norm violations and intergroup relations.* Oxford, UK: Clarendon Press.

Dyal, J. A. (1984). Cross-cultural research with the Locus of Control construct. In H. M. Lefcourt (Ed.), *Research with the Locus of Control construct* (Vol. 3, pp. 209–306). New York: Academic Press.

Eibl-Eibesfeldt, I. (1989). *Human Ethology.* New York: Aldine de Gruyter.

Eldering, L., & Choenni-Gobardhan, S. (1990/1991). *Interventieprogramma's voor kinderen uit kansarme groepen* [Intervention programs for disadvantaged children]. Leiden, the Netherlands: DSWO Press.

Enriquez, V. G. (Ed.). (1990). *Indigenous psychologies.* Quezon City, the Philippines: Psychology Research and Training House.

Eysenck, H. J., & Eysenck, S. B. G. (1983). Recent advances in the cross-cultural study of personality. In J. N. Butcher & C. D. Spielberger (Eds.), *Advances in the study of personality assessment* (Vol. 2, pp. 41–69). Hillsdale, NJ: Erlbaum.

Girndt, T. (1995). *Provisional manual for a course on intercultural communication.* Report. Tilburg, the Netherlands: Tilburg University.

Hofstede, G. H. (1980). *Culture's consequences: International differences in work-related values.* London: Sage.

Howard, A., & Scott, R. A. (1981). The study of minority groups in complex societies. In R. H. Munroe, R. L. Munroe, & B. B. Whiting (Eds.), *Handbook of cross-cultural human development* (pp. 113–151). New York: Garland Publishing.

Jensen, A. R. (1980). *Bias in mental testing.* New York: Free Press.

Kagan, J., & Klein, R. E. (1983). Cross-cultural perspectives on early development. *American Psychologist, 38,* 947–961.

Kağıtçıbaşı, Ç. (1982). Old-age security value of children: Cross-national economic evidence. *Journal of Cross-Cultural Psychology, 13,* 29–42.

Kağıtçıbaşı, Ç. (1996). *Family and human development across cultures.* Mahwah, NJ: Erlbaum.

Kardiner, A., & Linton, R. (1945). *The individual and his society.* New York: Columbia University Press.

Keller, H. (1997). Evolutionary approaches. In J. W. Berry, Y. H. Poortinga, & J. Pandey (Eds.), *Handbook of cross-cultural psychology* (2nd ed., Vol. 1, pp. 215–255). Boston: Allyn & Bacon.

Keller, H., Schölmerich, A., & Eibl-Eibesfeldt, I. (1988). Communication patterns in adult-infant interactions in western and non-western cultures. *Journal of Cross-Cultural Psychology, 19,* 427–445.

Kessen, W. (1979). The American child and other cultural inventions. *American Psychologist, 34,* 815–820.

Kim, U., & Berry, J. W. (Eds.). (1993). *Indigenous psychologies: Research and experience in cultural context.* Newbury Park, CA: Sage.

Laboratory of Comparative Human Cognition (1983). Culture and cognitive development. In P. H. Mussen & W. Kessen (Eds.), *Handbook of child psychology* (Vol. 1, pp. 295–356). New York: Wiley.

Leseman, P. P. M. (1989). *Structurele en pedagogische determinanten van schoolloopbanen.* Rotterdam: Rotterdamse School Adviesdienst.

Levine, R. A. (1973). *Culture, behavior, and personality.* Chicago: Aldine.

Lumsden, C. J., & Wilson, E. O. (1981). *Genes, mind and culture: The coevolutionary process.* Cambridge, MA: Harvard University Press.

Luria, A. R. (1971). Towards the problem of the historical nature of psychological processes. *International Journal of Psychology, 6,* 259–272.

Mead, M. (1928). *Coming of age in Samoa.* New York: William Morrow.

Miller, J. G. (1997). Theoretical isues in cultural psychology. In J. W. Berry, Y. H. Poortinga, & J. Pandey (Eds.), *Handbook of cross-cultural psychology* (2nd ed., Vol. 1, pp. 85–128). Boston: Allyn & Bacon.

Munroe, R. H., & Munroe, R. L. (1996). Child development. In D. Levinson & M. Ember (Eds.), *Encyclopedia of cultural anthropology* (Vol. 1, pp. 193–199). New York: Henry Holt.

Munroe, R. L., & Munroe, R. H. (1997). A comparative anthropological perspective. In J. W. Berry, Y. H. Poortinga, & J. Pandey (Eds.), *Handbook of cross-cultural psychology* (2nd ed., Vol. 1, pp. 171–213). Boston: Allyn & Bacon.

Myers, R. (1992). *The twelve who survive.* London: Routledge.

Papousek, H., & Papousek, M. (1991). Innate and cultural guidance of infants' integrative competencies: China, The United States, and Germany. In M. H. Bornstein (Ed.), *Cultural appoaches to parenting* (pp. 23–44). Hillsdale, NJ: Erlbaum.

Peeters, H. F. M. (1996). *Psychology: The historical dimension.* Tilburg, the Netherlands: Syntax Publishers.

Pettigrew T. F., & Van de Vijver, F. J. R. (1991). Thinking both bigger and smaller: Finding the basic level for cross-cultural psychology. In P. J. D. Drenth, J. A. Sergeant, & R. J. Takens (Eds.), *European perspectives in psychology* (Vol. 3, pp. 339–354). New York: Wiley.

Philips, S. V. (1972). Participant structures and communicative competence: Warm Springs children in community and classroom. In C. B. Cazden, V. P. John, & E. D. Hymes (Eds.), *Functions of language in the classroom* (pp. 370–394). New York: Teachers College Press.

Piaget, J. (1966). Nécessité et signification des recherches comparatives en psychologie génétique [Necessity and significance of comparative research in genetic psychology]. *International Journal of Psychology, 1*, 3–13.

Poortinga, Y. H. (1992). Towards a conceptualization of culture for psychology. In S. Iwawaki, Y. Kashima, & K. Leung (Eds.), *Innovations in cross-cultural psychology* (pp. 3–17). Amsterdam: Swets & Zeitlinger.

Poortinga, Y. H. (1997). Towards convergence? In J. W. Berry, Y. H. Poortinga, & J. Pandey (Eds.), *Handbook of cross-cultural psychology* (2nd ed., Vol. 1, pp. 347–387). Boston: Allyn & Bacon.

Poortinga, Y. H., & van der Flier, H. (1988). The meaning of item bias in ability tests. In S. H. Irvine & J. W. Berry (Eds.), *Human abilities in cultural context* (pp. 166–183). New York: Cambridge University Press.

Rebelsky, F. (1967). Infancy in two cultures. *Nederlands Tijdschrift voor de Psychologie, 22*, 379–387.

Rebelsky, F., & Daniel, P. A. (1976). Cross-cultural studies of infant intelligence. In M. Lewis (Ed.), *Origins of intelligence: Infancy and childhood* (pp. 279–297). London: Wiley.

Schliemann, A., Carraher, D., & Ceci, J. (1997). Everyday cognition. In J. W. Berry, P. R. Dasen, & T. S. Saraswathi (Eds.), *Handbook of cross-cultural psychology* (2nd ed., Vol. 2). Boston: Allyn & Bacon.

Scribner, S. (1979). Modes of thinking and ways of speaking: Culture and logic reconsidered. In R. O. Freedle (Ed.), *New directions in discourse processing* (pp. 223–243). Norwood, NJ: Ablex.

Scribner, S., & Cole, M. (1981). *The psychology of literacy.* Cambridge, MA: Harvard University Press.

Segall, M. H., Campbell, D. T., & Herskovits, M. J. (1966). *The influence of culture on visual perception.* Indianapolis: Bobbs-Merrill.

Segall, M. H., Dasen, P. R., Berry, J. W., & Poortinga, Y. H. (1990). *Human behavior in gobal perspective.* New York: Pergamon/Allyn & Bacon.

Serpell, R. (1993). *The significance of schooling: Life-journeys in an African society.* Cambridge: Cambridge University Press.

Serpell, R., & Hatano, G. (1997). Education, schooling, and literacy in a cross-cultural perspective. In J. W. Berry, P. R. Dasen, & T. S. Saraswathi (Eds.), *Handbook of cross-cultural psychology* (2nd ed., Vol. 2). Boston: Allyn & Bacon.

Shweder, R. A. (1990). Cultural psychology_what is it? In J. W. Stigler, R. A. Shweder, & G. Herdt (Eds.), *Cultural psychology: Essays on comparative human development* (pp. 1–43). Cambridge: Cambridge University Press.

Sinha, D. L. (1997). Indigenizing psychology. In J. W. Berry, Y. H. Poortinga, & J. Pandey (Eds.), *Handbook of cross-cultural psychology* (2nd ed., Vol. 1, pp. 129–169). Boston: Allyn & Bacon.

Super, C. M., & Harkness, S. (1986). The developmental niche: A conceptualization at the interface of child and culture. *International Journal of Behavioral Development, 9*, 545–569.

Super, C. M., & Harkness, S. (1997). The cultural structuring of child development. In J. W. Berry, P. R. Dasen, & T. S. Saraswathi (Eds.), *Handbook of cross-cultural psychology* (2nd ed., Vol. 2). Boston: Allyn & Bacon.

Valsiner, J., & Lawrence, J. (1997). In J. W. Berry, P. R. Dasen, & T. S. Saraswathi (Eds.), *Handbook of cross-cultural psychology* (2nd ed., Vol. 2). Boston: Allyn & Bacon.

van de Koppel, J. M. H. (1983). *A developmental study of the Biaka Pygmies and the Bangandu.* Lisse, the Netherlands: Swets & Zeitlinger.

Van de Vijver, F. J. R., & Poortinga, Y. H. (1982). Cross-cultural generalization and universality. *Journal of Cross-Cultural Psychology, 13*, 387–408.

Vygotsky, L. S. (1978). *Mind in society: The development of higher social processes.* Cambridge, MA: Harvard University Press.

Whiting, J. W. (1974). A model for psychocultural research. *Annual report.* American Anthropological Association: Washington DC.

Whiting, B. B., & Whiting, J. W. (1975). *Children of six cultures: A psychocultural analysis.* Cambridge, MA: Harvard University Press.

Williams, J. E., & Best, D. L. (1982). *Measuring sex stereotypes: A thirty nation study.* London: Sage.

Woodhead, M. (1996). *In search of the rainbow: Pathways to quality in large-scale programmes for young disadvantaged children.* The Hague, the Netherlands: Van Leer Foundation.

CHAPTER THREE

Theoretical Conceptions of Human Development
Robert Serpell

"There is nothing so practical as a good theory"

Kurt Lewin, cited in McGuire, 1973, p. 447

Hoping to support this proposition, I attempt in this chapter to identify the major theoretical constructs of developmental psychology that have practical relevance to the design of educational intervention programs for the early childhood years. My presentation of the constructs is organized in terms of a rough taxonomy with respect to their characterization of context, of development, and of the modes of interaction between the developing individual and the context. This approach has the attraction of specifying key variables for the design of an intervention program that can also be used to focus the attention of program personnel during their training. It does, however, run the risk of appearing to simplify the theories from which these constructs are derived and opens me to the charge of eclecticism.

I run these twin risks willingly, because I am convinced that intervention programs need to make their techniques intelligible both to the various personnel deployed in their implementation and to the people for whose children's welfare they are intended. If explaining the significance of a particular theoretical construct to either of these audiences requires selective simplification of the theory, that may be a necessary price to pay for its practical validation. Others may argue that this is not essential. After all, the scientific bases of modern medical and engineering technology are seldom fully understood by the majority of those who benefit from their application. In my view, however, this analogy is false, since psychological intervention programs (be they educational or therapeutic) must, for both epistemological and ethical reasons, rely on the conscious, voluntary participation of their recipients in the technical details of the program (Serpell, 1990).

The expert paradigm that informs certain clinical interventions with special populations extracts the patient from her normal social context and replaces it with an artificial one, structured in such a way as to optimize the conditions for the amelioration of the patient's condition. Whether this is ever a legitimate strategy for the enhancement of a child's developmental opportunities need not concern us here: it is clearly both impracticable and politically unacceptable as a method for the enhancement of developmental opportunities in a large section of society. That goal can only realistically be addressed by working with and through the children's existing families. Thus, as Eldering (1990/91, p. 58) has noted, "focusing on the effects of a program on children and at the same time blaming the parents for the educational arrears of their children, without studying how to change attitudes and parental behavior, reflects a short-sighted view in policy, in research, and in public debate."

In the first sections, I present a set of alternative theoretical conceptions of human development in context, ordered to some extent as a cumulative progression of insights. Each successive model transcends some of the limitations of its predecessor, while incorporating some of its strengths. Piagetian and Information Processing theories describe the complex and constructive nature of representation in ways that enrich our understanding of cognitive development beyond the scope of conditioning and differentiation theories. Theories of context as a system incorporating the developing individual capture a wider range of environmental processes than those identified in theories of context as external stimulation. By doing so, they do not necessarily invalidate microlevel accounts of how the developing child explores and represents the world, but they heighten our awareness of the sociocultural and historical parameters that constrain and complicate the long-term consequences of any single, planned intervention. Finally, theories that focus on the system of meanings woven into the sociocultural context link back with the constructive nature of representation to make it clear that the system is open to deliberate change by its participants, albeit only gradually, and often with great difficulty.

Then I discuss some of the implications of these theories for the early development of literacy and the design of educational interventions to promote it. In the final section I review the exemplary programs described elsewhere in this volume and consider the extent to which they have incorporated these theoretical principles.

CONTEXT AS EXTERNAL STIMULATION

The taxonomy of theoretical conceptualizations presented in Table 3-1 first divides the field broadly into those theories that treat context as a form of external stimulation and those that treat it as an incorporating system.[1] Each of the models I will discuss postulates one or more particular dimensions along which human behavior or cognition develops, and advances a corresponding formulation of the interaction between cognitive development and its context. A classic interpretation in the first of these traditions is Waddington's metaphor of the landscape which the developing organism must navigate in order to achieve development as progress (McCall, 1981). This image has given rise to the notion of "canalization," where biological constraints in certain phases of ontogenesis are said—like the banks of a canal in which the rolling-ball organism could get trapped—to restrict the range of behavioral changes that can be induced by contextual variation. This, and other spatial elaborations of the landscape metaphor, are powerful interpretive constructs and also strangely unidirectional, in that the organism merely rolls over the terrain with its direction of progress getting steered by the inclines, bumps, and gullies, without any kind of interactional negotiation.

Behaviorists in the tradition of Skinner (1953) have focused in particular on the concept of "reinforcement contingencies": positive or negative consequences of a given behavior that increase or reduce the probability of that behavior recurring in the future. The interactive process through which these contingencies are said to influence the pattern of development is sometimes called "shaping" the organism's behavior, resulting in a "fit" between the individual's behavioral dispositions and the demands of the environment. An elaboration of this perspective by Bandura (1977) adds "imitation" to the list of interactive processes, and generates the concept of "mastery" of target

Table 3-1. Theoretical Models and Metaphors

Nature of Context	Modes of Interaction	Dimensions of Development
External Stimulation		
Reinforcement Contingencies	Shaping Imitation	Fit Mastery
Information: terrain, objects, behavior of others (speech, etc.)	Affordance	Differentiation
Physical world (laws of natural science: social conventions, laws, etc.)	Exploration Representation Schematization Construction Encoding	Adaptation Comprehension Equilibration Reorganization Efficiency Automatization Metacognition
Incorporating System of Social Activity		
	Socialization	Integration
Routines	Guided Participation	Repertoire expansion
Practices (x technology)	Apprenticeship	Role change Legitimation Centralization
Institutions		Incorporation
Incorportating System of Cultural Meaning		
Symbolism	Internalization	Competence
Language (grammar, lexicon, pragmatics)	Intersubjectivity Negotiation	Participatory Enculturation
	Co-construction Discourse	Appropriation
Technology	Goal formation	Appropriation

Source: Adapted from L. Eldering & P. Leseman (1993), Early intervention and culture, UNESCO, Paris. By permission of the editors.

behaviors or skills as a developmental outcome. The organism, according to these closely allied perspectives, emits behavior spontaneously and over the course of development comes increasingly under the control of external contingencies. Interpretations of children's development with these biological and behaviorist models tend to eschew the notion of intentionality. This simplifying assumption is sometimes acceptable to caregivers of very young or seriously impaired children, but tends to be counterintuitive for those who are able to communicate verbally with the child as a person.

According to James Gibson (1979) and Eleanor Gibson (1982), context is characterized by information that is apprehended by the organism in terms of "affordances": stimulus features that are functionally related to various aspects of the organism's behavioral repertoire. Long before they learn analytically to describe the appearances of objects in terms of shape, color, and size, children perceive an object in terms of what potential actions it affords, such as grasping it, crawling under it, walking over it, etc. Development takes the form of increasing sensitivity to this information in the environment regarding the interactive potential of objects, of terrain, of the behavior of others (including their speech), and so on. These phenomena are initially apprehended in a relatively global manner, and through development become increasingly "differentiated" in the individual's perception of the world.

Perhaps the most influential of all developmental theories has been Piaget's (1971) genetic epistemology. The context of development in Piaget's theory is principally conceived as a physical world (governed by laws of natural science) with which the organism interacts by exploration, resulting in progressively fine-tuned adaptation, although it also includes a social world governed by societal conventions and laws. A particularly important theoretical construct in Piaget's theory that sets it apart from the others discussed so far is the interactive process called "representation," which first appears in the course of normal development toward the end of the first year of life. Representation generates a new layer of cognition beyond that which is characterized by sensori-motor interaction with the physical world, and this makes possible more abstract and powerful forms of comprehension, including those mediated through language. Neisser (1976) has advanced a synthesis of the ideas of Gibson and Piaget, focusing on the construct of a "schema," which plays an important part in Piaget's account of how representation occurs as well as featuring prominently in cognitive theories of memory (Bartlett, 1932). A schema is a preliminary, imprecise, selective analogue to a phenomenon in the real world, and Neisser suggests that it serves to guide the organism's exploratory search of the physical world. The search generates information that must eventually be incorporated (or, as Piaget would say, "assimilated") in a revision of the schema before it is used again in the "perceptual cycle" to guide further exploration.

Whereas Gibson stressed the process of differentiation as the key to increasing understanding of the world, Piaget argued that the child must construct a representation and then test it against reality. This testing forces the child to make adjustments (or "accomodations") to her schematic representations of the world, which in turn imply further adjustments to other parts of the child's overall understanding. A higher order process driving development is thus termed "equilibration," which generates increasingly abstract and general explanatory constructs to cover consistently all aspects of the child's experience.

The most recent cohort of developmental theories to focus primarily on a view of context as external stimulation from the physical world are known as Information Processing theories (Siegler, 1991). The basic interactive process in these theories is termed "encoding," a computer-processing metaphor for the topic addressed by the concepts of representation and schematization discussed above. The developmental outcome is some form of reorganization of the information stored in a coded form in the mind (or the brain). Developmental progress is construed in terms of the efficiency with which the mental organization permits the child to process information. One appealing account of how such efficiency is achieved is termed "automatization" (Sternberg, 1984), through which a complex series of cognitive operations becomes subsumed under a routine that can be performed as a whole without reflection. Another hypothesis about developmental progress that has featured prominently in the Information Processing tradition is that it involves increasing amounts of metacognitive awareness and skill, with the child becoming able to think and talk about her own mental processes such as attention and memory and to plan strategically how to optimize their deployment (Flavell, 1979).

A vast body of detailed, empirical research on cognitive development has been conducted within one or other of the theoretical frameworks outlined above. Yet the applicability of its findings to intervention programs working with and through children's families is seriously constrained by the artificiality of the social and/or physical arrangements under which the research was undertaken. Until quite recently, many laboratories achieved their control over extraneous variables by recourse to procedures that are ecologically unrepresentative for most of the world's population (LCHC, 1983).

CONTEXT AS AN INCORPORATING SYSTEM

Another whole family of theories has been advanced, partly in reaction to this problem of ecological validity, and partly to correct an excessive emphasis on properties of the physical world as defining the context of child development. These theories conceptualize the context of child development as an incorporating system of social activity (Bronfenbrenner, 1979). The interaction between the organism and context is construed as a process of socialization, whose developmental outcome is some form of integration into the social system. The structure of the context according to such theories comprises sociocultural "routines," "practices," and "institutions," which are organized in a series of nested layers comprising microsystems of social relationships within mesosystems (such as families, schools, and neighborhoods), which in turn are circumscribed by macrosystemic factors (such as administrative bureaucracies, governmental policies, and cultural ideologies).

Routines include recurrent ways of interacting for social purposes, such as greeting, scolding, or testing a child's incipient command of language (Peters & Boggs, 1986). The developing child may be said to interact with this contextual structure through the process of guided participation (Rogoff, 1990), resulting in a gradual expansion of her behavioral repertoire. At a somewhat larger scale of analysis, more immediately accessible to an indigenous informant, a social system is structured in terms of culturally specific practices, in which the developing child participates in ways that are both "legitimate" and yet "peripheral" (Lave & Wenger, 1991), for example, when a young child is helping a parent to bake a cake, or to service the family car. One metaphor for the developmental changes over time in the forms of such participation is "apprenticeship" (Rogoff, 1990). According to this theoretical perspective, the transition of a child who graduates from the status of novice to that of expert is defined not so much in terms of what she knows about a particular domain (and the elaboration of the individual's cognitive repertoire) as in terms of her changing social role in the activity, which becomes more legitimate and more central.

The practice perspective on development (Goodnow, Miller, & Kessel, 1995) also acknowledges the socially organized and historically accumulated structure of technology. Thus, Scribner and Cole (1981) argue that the acquisition of literacy cannot be understood exclusively in terms of perceptual and linguistic processes mediating the "extraction of meaning from print" (Gibson & Levin, 1975). It also requires an account of the social purposes for which the practices of writing and reading are undertaken by literate members of the society into which the aspiring initiate is being socialized. Even in a single society, becoming literate can entail quite different patterns of skill depending on the particular form of the practice. This notion has been elaborated in a productive way for sociocultural variations in the kinds of emergent literacy that children bring to school from their home environments in the United States (Heath, 1983). At a still higher-order level, social practices are organized by institutional factors, and the developmental outcome of social participation may be construed as incorporation into the life of the institutions. Thus in most contemporary, industrialized societies, the course of child development includes incorporation into the structure of a succession of educational institutions as a student at various levels of schooling. From this perspective, the individual's developmental status is indexed by such institutional markers as age-for-grade, completion of the mandated curriculum (versus dropping out), or the type and level of post-basic educational credentials attained (e.g., technical/academic, two-year/four-year college degree, master's/doctoral degree; etc.). The relatively unschooled person is thus socially stigmatized as developmentally incomplete (Serpell, 1993a).

An influential formulation that sets out to integrate the notion of context of child development as a social system with conceptions in terms of external stimulation is Super and Harkness's (1986) concept of the developmental niche: an integrated eco-sociocultural system to which a child is expected to adapt in the course of development. They distinguish three components of the niche: (1) "the physical and social settings in which the child lives;" (2) "customs of child care and child rearing" (which would feature in the present taxonomy as cultural practices), and (3) "the psychology of the caretakers," or ethnotheories of caregiving (Harkness & Super, 1992, this volume; Serpell et al., 1997), that is to say, the implicit theoretical ideas that inform the decisions made by those responsible for the care and upbringing of children in a given sociocultural group.

This last component illustrates a distinct subtheme among the theoretical perspectives on context as an incorporating system, where the focus is on the system of cultural meanings relating to child development that are shared among the participants in a sociocultural system. The idea that culture is best understood as a meaning-system has been elaborated in a variety of forms (D'Andrade, 1984; Quinn & Holland, 1987). One of the consequences is that the structure of the context of child development includes the symbolism distinctive to a particular culture. One version of cultural psychology construes all human action as informed by intentions and directed at mental representations (Shweder, 1990). It is these representations that constitute as forms of life in which humans participate, and through their participation the forms of life are constantly undergoing change. Representations are also embodied in various, relatively enduring, elements of culture that are passed on from one generation to the next (institutions, practices, artifacts, technologies, art-forms, texts, and modes of discourse). The interaction of the developing child with this system of meanings has been conceptualized as "internalization" (Vygotsky, 1978; Wertsch, 1985) eventuating in competence, and as "negotiation" (Ochs, 1990), or co-construction (Valsiner, 1991; Zukow, 1989) leading to participatory enculturation.

In the domain of language, an influential account of the earliest stages centers on the concept of "intersubjectivity" (Bruner, 1990; Trevarthen, 1980) that lays the groundwork, even before the ontogenetic appearance of speech, for the pragmatics of discourse, through which so much of human culture is appropriated.

Conceiving the outcome of development as appropriation combines the notion of intergenerational transmission with that of active participation by the child in her own enculturation, and also highlights the subjective sense of ownership that undergirds claims of authenticity by cultural insiders (Serpell, 1993b). In the case of mathematics, the process through which this appropriation of an inherited technology is achieved has been described as the emergence of goals in the course of participation in practices and the construction of strategies for attaining those goals involving the adaptation of preexisting form-function relationships (Saxe, 1991). To the extent that the child perceives the goals of a given task as factitious and/or imposed by others, rather than emerging from her own spontaneous activity, the educational process may be regarded as inauthentic and unlikely to engage intrinsic motivation. This argument lies at the root of a growing movement in educational circles to ground education in activities that resonate with the cultural meaning-system of the child's home environment (Tharp, 1989).

LANGUAGE DEVELOPMENT AND EMERGENT LITERACY

One important source of complexity in the analysis of context as an incorporating system of cultural meaning arises from the sociolinguistic phenomena of multilingualism (see also Verhoeven, this volume). In many societies around the world, children routinely grow up learning more than one distinct variety of language within the home setting. When two or more linguistic varieties coexist within a single, integrated social system, certain patterns of organization regularly recur. At the societal level, some form of stratification tends to occur among various domains of discourse with a particular variety preferred for each domain. At the level of the individual, selection of which variety to deploy is governed by a complex set of criteria that include not only the presumed linguistic competence of the persons addressed but also the social connotations of using a particular variety for a particular topic in a particular context (Gumperz, 1982; Ochs, 1990). Moreover, this patterning of code selection is closely related to the subtle differentiation of genres and registers of speech that have been documented in so-called "monolinguistic" speech communities (Halliday, 1975). One area of emerging consensus is that the conditions of social organization under which a child encounters different varieties of language can exercise a crucial influence on the success with which she or he masters each of them (Riegel & Freedle, 1976).

The growing competence of a child to express meaning and communicate with others is judged in most contemporary societies with reference to both oral language and literacy. Many school curricula display a preoccupation with children's mastery of various formal aspects of language and script, such as grammar, vocabulary, decoding, and spelling. Yet, as Snow (this volume) explains, literacy involves much more than this. Indeed, many educators think of it as a kind of torch that empowers the mind with enlightenment and liberates it from ignorance (Serpell & Hatano, 1997). Many researchers have sought to identify the crucial parameters of this process with a view to including them in the design of educational intervention.

A valuable line of theory for relating preliterate aspects of linguistic competence to the early stages of acquisition of literacy centers on the capacity to construct narrative. Peggy Miller and her colleagues (1987, 1990) have documented a variety of ways in which adult caregivers communicate cultural norms to young children through narrative. And Heath (1983) has argued that subcultural variations in the preferred forms of narrative have a major impact on the relative ease with which they cope with the demands of the early school curriculum. In contemporary middle-class Western societies, this cognitive resource is instantiated in a widespread cultural practice of adults reading storybooks to and with their children, beginning well before they are enrolled in school. Considerable research has been addressed to the developmental potential of this practice, as an opportunity for generating expansion of the child's behavioral repertoire and competence in the symbolic system of the culture, as well as a form of specific orientation toward the demands of a literate school curriculum (Sulzby & Teale, 1991; Wells, 1986).

The activity of joint storybook reading can be conceptualized as guided participation of the child in a routine that gives rise to a process of co-constructive enculturation. The ways in which this and other culturally packaged routines are used by parents to structure their child's home experiences in the preschool years appears to influence the pattern of the child's emergent literacy. In our longitudinal study in Baltimore, we found that families varied with regard to the relative emphasis they placed on three complementary cultural themes in contemporary Western society about the nature of literacy: that it is a source of entertainment, a set of skills to be deliberately cultivated, and an integral ingredient of everyday life. Middle-income families tended to place greater emphasis on the entertainment theme, and across both these and lower-income families of African American and European American ethnicity, children in whose niche greater emphasis was placed on the entertainment theme performed at a higher level on several measures of emergent literacy (Baker et al., 1996).

For Snow (this volume), like Bernstein (1970), Goody (1977), and Olson (1994), the distinctive character of written language arises from its capacity to communicate with distant audiences without the use of verbal or paralinguistic interaction to negotiate a shared understanding of context. Explicitness of verbal reference thus holds a privileged status in the production and interpretation of written texts. Patterns of oral communication that cultivate this style of discourse are therefore deemed to afford optimal opportunities for early literacy development: these include certain types of communicative activity, such as extended narrative, dramatization, and problem-solving discussion. Snow further contends that the impact of these activities on literacy development is mediated by the mastery of "certain formal aspects of the language system," including verb tenses, aspects and moods, specialized vocabulary, and relational connectives.

Substantial empirical evidence has accumulated to substantiate the influence on literacy development in Western societies of certain types of discourse in children's home and school experience (Leseman, this volume; Snow, this volume; Wells, 1986). However, the theoretical grounding of this research is open to question in light of the extraordinary diversity of cultural practices associated with both language socialization (Schieffelin & Ochs, 1986) and literacy (Serpell & Hatano, 1997) across the full gamut of human societies. Thus, while joint storybook reading and dinnertime conversation may hold significant power to enculturate children into the mainstream of American literacy, their potential as mechanisms for cultivating literacy, let alone generating cognitive enlightenment, may be critically constrained by the contextual peculiarities of that particular cultural system.

In an intervention study, Goldenberg, Reese, and Gallimore (1992) attempted to generate cultural practices within low-income Hispanic families in California that would be conducive to the cultivation of early literacy development. In this study, first-grade children were sent home with a set of Spanish-medium storybooks (libros) designed to be read as entertaining literature. Observations suggested that these *libros* were used in a more formally didactic manner than the researchers had intended, and parents expressed a preference for more skills-oriented workbooks over the storybooks. Nevertheless, the group of children assigned *libros* (who also read these storybooks at school) achieved greater progress in school literacy than those assigned workbooks. The mixed results of this attempt to engineer cultural change pose a complex challenge for intervention policy: under what circumstances is it appropriate to prescribe new cultural practices for "other people's children"? (Delpit, 1988; cf., Thompson, Mixon, & Serpell, 1996.)

INSTRUCTIONAL APPLICATIONS

In the field of emergent literacy, the theoretical ideas of Vygotsky (1978) have been influential not only at the level of conceptualizing the historical and sociocultural parameters of literacy as a cultural resource, but also for the microlevel analysis of instructional processes (Cole, 1985). The zone of proximal development ("zpd," or "zoped") is defined as the range of behaviors in a developmental sequence that lie within the competence of an individual to perform with assistance, and which are likely soon to come within the individual's competence for unassisted performance. One very general instructional principle that has been derived from the concept of the zoped is the need for the teacher to adjust her instructional interventions dynamically to the evolving competence of each individual learner. Rather than categorizing the child's existing knowledge and skills and comparing them to a predetermined set of curricular outcomes, the most effective mode of instruction will involve "in-flight" decision-making about the optimal match between the learner's latest performance and the teacher's next intervention.

Tharp and Gallimore (1988) have articulated a number of ways in which a teacher can be prepared for this demanding pattern of individualized and contextually-sensitive instruction. The general approach is for the teacher and student to engage in an "instructional conversation," in which the teacher seeks to weave new information into the student's existing mental structures. A concrete example is the "experience-text-relationship" method for teaching reading: the teacher first assists the child to prepare her existing relevant systems of understanding grounded in prior experience, next explains the structure of the information in the text, and then focuses on bringing the child's prior experience and the present text into a relationship, weaving them into the meaning of the ongoing educational discourse.

Other strategic constructs that have featured in the literature emanating from this theoretical perspective are scaffolding (Wood, Bruner, & Ross, 1976) and prolepsis (Stone, 1993), techniques designed to support and extend the child's cognitive activity within her zone of proximal development.

In the preschool period, Klein and her colleagues (Klein & Alony, 1993) have articulated a mediational approach to quality teaching that involves five serially organized phases: focusing a reciprocal awareness of intentionality; arousing an affective appreciation of meaning; expanding the child's cognitive awareness beyond the satisfaction of immediate needs; rewarding specific components of the child's behavior with a view to generating feelings of competence; and mediated regulation, designed to establish a correspondence between the child's conscious interests and the requirements of a task.

Because of the discipline's organismic preoccupations, educational applications of theories from developmental psychology tend to focus on pedagogical process: the sequence of steps into which instruction is segmented is organized in terms of how a learner can grow. In practice, this processual analysis needs to be mapped onto a curriculum structure for the presentation of a body of cultural knowledge.

THEORETICAL FOCUS IN THE DESIGN OF INTERVENTION PROGRAMS

In the preceding paragraphs, I have sketched a number of different theoretical perspectives on the context of human development, the dimensions along which we should evaluate the outcomes of development, and the processes of interaction between the developing child and context that generate development. Early childhood intervention programs are an attempt to modify the context with a view to enhancing the course of development. Thus, theory should in principle be helpful in deciding what kind of contextual modification is most appropriate for achieving the desired developmental outcomes. In practice, however, early education programs in the real world tend to deviate in a number of ways from the precise implications of any one of the theoretical models presented above. In this section I will discuss several different lines of reasoning about such deviations, under the following headings:

- Incomplete or eclectic assimilation of theory into practice

- Organizational adaptability as a pragmatic requirement of going to scale

- Multiple goals as a reflection of systemic interdependency

I will illustrate my analysis with reference to the four exemplary programs presented elsewhere in this volume: Home Intervention Project for Preschool Youngsters (HIPPY), Success for All (SFA), Turkish Early Enrichment Project (TEEP), and Integrated Child Development Services (ICDS).

Incomplete or Eclectic Assimilation of Theory into Practice

The insights of Piagetian, Information Processing, and neo-Vygotskyan theories about the nature of cognitive processing have been incompletely assimilated into the pedagogical practices of many schools and preschools. For instance, Muralidharan and Kaul (this volume) state that in India the curriculum advocated for the preschool education component of Integrated Child Development Services rests on a "progressive" theoretical framework, influenced by Piaget, with "a visible emphasis on cognitive stimulation and active learning through concrete experiences," aiming to promote a wide range of dimensions of development that include the notions of comprehension, repertoire expansion, and role change. Yet the evaluation and impact studies of ICDS that they cite focus on mastery of skills that are firmly grounded in the school curriculum (rote counting, color identification and naming, and crayon manipulation), and on behavioral fit (school adjustment, and improving retention in Grades One and Two). Moreover, they note that many Anganwadis are succumbing to parental or community pressures to concentrate on direct instruction of the "Three Rs (reading, 'riting, 'rithmetic)."

In the case of Success for All, the main criteria for evaluation presented by Slavin and Madden (this volume) are "reading performance outcomes" on standardized tests, reflecting the focus of the program on "direct instruction." The content of the reading program, however, includes not only teaching for mastery of letter sounds, decoding, and vocabulary, but also participatory opportunities for cooperative learning designed to expand the child's repertoire of metacognitive strategies such as prediction and summarization, and fostering the appropriation of a cultural meaning-system through engagement in joint storybook reading and story-related writing. These higher-order aspects of emergent literacy may well be more predictive of the longer-term significance of formal education in the children's lives than the more tangible indices of scholastic achievement emphasized in most formal systems of school accountability.

How should we interpret such ambiguities? Do they reflect an unrealistic desire to "have one's cake and eat it too," by rhetorically acknowledging several prestigious sources of ideas without addressing the possibility of internal inconsistencies? Educational programming in the real world tends to be heavily influenced by implicit institutional constraints and by explicit demands for accountability to particular constituencies. Rather than basing their decisions on formal scientific reasoning, program managers may often be tempted to invoke theoretical ideas eclectically to support their commitments to pragmatic and political goals. Or does the incomplete match between theory and practice arise from a type of explanatory insight more readily available to service practitioners than to academic researchers, concerning the multifaceted nature of real-world problems?

The integrated design of SFA reflects a pragmatic approach that concurrently focuses several, theoretically distinct strategies on the children. This is arguably the most ethically responsible approach, since it leaves no stone unturned in its commitment to helping the children. From the standpoint of empirical research, however, this composite, multimethod strategy makes it hard to evaluate what the key to its effectiveness is, or conversely, to identify areas that need improvement. As Slavin and Madden (this volume) point out, rigorous assessments of the impact of an early interaction program over a substantial number of cohorts are very rare. The consistency with which gains were documented for SFA thus provides unusually impressive evidence of resilience of the program. However, this should not blind us to the fact that the gains reported are quite modest (about half of one standard deviation, or half a grade level) and differ, by their own account, very little from those of a theoretically quite different type of interaction, Reading Recovery.

Organizational Adaptability as a Pragmatic Requirement of Going to Scale

Educational programs such as HIPPY and SFA are often conceptualized as a kind of blueprint for social action, analogous to the engineering drawing that guides the construction of a bridge, an idealized model whose impact in the real world will depend on accurate implementation of its every detail. The various elements of the program are organized in a hierarchically ordered conceptual framework. At the top of the list, the curriculum and materials define the core, or essence, of the program. Next, issues such as personnel training feature as subsidiary factors necessary to ensure efficient delivery of the program, followed by the recruitment of participants necessary for targeting appropriate program beneficiaries. Finally, at the bottom of the list come the administrative arrangements for coordination and publicity. Even when issues lower on the list are identified by evaluators as critical to the impact of the program, their influence tends to be interpreted in common-sense, rather than theoretical, terms, as if they were somehow extraneous to the essential activity of education which centers on the interaction of an isolated individual with specific stimuli. For instance, HIPPY (the Home Intervention Program for Preschool Youngsters) is conceptualized by Kağıtçıbaşı (this volume) as the "cognitive training" component of the Turkish Early Enrichment Project. Explicit procedures were taught via programmed instruction to the children's mothers, to whom responsibility was delegated for implementing a prestructured pattern of stimulation of the child. Likewise, in the Dutch case presented by Eldering and Vedder (this volume), implementation of HIPPY is analyzed as a process in which paraprofessionals first familiarize mothers with a curriculum structured in terms of weekly materials and activities, and then monitor the progress of mother and child through the program.

Yet, as Korten (1980) has explained, in order for a social intervention program to "go to scale" (Myers, 1992) from a pilot project to a general cultural practice sustained by public policy, it is seldom effective to push for implementation of an idealized blueprint. Widespread appropriation of a programmatic concept is more likely to come about through a gradual "learning process approach." This calls for "organizations with a well-developed capacity for responsive and anticipatory adaptation—organizations that (a) embrace error; (b) plan with the people; and (c) link knowledge building with action." (Myers, 1992, p. 498). It may be that social scientists can best facilitate such a complex process by encouraging flexible adaptation of theoretical constructs. Certainly, going to scale without sacrificing the focus of educational innovations requires engineering a supportive administrative environment. The practical value of bringing administrative procedures into harmony with educational goals may give rise to the confounding of variables in ways that pose a difficult challenge for analytical research.

For instance, Slavin and Madden (this volume) place considerable emphasis on the fact that SFA is particularly effective with the lower achieving quartile of students, supposedly preventing them from being relegated to special education streams. Yet, as they acknowledge, there are two components to this effect: raising the level of attainment of these children, and deterring administrators from special educational placement decisions. Since the guiding philosophy of SFA includes a strenuous determination to prevent special education placement, it is difficult to interpret this aspect of the program's claims to effectiveness. Is it principally a matter of consistent implementation of policy, or is there a real impact on the cognitive development of the children in question? Consistent with its pragmatic and politically committed orientation, the program assigns the most qualified tutors to the children with the most conspicuous initial difficulties. This deliberately differential distribution of what the evaluation shows to be one of its most powerful resources (one-on-one tutoring) may partly explain the relatively greater benefits derived from the program by the lowest-achieving students.

Multiple Goals as a Reflection of Systemic Interdependency

One of the consequences of adopting a systemic theoretical perspective on context and its interaction with development is to enhance the salience of factors that might otherwise be construed as extraneous, incidental features of implementation. The developmental outcomes on which attention is focused involve social relations, and the processes conducive to their attainment require mutual understanding among students, teachers and other agents of socialization. Cognitive competence is thus defined in relation to the full range of contextual factors that constitute the practice.

An independent evaluation of SFA by Smith, Ross, and Casey (1996) found some confirmatory evidence that the program "can typically be replicated successfully at distant locations from and with monitoring by, the program developers" (p. 351). But their results were "not as strong and consistent as those obtained in the original series of SFA evaluations performed by the developers" (p. 351). One of the future lines of research suggested by these evaluators is to broaden the systemic conceptualization of outcomes, situating them relative to sociocultural context, and to examine the impact of SFA on "broader definitions of literacy" (p. 351), including not only variables such as listening comprehension, writing, and self-perception as a reader, but also dimensions of social participation such as use of libraries; writing to the newspaper; and joining recreational, religious, or political associations that conduct much of their business in writing.

The cross-national analysis by Eldering and Vedder (this volume) clearly illustrates the fact that what are nominally two cases of "the same program" may in reality be very different given the details of their sociocultural instantiation. In the Turkish case (TEEP) described by

Kağıtçıbaşı (this volume), factory-worker mothers were given time off at the factory to meet in groups and discuss in their indigenous language how to apply the HIPPY routines with their children in preparation for a national, Turkish-medium school curriculum. In the Netherlands, Turkish immigrant housewife mothers were visited at home by a fellow-Turkish immigrant paraprofessional who presented in Turkish the HIPPY routines as "self-explanatory." But the children were being prepared for enrollment in a Dutch-medium school curriculum. Even when depicted in such broad strokes, the different significance of the linguistic medium of early education is immediately apparent. Furthermore, a major index of the efficacy of HIPPY in Kağıtçıbaşı's study was the degree to which children enrolled in the program later stayed on in school beyond the age of 11. This behavior holds quite different significance in the two societies. In the Netherlands, a full secondary education is available and compulsory for all children. Turkey, on the other hand, shares with many parts of the Third World the phenomenon that a large proportion of students, especially girls, leave school after only a few years of schooling, a topic that is beset with economic and political complexities. Sadly, many students who withdraw prematurely from schools in these societies do so believing that they have failed due to inadequacies of their own intellect, although there are good reasons to believe that their cognitive mismatch with the curriculum is confined to relatively specific task demands (Serpell, 1993a).

The nested organization of systems of social activity (families and schools, within neighborhoods and districts, within nations and their public policies) and the relativity of symbolic meanings to particular cultural frameworks of interpretation (narratives; curricula; and ideologies of work and play, gender roles, intergenerational relations, etc.) demand that the impact of an enterprise as complex as an early education program be appraised quite differently in each particular sociocultural setting. The first step of such an appraisal, as Eldering and Vedder note, should be to specify the goals of the intervention. Their list of alternative dependent variables illustrates the wide range of possible, positive outcomes of early education programs—school readiness, the child's intellectual development, family empowerment, or quality of cooperation between parents. From the perspective of theoretical formulations of the type schematized in the top half of Table 3-1, family empowerment and cooperation among families might plausibly be construed as "extraneous" variables, perhaps supportive of, but not intrinsic to, the developmental goals of intervention. However, from the type of perspective represented in the lower part of the table, where the child's development is conceptualized as a progressive integration within an system of social relations and appropriation of a system of cultural meanings, such sociocultural processes appear more central to the explicit goals of intervention.

One possible articulation of the interrelations among social and cognitive processes is the "virtuous circle" of mutually sustaining interactions among children, parents, and teachers, postulated by Schweinhart, Weikart, and their colleagues, cited by Kağıtçıbaşı (this volume). These authors' long-term follow-up studies of High/Scope Perry Preschool Project in the United States have found that children enrolled in the program grow up with a strong commitment to schooling and an enduring positive valuation of education, as well as manifesting positive social adjustment to institutions (such as school, family, and law), even when there is little or no evidence of enhancement of their cognitive capacity (as indexed by IQ). These findings are consistent with the enhanced self-esteem and persistence in school among graduates of the TEEP program in Turkey. The concept of systemic interdependency embraces such phenomena as indicative of successful intervention.

This more systemic perspective has important methodological implications for the design of educational intervention programs. Rather than conceiving of parents as strategically placed agents to whom the implementation of a prestructured program of external stimulation can be assigned by a simple administrative act of delegation, the context is construed as a system with its own internal principles of organization whose adult members need to be recruited as voluntary participants in the reorganization of their community— adopting new practices, establishing new institutions, and in the process generating new systems of meanings to inform, justify, and sustain their collective changes in behavior.

This dimension of context is more explicitly acknowledged in Kağıtçıbaşı's (this volume) account of TEEP than in the accounts of ICDS, SFA, and the Netherlands application of HIPPY. The "holistic view of the child and the mother" favored by the ICDS involves recognizing "the importance of maternal well-being for the healthy development of the children," but no intrinsic connection is articulated between the mother's beliefs and intentions and the developmental agenda set for the child. "Community participation and involvement before the scheme is launched" is advocated as a means of ensuring local material support, rather than a philosophically essential condition for the viability of the enterprise of intervention. In SFA, a Family Support Team seeks "to make families comfortable in the school," and "trains the parents to fulfill numerous volunteer roles within the school." But the examples cited are relatively peripheral to the educational process: "providing a listening ear to emerging readers," and "helping in the school cafeteria."

In the Netherlands' application of HIPPY, periodic group meetings were held to "enable mothers to share their experience with the program and their problems, to learn the experience of others, and to internalize through active discussion some of the program's objectives." In TEEP, this component of the intervention was conceived as "mother enrichment." Group discussion sessions were aimed at "empowerment of the mothers in coping with problems and attending to their children's needs," through a combination of reinforcing indigenous cultural values such as "close-knit family ties" and "relatedness values," and promoting a new element of child rearing, namely, the cultivation of autonomy. Many of the attitudinal changes reported as outcomes seem attributable to a set of systemic interdependencies among parental and child values, aspirations, and practices. Parents' expectations of educational attainment for their child became more ambitious, children stayed on in school longer and perceived their mothers as having been more supportive, and mothers looked more favorably on their adolescent child's social integration.

CONCLUSION

The differences of focus that I have cited among the four exemplary programs partly reflect differences in their historical evolution, which gave rise to variations in the order of priorities among the various levels at which operational issues are formulated. For instance, each of the programs eventually aspires to influence a large number of children at many different sites. But the massive scale of ICDS was an initial premise, whereas replication and diffusion are perceived as a second phase of program development for HIPPY and SFA.

Some laboratory scientists are currently impressed by the biological constraints on human development, and point to genetic engineering as an emergent source of new intervention technology. Many economic development theorists are preoccupied with external

62   *Robert Serpell*

constraints imposed by variations in the material environment, and emphasize the elimination of environmental deprivation as the key to intervention strategy. Yet many case studies of outstandingly perceptive, creative, and compassionate persons who developed against a background of very adverse conditions attest to the extraordinary plasticity and resilience of human development. Moreover, both the genetic and economic perspectives tend to pay insufficient attention to the essential purposiveness of human behavior.

Educational intervention is rooted in philosophical optimism about the capacity of humans to ameliorate their condition. In order to construct an agenda responsive to this perspective, theoretical accounts of developmental context need to focus on processes of social participation. Coordination of many people in a joint endeavor calls for a set of common principles. If these are conceived mechanically and imposed from above, individual agents tend to become alienated from their roles in the system. Thus, in my view, the co-construction of goals in terms of a system of shared meanings provides an optimal entry point for the design of ameliorative programs of human development.

NOTES

1. In the interest of focus, I have omitted from the taxonomy theories that are primarily concerned with the development of personal identity. But I recognize that this may have deprived my analysis of certain valuable resources, such as the notions of thematic preoccupations and crises (Erikson, 1963).

REFERENCES

Baker, L. B., Sonnenschein, S., Serpell, R., Scher, D., Fernandez-Fein, S., Munsterman, K., Hill, S., Goddard-Truitt, V., & Danseco, E. (1996). Early literacy at home: children's experiences and parents' perspectives. *The Reading Teacher, 50* (1), 70–72.
Bandura, A. (1977). *Social learning theory.* Englewood Cliffs, NJ: Prentice Hall.
Bartlett, F. C. (1932). *Remembering.* Cambridge: Cambridge University Press.
Bernstein, B. (1970). *Class, codes and control, I.* London: Routledge & Kegan Paul.
Bronfenbrenner, U. (1979). *The ecology of human development.* Cambridge, MA: Harvard University Press.

Bruner, J. S. (1990). *Acts of meaning.* Cambridge, MA: Harvard University Press.

Cole, M. (1985). The zone of proximal development: Where culture and cognition create each other. In J. V. Wertsch (Ed.), *Culture, communication, and cognition: Vygotskian perspectives* (pp. 146–161). Cambridge: Cambridge University Press.

D'Andrade, R. (1984). Cultural meaning systems. In R. A. Shweder & R. Levine (Eds.), *Culture theory: Essays on mind, self and emotion.* Cambridge: Cambridge University Press.

Delpit, L. D. (1988). The silenced dialogue: Power and pedagogy in educating other people's children. *Harvard Educational Review, 58,* 280–298.

Eldering, L. (1990/91). Intervention programmes for preschoolers from immigrant families: The Dutch case. In N. Bleichrodt & P. J. D. Drenth (Eds.), *Contemporary issues in cross-cultural psychology* (pp. 50–63). Amsterdam: Swets & Zeitlinger.

Erikson, E. H. (1963). *Childhood and society.* New York: Norton.

Flavell, J. H. (1979). Metacognition and cognitive monitoring: A new area of cognitive-developmental inquiry. *American Psychologist, 34,* 906–911.

Gibson, J. J. (1979). *The ecological approach to visual perception.* Boston: Houghton-Mifflin.

Gibson, E. J. (1982). The concept of affordances: The renascence of functionalism. In A. Collins (Ed.), *The concept of development: The Minnesota Symposia on Child Development* (Vol. 15, pp. 55–81). Hillsdale, NJ: Erlbaum.

Gibson, E. J., & Levin, H. (1975). *The psychology of reading.* Cambridge, MA: MIT Press.

Goldenberg, C., Reese, L., & Gallimore, R. (1992). Effects of literacy materials from school on Latino children's home experiences and early reading achievement. *American Journal of Education, 100,* 497–536.

Goodnow, J. J., Miller, P., & Kessel, F. (Eds.).(1995). *Cultural practices as contexts for development.* San Francisco: Jossey-Bass.

Goody, J. (1977). *The domestication of the savage mind.* Cambridge: Cambridge University Press.

Gumperz, J. J. (1982). *Discourse strategies.* Cambridge: Cambridge University Press.

Halliday, M. A. K. (1975). *Learning how to mean: Explorations in the development of language.* London: Arnold.

Harkness, S., & Super, C. M. (1992). Parental ethnotheories in action. In E. E. Sigel, A. V. McGillicuddy-DeLisi, & J. J. Goodnow (Eds.), *Parental belief systems: The psychological consequences for children* (2nd ed., pp. 373–391). Hillsdale, NJ: Erlbaum.

Heath, S. B. (1983). *Ways with words.* Cambridge: Cambridge University Press.

Klein, P. S., & Alony, S. (1993). Immediate and sustained effects of maternal mediating behaviors on young children. *Journal of Early Intervention, 17,* 177–193.

Korten, D. (1980). Community organization and rural development: a learning process approach. *Public Administration Review, 40,* 480–511.

Lave, J., & Wenger, E. (1991). *Situated learning: legitimate peripheral participation.* Cambridge: Cambridge University Press.

LCHC (1983). Culture and cognitive development. In P. H. Mussen & W. Kessen (Eds.), *Handbook of child psychology, Vol 1: History, theory and methods.* New York: Wiley.

McCall, R. B. (1981). Nature-nurture and the two realms of development. *Child Development, 52,* 1–12.

McGuire, W. J. (1973). The Yin and Yang of progress in social psychology: Seven koan. *Journal of Personality and Social Psychology, 26(3),* 446–456.

Miller, P., Potts, R., Fung, H., & Hoogstra, L. (1990). Narrative practices and the social construction of self in childhood. *American Ethnologist, 17,* 292–311.

Miller, P., & Sperry, L. L. (1987). The socialization of anger and aggression. *Merrill-Palmer Quarterly, 33,* 1–31.

Myers, R. (1992). *The twelve who survive: Strengthening programs of early childhood development in the Third World.* London and New York: Routledge.

Neisser, U. (1976). *Cognition and reality.* San Francisco: Freeman.

Ochs, E., (1990). Indexicality and socialization. In J. W. Stigler, R. A. Shweder, & G. Herdt (Eds.), *Cultural Psychology.* Cambridge, MA: Harvard University Press.

Olson, D.R. (1994). *The world on paper.* Cambridge: Cambridge University Press.

Peters, A. M., & Boggs, S. T. (1986). Interactional routines as cultural influences upon language acquisition. In B. B. Schieffelin & E. Ochs (Eds.), *Language socialization across cultures.* Cambridge: Cambridge University Press.

Piaget, J. (1971). *The construction of reality in the child.* New York: Ballantine.

Quinn, N., & Holland, D. (1987). Culture and cognition. In D. Holland & N. Quinn (Eds.), *Cultural models in language and thought*. Cambridge: Cambridge University Press.

Riegel, K., & Freedle, R. (1976). What does it take to be bilingual or bidialectal? In D. S. Harrison & T. Trabasso (Eds.), *Black English: A seminar* (pp. 25–44). Hillsdale, NJ: Erlbaum.

Rogoff, B. (1990). *Apprenticeship in thinking*. New York: Oxford University Press.

Saxe, G. B. (1991). *Culture and cognitive development: Studies in mathematical understanding*. Hillsdale, NJ: Erlbaum.

Schieffelin, B. B., & Ochs, E. (Eds.). (1986). *Language socialization across cultures*. Cambridge: Cambridge University Press.

Scribner, S., & Cole, M. (1981). *The psychology of literacy*. Cambridge, MA: Harvard University Press.

Serpell, R. (1990). Audience, culture and psychological explanation: A reformulation of the emic-etic problem in cross-cultural psychology. *Quarterly Newsletter of the Laboratory Comparative Human Cognition, 12*(3), 99–132.

Serpell, R. (1993a). *The significance of schooling: Life-journeys in an African society*. Cambridge: Cambridge University Press.

Serpell, R. (1993b). Interface between socio-cultural and psychological aspects of cognition. In E. Forman, N. Minick, & A. Stone (Eds.), *Contexts for learning: sociocultural dynamics in children's development*. New York: Oxford University Press.

Serpell, R., & Hatano, G. (1997). Education, schooling, and literacy. In J. W. Berry, P. R. Dasen, & T. S. Saraswathi (Eds.), *Handbook of cross-cultural psychology,* (2nd ed., Vol. 2, pp. 345–382). Boston: Allyn & Bacon.

Serpell, R., Sonnenschein, S., Baker, L., Hill, S., Goddard-Truitt, V., & Danseco, E. (1997). *Parental ideas about development and socialization of children on the threshold of schooling*. National Reading Research Center Reading Research Report No. 78. Athens, GA: Universities of Maryland and Georgia.

Shweder, R. A. (1990). Cultural psychology: What is it? In J. W. Stigler, R. A. Shweder, & G. Herdt (Eds.), *Cultural psychology*. Cambridge: Cambridge University Press.

Siegler, R. (1991). *Children's thinking*. Englewood Cliffs, NJ: Prentice Hall.

Skinner, B. F. (1953). *Science and human behavior*. New York: Macmillan.

Smith, L. J., Ross, S. M., & Casey, J. (1996). Multi-site comparison of the effects of Success for All on reading achievement. *Journal of Literacy Research, 28* (3), 329–353.

Sternberg, R. J. (1984). Towards a triarchic theory of intelligence. *The Behavioral and Brain Sciences, 7*, 269–315.

Stone, A. (1993). What's wrong with the metaphor of scaffolding? In E. Forman, N. Minick, & A. Stone (Eds.), *Contexts for learning: Sociocultural dynamics in children's development*. New York: Oxford University Press.

Sulzby, E., & Teale, W. (1991). Emergent literacy. In R. Barr, M. L. Kamil, P. Mosenthal, & P. D. Pearson (Eds.), *Handbook of reading research* (Vol. 2, pp. 727–758). New York: Longman.

Super, C., & Harkness, S. (1986). The developmental niche: A conceptualization at the interface of child and culture. *International Journal of Behavioral Development, 9*(4), 545–569.

Tharp, R. G. (1989). Psychocultural variables and constraints: Effects on teaching and learning in schools. *American Psychologist, 44*, 349–359.

Tharp, R. G., & Gallimore, R. (1988). *Rousing minds to life: Teaching, learning, and schooling in social context*. New York: Cambridge University Press.

Thompson, R., Mixon, G., & Serpell, R. (1996). Engaging minority students in reading: focus on the urban learner. In L. Baker, P. Afflerbach, & D. Reinking (Eds.), *Developing engaged readers in school and home communities* (pp. 43–63). Mahwah, NJ: Erlbaum.

Trevarthen, C. (1980). The foundations of intersubjectivity: Development of interpersonal and cooperative understanding of infants. In D. R. Olson (Ed.), *The social foundations of language and thought: Essays in honour of Jerome S. Bruner*. (pp. 316–342). New York: Norton.

Valsiner, J. (1991). Social co-construction of psychological development from a comparative-cultural perspective. In J. Valsiner (Ed.), *Child development within culturally structured environments*, Vol. 3. Norwood, NJ: Ablex.

Vygotsky, L. (1978). *Mind in society: The development of higher psychological processes*. Cambridge, MA: Harvard University Press.

Wells, G. (1986) *The meaning makers: Children learning language and using language to learn*. Portsmouth, NH: Heineman.

Wertsch, J.V. (1985). *Vygotsky and the social formation of mind*. Cambridge, MA: Harvard University Press.

Wood, D., Bruner, J. S., & Ross, G. (1976). The role of tutoring in problem-solving. *Journal of Child Psychology and Psychiatry, 17*, 89–100.

Zukow, P. G. (1989). Siblings as effective socializing agents: Evidence from central Mexico. In P. G. Zukow (Ed.), *Sibling interaction across cultures: theoretical and methodological issues* (pp. 79–105). London: Springer-Verlag.

From Parents' Cultural Belief Systems to Behavior[1]

Sara Harkness and *Charles M. Super*

In recent years, there has been increasing recognition that much of children's learning and development takes place in the context of participation in culturally constituted practices. From sleeping and the regulation of state in infancy (Morelli, Rogoff, Oppenheim, & Goldsmith, 1992; Super et al., 1996), to early language acquisition through verbal routines (Harkness, 1988; Ochs & Schieffelin, 1984), to familiarization with literacy through the bedtime story in early childhood (Heath, 1986) and learning math through selling Girl Scout cookies in middle childhood (Rogoff, Baker-Sennett, Lacasa, & Goldsmith, 1995), children's participation in cultural practices is now recognized as forming both the medium and the substance of learning and development.

Inherent but rarely documented in this interactionist approach is a further recognition that children's culturally structured learning experiences are set within a larger framework of daily life that is also organized. Opportunities for child "novices" to interact with adult "experts" are influenced by individual characteristics such as the personality and educational background of caretakers, and by immediate physical aspects of the surroundings such as the type of dwelling the family lives in and the activity schedules of others who live there. But more generally, these opportunities are organized by the way that such factors interact with each other as a system. Furthermore, the organization of any particular aspect of a child's environment gains power insofar as it is replicated in a variety of different settings, such as school, community, and recreational settings. In order to understand the development effects of any one kind of learning experience, then, it is necessary to consider it not only in its *own* cultural context, but also as part of a larger system of culturally organized experience.

In this chapter, we present a theoretical framework, the "developmental niche," that has been formulated for studying the cultural structuring of children's environments (Harkness & Super, 1992; Super & Harkness, 1986). In our most recent work with this model, we have focused on the role of parents' cultural belief systems (or parental ethnotheories) as a component of the niche, and how these are represented in the ways that parents organize their children's everyday experience. We propose that understanding the role of parents' cultural belief systems and their relationship to behavior is a key to developing successful intervention programs to support children's literacy development in the early years of life.

CULTURE AND THE DEVELOPMENTAL NICHE

The concept of culture—central to the field of anthropology, and increasingly to the field of human development—may be the most controverted of any basic construct in the social sciences. "Culture" has been used to signify a wide range of different things, including place, context, a set of shared beliefs and practices, a basis for communication, and a set of internal representations. It has been conceptualized both as shared personal characteristics and as a system for the organization of diversity (Wallace, 1961). As a contextual feature that predicts individual behavior, it is logical to ask, as the Whitings did in the introduction to their landmark study *Children of Six Cultures*, "If you want to predict the behavior of a preadolescent child, which would it be most important to know: his or her sex, age, birth order, the culture into which he was born, or the situation he was in at the moment you made your prediction?" (Whiting & Whiting, 1975, p. 11). The answer may well be the "cultural place," as Weisner has suggested (Weisner, 1996). Likewise, cross-cultural research by Bornstein and his colleagues has demonstrated that reliable group differences in maternal behavior and child developmental measures in different countries can be found even when other "background" variables such as urbanization, education and occupation of parents are held constant (Bornstein et al., 1992).

Powerful though "culture" as an external, independent variable is for predicting individual behavior, however, there has been general agreement that the concept includes internal, cognitive, and affective dimensions as well. Thus, for example, the cultural anthropologist Clyde Kluckhohn wrote "the essential core of culture consists of traditional (i.e., historically derived) ideas, and especially their attached values" (Kluckhohn, 1945/1962, p. 73). For the Whitings, likewise, culture must be seen not just as a predictor variable, but rather as the shared symbolic determinants of behavior (Whiting & Whiting, 1960). Recognition of the internal, symbolic aspects of culture has led, in turn, to an interest in language and discourse as a medium of culture construction and transmission, in which cultural "messages" are conveyed and interpreted by individual participants. Miller and Hoogstra (1992, p. 84) have suggested that these processes are essential to children's learning of their cultures:

> Although cultures differ in the extent to which they privilege talk as a defining property of social life, it is probably safe to assume that talk is a pervasive, orderly, and culturally organized feature of social life in every culture . . . It follows from this premise that becoming culturally competent entails becoming a competent speaker. Because talk comes packaged with nontalk, several aspects of nontalk must be acquired along the way toward full participation in society. That is, children have to learn how to interweave nonverbal systems such as gesture, gaze, and paralanguage with the verbal. They have to learn when not to talk and how and when to listen. Also, and critically important, they need to learn to detect and interpret the unspoken assumptions that lie behind talk, requiring complex processes of social inferencing.

The idea of cultural "messages" that are communicated, perhaps renegotiated, internalized, and perhaps reconstructed has its own history (e.g., Goodnow, 1996; Mead, 1930/1966; Shweder, Jensen, & Goldstein, 1995). This perspective is vitally important for understanding culture change and individual variability within culturally defined groups. But the idea of "messages," in turn, requires a concept of the cognitive structures that are communicated, by whatever means. Cognitive anthropologists have introduced the term "cultural models" to signify these structures. As described by Quinn and Holland, cultural models are shared understandings that "frame experience, supplying interpretations of that experience and inferences about it, and goals for action" (Quinn & Holland, 1987, p. 6). As this definition implies, and as D'Andrade (1990; 1992) has argued, cultural models are important not only for representing the ways that things *are*, but why they are that way and how they *should* be. In essence, he suggests, cultural models are schemas that have motivational properties.

Although the ideas of culture as external context and culture as internal representations have been contrasted with each other, and have further been associated with a more general historical shift toward cognitive approaches across several behavioral sciences (D'Andrade, 1992), it seems clear that a variety of formulations continue to be useful. Further, although these various ideas of culture seem in some ways opposed to each other, they share a central assumption: the idea of systematicity. Culture, in all these views, is not a random collection of social settings, customary practices, or beliefs and values, but rather an organized and meaningful system. The fact that the system can be viewed in its external manifestations as well as investigated through its internal representations makes the idea of culture a complex construct, yet one that is necessary for analyzing human development in context.

The theoretical framework of the "developmental niche" draws from all these concepts of culture in order to understand processes of child development as they are interwoven with the child's acquisition of cultural knowledge (Super & Harkness, 1986). We conceptualize the developmental niche in terms of three major subsystems that operate together as a larger system, and each of which interacts conditionally with other features of the culture (see Figure 4-1). The first of these subsystems is constituted by the physical and social settings in which the child lives, including elements such as the size and composition of the household and daily routines of its members. Is the child born into a family with a mother, father, and one older sibling, or into a family that includes many siblings and half-siblings? Is the child cared for primarily by the mother for the first five years of life, or is the child herself a caretaker for a younger sibling by the time she reaches the age of 4 or 5? What kinds of activities engage the adults in the child's experienced world: weaving clothing for the family, planting and weeding crops, watching TV, or mowing the lawn? Is the child's day structured around a regular schedule of activities, meals, and rest, or does it vary depending on the differing activities of others?

Insofar as the behavior of parents and other caretakers is recurrent and meaningful to the participants, it represents the second component

The Developmental Niche

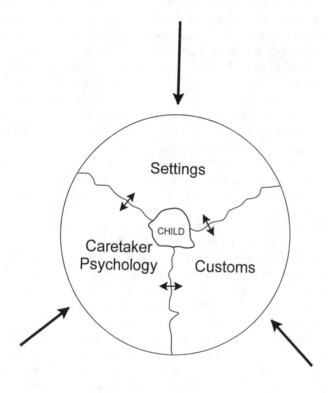

Figure 4.1. The developmental niche and its interacting systems.

of the niche, customs or practices of care. Such customs may or may not have explicitly recognized meanings for the caretakers; quite often, in fact, they are so commonly used by members of the community, and so thoroughly integrated into the larger culture, that they do not need individual rationalization and are not necessarily given conscious thought. Sleeping arrangements for infants are one example: although they vary radically across cultures, it is common for members of any given culture to assume that their own practices—whether co-sleeping with babies or use of a crib from the newborn period, for example—are the morally right and naturally mandated approach (Abbott, 1992; Morelli et al., 1992). Specific customs of care can also be organized into larger constellations, however, and in some cases these are labeled. One such example is the "three R's" of Dutch child rearing: *rust* (rest), *regelmaat* (regularity), and *reinheid* (cleanliness) (Super et al., 1996). For middle-class parents of young children in the town of Bloemenheim (a pseudonym), the Netherlands, whom we studied in 1992, the "three R's" were an important principle whose application the parents had themselves experienced in their childhood years, had carried over into the organization of adult life, and had heard further reinforced by health professionals in the universal well-baby clinics (*Consultatiebureaus*).

As is evident in the above examples, the developmental niche framework asserts that regularities in both the physical and social settings of daily life, and in customs or practices of care, carry cultural meanings that are evident to the growing child. But what is the origin of these systems? From the point of view of the child, the parents are an important source, as they mediate the child's experience of daily life through management of settings and implementation of customs. As Beatrice Whiting (1980) pointed out, parents may be most powerful as socializers of their children not through their own interactions with children, but rather in the ways that they assign children to different kinds of settings. While the Whitings (1975) have suggested that parental assignment of children to settings is primarily a function of their own social and economic environments (e.g., the organization of adult work life and gender roles), we have become increasingly interested in parents' cultural belief systems as organizers of parental action. This approach recognizes the diverse economic, social, and historical origins of parental thinking, but focuses on its directive function in structuring the child's immediate environment. Thus, within the culturally structured context of the individual family, we assign a leading role to parental ethnotheories as part of the third component of the niche, the psychology of the caretakers.

PARENTAL ETHNOTHEORIES

The study of parental beliefs has received increasing attention in recent years from scholars across a wide variety of disciplines (Goodnow & Collins, 1990; Goodnow, Miller, & Kessel, 1995; Sigel, McGillicuddy-DeLisi, & Goodnow, 1992; Smetana, 1995). Goodnow (1996) suggests that parents' ideas can be studied as an interesting form of adult cognition and development, as a way to understand parental action, as an aspect of "context" in child development research, and as a way to approach the issue of intergenerational continuity and change. As research on parental beliefs has grown, so also has the recognition that many of parents' ideas about children and their development are shared by social groups, and that differences across groups cannot be reduced to differences in socioeconomic status, place of residence, or other kinds of universal variability (Harwood, Miller, & Irizarry, 1995). Thus the need for a construct such as parents' *cultural* belief system, or parental ethnotheories (Harkness & Super, 1996).

We conceptualize parental ethnotheories as cultural models that parents hold regarding children, families, and themselves as parents. Parental ethnotheories are made up of component beliefs that are often implicit, taken-for-granted ideas about the "right" or natural way, and these component beliefs support each other as a system; they are also emotionally meaningful, and they provide a basis for individual parents to evaluate their own or others' goodness or competence as parents. Parental ethnotheories may be derived from a wide array of sources in the culture, including the media (Lightfoot & Valsiner, 1992), general cultural themes, reflection on the remembered past, and formal and informal sources of advice (Harkness, Super, & Keefer, 1992). Because parental ethnotheories are constituted in the process of raising particular children in specific contexts, they inevitably grow and change over the course of parenting. Finally, parental ethnotheories, like other cultural models related to the self, provide not only representations of the way things are and the way they ought to be, but also goals for action (D'Andrade, 1992).

The connection between cultural models and goals for action is an important one, as it lays the foundation for studying the relationships between parental ethnotheories and behavior. In contrast to other theorists, who have proposed that behavior is the direct outcome of environmental features or constraints such as socioeconomic status, we propose that parental customs and practices are instantiations of ethnotheories, which can be observed at the behavioral level. The link from ideas to behavior in any given instance, however, is complex. As indicated in Figure 4-2, we imagine parental ethnotheories as organized both hierarchically and laterally. At the top of the hierarchy are general implicit cultural models of the child and the family, which are closely linked to each other (as well as to other domains not represented here). These implicit cultural models cannot be directly accessed in their "pure" form, although we can gain some insights into their qualities through parental discourse in interviews, or responses to other kinds of research measures such as questionnaires. For example, parents' talk about their children's intelligence and personality, and about customs of care such as "quality time" and "family time," provide building blocks for the construction of the basic implicit cultural model. A caveat here, of course, is that parents in the context of interviews or questionnaires may provide what they imagine to be the interviewer's desired response rather than their own real ideas. Standard precautions for avoiding bias should always be used, and multiple methods can provide greater confidence in the validity of interpretations.

In contrast to general cultural models, customs and practices of care seem to be relatively easy for parents to explain. Again, a caveat is in order: explanations of the importance of a given custom (for example, bedtime routines) are more easily provided in a cross-cultural framework, which is easily achieved if the interviewer is a member of a different culture. If this is not the case (as, for example, in our earlier research with middle-class American parents), it may be necessary to introduce a moment of artificiality into the conversation by asking parents to explain and justify something that both parent and interviewer may take for granted. The link from ideas to behavior is now ready to be made, but several intervening factors may change the outcome from what the researcher might predict: among the most important of these are individual characteristics of the parent, characteristics of the child (including birth order, gender, and temperament), features of the immediate situation, competing cultural models that would push the outcome toward a different end, and the perceived relevance of the cultural model to that situation from the perspective of the parents themselves. We should therefore not expect a

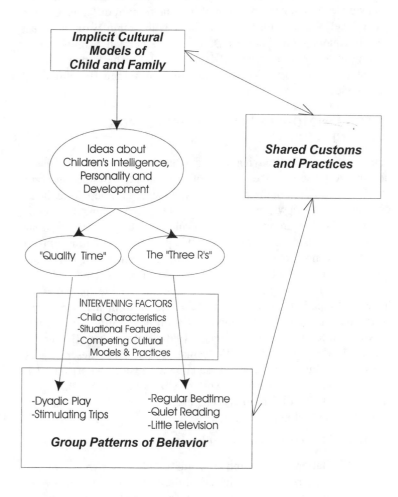

Figure 4-2. Parental ethnotheories and how they are organized.

perfect correspondence between ideas and particular instances of behavior, but on average, if ideas do have directive force in parental behavior, we should see evidence of it in the form of differences at the group level. We will illustrate these ideas with examples of our recent research among middle-class Dutch and American parents before turning to the issue of how the developmental niche framework and parental ethnotheories are relevant to issues in early childhood intervention and education programs.

CULTURAL MODELS IN PARENTS' DESCRIPTIONS OF THEIR CHILDREN

A new technique for studying parents' ethnotheories of the child that is proving very useful is the analysis of how parents describe their own children or children in their community, whether in group discussions, open-ended interviews, or in response to direct questioning. Collection of this kind of data in several different cultural settings has given strong support to the theoretical assumption that parents' descriptions of their children are not completely individualistic productions, but rather reflect culturally shared ideas about which aspects of child behavior and personality are significant and/or desirable. The technique as we have developed it complements the work of Kohnstamm and his colleagues on the five factor model of adult personality as a possible universal reference frame (Digman, 1990; Kohnstamm, Halverson, Havill, & Mervielde, 1996). The semantic space they describe may prove to be robust across cultures, and it may be generally organized as they anticipate, but our current work examines how within that space specific cultures differentially emphasize, connote, and elaborate domains of special importance.

Briefly, our method consists of four main steps:

1. Elicitation of descriptive words or phrases (which we call descriptors) about children, through parental interviews or discussions with members of a defined social group or community of interest.

2. From the full list of descriptors, selection of a subset (usually 12 to 16) based on their frequency of occurrence in discourse, their apparent significance to parents in the community, and their distribution across the widest possible domains of meaning.

3. Construction and application of a triads test questionnaire based on the selected descriptors with a sample of parents in the community.

4. Analysis of the results using multidimensional scaling, cluster analysis, and consensus analysis to explore the organization of meaning and the degree of community consensus about that structure (for a fuller description of the methodology, see Harkness, Super, van Tijen, & van der Vlugt, 1994).

The results of this technique as applied to a sample of parents of children from six months to eight years of age in the town of Bloemenheim are shown in Figure 4-3. The descriptors are arranged here largely in two parallel rows distributed diagonally across the page. Two dimensions are evident. The first (going from upper right to lower left) contrasts social and individual qualities, with clever (*slim*), persistent (*vasthoudend*), strong-willed (*sterke wil*), self-reliant (*zelfstandig*), enterprising (*ondernemend*), and active (*actief*) on one side in contrast to verbal (*verbaal*), open (*open*), sociable (*sociaal*), sweet (*lief*), and cheerful (*vrolijk*) on the other. Close to the median on this contrast but tying down the ends of the second dimension (upper left to lower right) are cautious (*afwachtend*) and impulsive (*impulsief*), signaling a dimension of contrast between impulsivity and inhibition. Interpretation of this second dimension is supported by the close proximity of active and enterprising to impulsive; the proximity of verbal to the opposite end of this dimension is less obvious, but suggests that parents may think of children's talking as contrasted with being physically active. Cluster analysis of the triads test results was also carried out; the circles on Figure 4-3 show descriptors clustered together at an intermediate level of association (.59). At this level of interpretation, the most striking results are the associations between clever, persistent and strong-willed in the inhibited/individual quadrant, and self-reliant, enterprising and active in the individual/active quadrant. A cluster of desirable social qualities (open, sociable, sweet, and cheerful) occupies the impulsive/social quadrant, while verbal is isolated in the remaining (inhibited/social) quadrant. Consensus analysis of these results confirms that parents in this sample were in strong agreement about the patterns of association and contrast among the descriptors. Of particular interest for the present context is how parents conceptualize children's intelligence. Interpretation of the

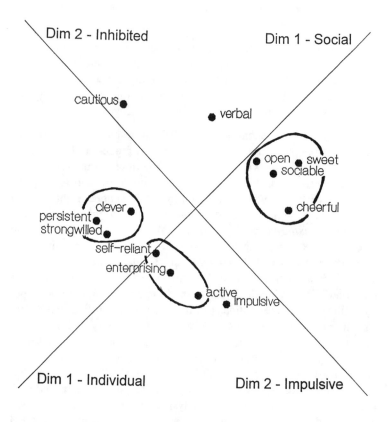

Figure 4-3. Analysis of how parents describe children in Bloemenheim. See text for describting method used.

Dutch results suggests that for these parents, intelligence is associated with enduring effort, directed by strength of will, and organized by clarity of purpose (another definition given by parents in talking about children's "will"). Intelligence, if this interpretation is correct, is not even necessarily related to verbal abilities; or, at least, talkativeness is not seen as an expression of intelligence.

In contrast to the Dutch cultural constructions of "intelligence," American parents in two distinct geographic areas (metropolitan Boston and central Pennsylvania) highlight the aggressive and competitive aspects of intelligence, and interpret many diverse aspects of behavior as manifestations of intelligence. An analysis of the frequency of this kind of descriptor in discourse by middle-class parents in the Boston area suggests that it is by far the most common of descriptors used by parents to talk about their own children, accounting for almost one-fifth of all descriptors (excluding immediate repetitions) in contrast to less than half of that for the Dutch parents. For American parents in central Pennsylvania, "smart" is closely associated with "athletic," a belief that captures both the competitive aspect of intelligence as a means of achieving success and also the local cultural model of athletic prowess as itself a demonstration of cultural supercompetence (Raghavan, 1993).

THE INSTANTIATION OF PARENTAL ETHNOTHEORIES IN CUSTOMS AND PRACTICES OF CARE

How do parents convey their ideas about desirable development to their children? Although they may occasionally express their hopes and fears directly, more often these are communicated implicitly, through repeated actions and routines. Moreover, parents' cultural belief systems, like other aspects of the child's developmental niche, are likely to be experienced by parents as the "normal" or "natural" way to think and act. Thus it is that customs or practices of care take on particular significance as vehicles for parents to express, or instantiate cultural beliefs, often themselves unexamined, through actions.

For parents in Bloemenheim, customs of care regarding the development of intelligence were a topic often discussed in interviews. The advice voiced by many was, "You must not push!" Parents who were somewhat familiar with American culture liked to make the distinction between this stance and what they saw as the American way, leading to overstimulation of the child and the inevitable resulting resistance by the child. So what could a parent in Bloemenheim do to encourage the optimal development? A theme emphasized by many parents was the importance of "regularity" (*regelmaat*). Through the provision of an environment characterized by regular schedules and rules, parents explained, children would naturally learn about "where they stood," or about their own place in their social world. Secure within the "borders" (*grenzen*) set by this regularity, children would then be free to explore their own interests and develop their own competencies. Regularity, in this cultural view, had the essential function of providing the scaffolding upon which new experiences could be assimilated and knowledge could be built. In this regard, parents of older children, especially, referred to the importance of children developing an ability to entertain themselves and to apply to all tasks a focused attentiveness.

American parents' concerns about the development of intelligence centered on rather different customs. For the Cambridge parents, the primary issue seemed to be the provision of sufficiently stimulating environments for children, including attention and interaction with the parents themselves. Children were perceived as needing and even demanding stimulation. As one father put it, "Aaron's a very active child. He needs to be very active. He needs to play with children who are at a certain level of sophistication . . . On weekends we've got to take him to a museum or a park or something or he'll be impossible". Parents also expressed the idea that they themselves should be frequently, and intensely, involved in interaction with their children— an activity regarded as important for the child's emotional as well as cognitive development. Ideally, parents felt, they should spend special time or quality time with the child, undistracted by other needs such as the competing demands of another sibling or housework.

FROM BELIEFS AND CUSTOMS TO BEHAVIOR

It seems clear that the Cambridge and Bloemenheim parents held somewhat differing cultural beliefs about children and their needs, and that these beliefs were instantiated by differing cultural customs and practices of care. That is, parents perceived themselves as structuring their child's daily lives and interacting with their children in accordance with culturally defined beliefs. But what of their actual behavior? Leaving aside the possibility that parents were telling us mainly what they believed we wanted to hear rather than what they really thought, it is still possible that the behavioral profiles of the two groups might not be consistent with the differences in beliefs and customs. That is, parents might carry out similar behavior but simply not bestow it with the same significance. However, a strong model of the belief-behavior connection would hypothesize that differences in beliefs would be mirrored by actual behavioral differences.

In order to test whether this was the case for the Bloemenheim and Cambridge parents, we compared several kinds of behavior as recorded in the parental diaries. From the diaries kept by parents of children at 18 months, 3 years, and 4.5 years, we derived several measures of "stimulation": television-watching, book-reading, playing with a parent, and "cultural" outings. Each of these has somewhat different qualities. Television-watching was considered stimulating in the sense of arousing by parents in both Cambridge and Bloemenheim; additionally, certain programs such as Sesame Street (which is available in both countries) were considered stimulating for cognitive development. According to both groups of parents, but especially the Bloemenheim parents, television-watching could also easily *over*stimulate children and should be curtailed for that reason. It is interesting, in this context, that Sesame Street was programmed to last only 15 minutes in the Netherlands in contrast to an hour in the United States. Book-reading is, of course, the epitome of an exercise in literacy development. However, it is also a quiet and, if done alone, focused and independent activity. Playing with a parent is in part a reflection of the parent's ideas about the importance of this activity (in the American case, important for cognitive growth), though it can also reflect individual differences in children's demands. Outings with the child, including sight-seeing, trips to the library, and trips to museums, presumably reflect parents' interest in providing educationally stimulating activities for their children. Based on differences between the Cambridge and Bloemenheim parents' concerns with stimulation, we would expect the Cambridge children to be more involved in at least three of these activities, and possibly in reading as well; but our prediction here is less certain, given the dual quality of this behavior.

Table 4-1 compares the two samples of children in terms of both the occurrence and average duration of the various activities related to "stimulation." As can be seen, the children differ significantly with regard to all four measures. The most striking difference, in its absolute magnitude, is the amount of time that parents report their child playing with one or both of them: more than a third of the child's waking time, for the Cambridge children, compared to only about 14 percent of the time for the Bloemenheim children. This difference in parents' time playing with their children is consistent with an earlier result (Super et al., 1996) of comparisons between a sample of 6-month-old infants in Bloemenheim and infants in Cambridge, in which we found that the American mothers talked more to their babies and touched them more. The American babies, correspondingly, were more often in higher states of arousal. Both these sets of results suggest that the American parents were engaged in a higher rate of socially stimulating interaction with their children. Television-watching was also found to account for a significantly longer time in the Cambridge children's days, although the frequency of watching was not so different. Stimulating cultural outings were found to be more frequent and of longer duration for the Cambridge children. In contrast to these three measures, book-reading was significantly higher for the Bloemenheim children in terms of both time and frequency. In light of interview material, this difference presumably reflects a salience for the Bloemenheim parents of this activity's focused and calming qualities.

In Table 4-2, we compare the Cambridge and Bloemenheim children on measures of regularity in relation to bedtime and dinnertime. As reported previously (Super et al., 1996), the Bloemenheim children had earlier and more regular bedtimes than the Cambridge children. This is true both at the group level and at the individual level: that is, there was less variability within the group in terms of bedtime, and there was also less variability within individual children on different days. The same pattern of greater regularity among the Bloemenheim children appears in relation to dinnertime, which varies from before 5:00 to almost 8:00 for the Cambridge sample, whereas variability in the Bloemenheim sample is from about 5:30 to 7:00. As with bedtimes, dinnertimes are also significantly more regular for individual children in the Bloemenheim sample.

In summary, then, it appears that there are significant differences between the Cambridge and Bloemenheim parents at the group level, and that these correspond to a large extent to the predictions we had made regarding stimulation and regularity. The notable exception to this pattern of results is book-reading. Our impression in informal home observations was that young children in Bloemenheim had developed a remarkable capacity for entertaining themselves quietly and independently. With television-watching strictly curtailed, children

Table 4-1. Children's Activities in Cambridge and Bloemenheim

	Cambridge		Bloemenheim	
	Percent of Waking Hours	Episodes per 24 Hours	Percent of Waking Hours	Episodes per 24 Hours
Watch television	5.2**	.73	3.1**	.63
Read book	.6**	.13***	1.5**	.52***
Play with parent	35.2***	3.64***	13.7***	2.14***
Stimulating outing[1]	1.7*	.10*	.7*	.06*

[1]Defined as: outing to an event, such as sight-seeing, visiting a library, or a museum

*$p < .05$, comparing the two samples.

**$p < .01$, comparing the two samples.

***$p < .001$, comparing the two samples.

Table 4-2. Regularity in Bedtime and Dinnertime in Bloemenheim and Cambridge

	Mean within Group	Standard Deviation within Individual	Standard Deviation
Bedtime			
Cambridge	8:16 *PM***	.67 hrs**	.61 hrs*
Bloemenheim	7:30 *PM***	.49 hrs**	.47 hrs*
Dinnertime			
Cambridge	5:56 *PM*	.57 hrs*	.51 hrs***
Bloemenheim	5:47 *PM*	.41 hrs*	.33 hrs***

*$p < .05$, comparing the two samples.

**$p < .01$, comparing the two samples.

***$p < .001$, comparing the two samples.

often engaged in activities such as book-reading, drawing, or other artwork. The American children, in contrast, seem not only to have spent more time watching TV, but also may have demanded, and received, more playtime with parents. One interesting aspect of this contrast is that it makes sense in terms of larger cultural themes of child rearing, even while contradicting a specific behavioral prediction.

IMPLICATIONS FOR EARLY INTERVENTION AND EDUCATION

In this chapter, we have suggested that parental beliefs, shaped and to a large extent shared within a culturally structured environment, are instantiated in customs and practices of care, and expressed in behavior. It follows from this perspective that any program that aims to change parental behavior—or the behavior of children—must take parents' ideas into account. The research we have discussed in this chapter was with groups that, in the eyes of their own cultures, were not in need of remediation. Nevertheless, we can draw some implications for the application of the perspective described here to early interventions and schooling for young children and their families.

First, in order to intervene effectively for the enhancement of literacy in the preschool years, it is essential to be familiar with parents' concepts of the child. Because, as we have noted, so many cultural beliefs about the nature of the child are unexamined assumptions about what is "normal," it is typically the case that interventionists may approach parents with *a priori* ideas about what kinds of beliefs parents have or ought to have. If the target group for intervention comes from a different cultural tradition, these assumptions are likely not to be shared—even if the group in question has been living in the present environment for some time. In such cases, communication between parents and teachers may be frustrating for both sides, resulting in parental withdrawal from further contact. Greenfield, Quiroz, and Raeff (in press), for example, have documented how parent-teacher conferences between immigrant Latino parents and their children's European American elementary school teachers are often founded on miscommunication resulting from different cultural orientations: whereas the teacher wants to highlight the child's individual accomplishments, the parents avoid focusing on a single child and draw attention to siblings or the whole family. In this case, it would be helpful if the teachers could recognize the parents' need to talk about the child from a more sociocentric, rather than individualistic, perspective.

In addition to being familiar with parents' cultural beliefs about children and the family, it is also essential to understand how these beliefs are instantiated in specific practices. Although this may seem like an obvious point, different cultural practices are in actuality often regarded through the lens of one's own culture with a resulting negative interpretation. In Bloemenheim, for example, a teacher in the local public elementary school suggested that Moroccan parents in the community "don't care about their children" because they would typically leave them free to play outside unsupervised during the after-school hours, expecting them to come home only for dinner. The Moroccan parents, for their part, were frustrated with teachers at the school for, in their view, refusing to take responsibility for disciplining the children adequately during the time they were at school and thus under the teachers' authority. In a similar vein, a study of Haitian children at public elementary schools in Massachusetts found that children's behavior problems in the classroom were related to differences in behavior management between the democratically oriented European American teachers and the more authoritarian disciplinary style that the parents used at home.

In considering issues of disparity in ideas and practices between home and school, it is important to differentiate those that are truly cultural from those that may represent problems in coping or dysfunctionality in ethnic or minority families, particularly those that are economically disadvantaged. Establishing effective communication and partnership in practices with such parents may be thwarted more by these issues than by underlying differences in beliefs about children. Poor families in the United States who are on welfare, unemployed and/or homeless, or burdened by drug and alcohol abuse problems or family violence may have cultural belief systems that are very similar to those of the middle class, but they have not had the opportunity to put them into practice. As the above examples suggest, overcoming differences in cultural belief systems and practices is not an easy task, especially when further complicated by issues of poverty and social discrimination. Cultural beliefs such as those that are instantiated in styles of communication or discipline are not just neutral cognitions about the nature of reality, they are also emotionally charged as motivators of behavior. Nevertheless, we suggest that educators and planners of interventions must take cultural beliefs and related practices into account in order to maximize the chances for success. How can this be done?

Logically, there are three possibilities: 1) educate parents in the cultural belief systems of the mainstream, 2) adapt to the beliefs and practices of the cultural group in question, and 3) use cultural intermediaries to negotiate the differences between the mainstream and the cultural minority group. All of these approaches have their merits. Parent education has sometimes been criticized as ethnocentric, but if combined with parent support groups, it may be perceived as empowering. Providing parents with new goals for their development may liberate parents from traditions that they experience as oppressive, even though they have remained tied to them. The second strategy, adaptation to parents' beliefs and practices, may sometimes also be feasible. For example, Greenfield, Quiroz, and Raeff (in press) cite the example of having an older sibling read to a younger child, thus fulfilling both the teacher's desire for the child to have more individual attention around literacy at home and the parents' need for the children to be helpful in the family context. Similarly, Weisner, Gallimore, and Jordan (1988) found that classroom strategies emphasizing group participation were more successful than the traditional individually oriented practices for Hawaiian children. Third, the use of bicultural persons as bridges between home and school (or intervention program) may be effective in "translating" ideas and practices from one group to the other. In this case, of course, it is essential that such persons be able to understand and articulate both cultural perspectives. Finally, we suggest that interventions using the perspective we have developed here are likely to be more successful the earlier they are begun in the development of parenting in parents. Interventions with parents of infants, or even expectant parents, have the advantage of capturing parental attention at a point when cultural belief systems and practices are in their formative stage of development and when attention to the child may be more intense. By laying a foundation of shared ideas and partnership in practice at this early stage, educators and others will be in an optimal position to guide parental behavior and enhance children's development for success in school and beyond.

NOTES

1. The original research discussed in this chapter was supported in part by grants from the Spencer Foundation, the William T. Grant Foundation, the

Carnegie Corporation of New York, and the National Science Foundation, USA (award number BNS 83–11084).

REFERENCES

Abbott, S. (1992). Holding on and pushing away: Comparative perspectives on an Eastern Kentucky child-rearing practice. *Ethos, 20,* 33–65.

Bornstein, M. H., Tamis-LeMonda, C. S., Tal, J., Ludemann, P., Toda, S., Rahn, C. W., Pecheux, M.G., Azuma, H., & Vardi, D. (1992). Maternal responsiveness to infants in three societies: The United States, France, and Japan. *Child Development, 63,* 808–821.

D'Andrade, R. G. (1992). Schemas and motivation. In R. G. D'Andrade & C. Strauss (Eds.), *Human motives and cultural models* (pp. 23–44). Cambridge: Cambridge University Press.

D'Andrade, R. (1990). Some propositions about the relations between culture and human cognition. In J. W. Stigler, R. A. Shweder, & G. Herdt (Eds.), *Cultural Psychology: Essays on comparative human development* (pp. 66–129). Cambridge: Cambridge University Press.

Digman, J. M. (1990). Personality structure: Emergence of the Five-Factor Model. In M. R. Rosenzweig & L. W. Porter (Eds.), *Annual review of psychology* (Vol. 41, pp. 417–440). Palo Alto: Annual Reviews.

Goodnow, J. J., & Collins, W. A. (1990). *Development according to parents: The nature, sources, and consequences of parents' ideas.* London: Erlbaum.

Goodnow, J. J., Miller, P. J., & Kessel, F. (Eds.), (1995). *Cultural practices as contexts for development.* New Directions for Child Development, Vol. 67. San Francisco: Jossey-Bass.

Goodnow, J. (1996). From household practices to parents' ideas about work and interpersonal relationships. In S. Harkness & C. M. Super (Eds.), *Parents' cultural belief systems: Their origins, expressions, and consequences.* New York: Guilford.

Greenfield, P. M., Quiroz, B., & Raeff, C. (in press). Cross-cultural conflict and harmony in the social construction of the child. In S. Harkness, C. Raeff, & C. M. Super (Eds.), The social construction of the child: Variability within and across settings. *Language Sciences, 10*(1), 53–67.

Harkness, S. (1988). The cultural construction of semantic contingency in mother-child speech. *Language Sciences, 10*(1), 53–67.

Harkness, S., & Super, C. M. (1992). The developmental niche: A theoretical framework for analyzing the household production of health. *Social Science and Medicine, 38*(2), 217–226.

Harkness, S., & Super, C. M. (1996). *Parents' cultural belief systems: Their origins, expressions, and consequences.* New York: Guilford.

Harkness, S., Super, C. M., & Keefer, C. H. (1992). Learning to be an American parent: How cultural models gain directive force. In R. G. D'Andrade & C. Strauss (Eds.), *Human motives and cultural models* (pp. 163–178). New York: Cambridge University Press.

Harkness, S., Super, C. M., van Tijen, N., & van der Vlugt, E. (1994). *What's in a descriptor: Parental concepts of children in Holland.* Unpublished manuscript.

Harwood, R. L., Miller, J. G., & Irizarry, N. L. (1995). *Culture and attachment: Perceptions of the child in context.* New York: Guilford.

Heath, S. B. (1986). What no bedtime story means: Narrative skills at home and at school. In B. B. Schieffelin & E. Ochs (Eds.), *Language socialization across cultures* (pp. 97–126). New York: Cambridge University Press.

Kluckhohn, C. (1945/1962). The concept of culture. In C. Kluckhohn (Ed.), *Culture and behavior* (pp. 19–73). New York: Free Press.

Kohnstamm, G. A., Halverson, C. F., Havill, V. L., & Mervielde, I. (1996). Parents' free descriptions of child characteristics: A cross-cultural search for the roots of the Big Five. In S. Harkness & C. M. Super (Eds.), *Parents' cultural belief systems: Their origins, expressions, and consequences* (pp. 27–55). New York: Guilford.

Lightfoot, C., & Valsiner, J. (1992). Parental belief systems under the influence: Social guidance of the construction of personal cultures. In I. E. Sigel, A. V. McGillicuddy-DeLisi, & J. J. Goodnow (Eds.), *Parental belief systems: The psychological consequences for children (Second Edmitive education).* New York: William Morrow.

Mead, M. (1930/1966). *Growing up in New Guinea: A comparative study of primitive education.* New York: William Morrow.

Miller, P. J., & Hoogstra, L. (1992). Language as tool in the socialization and apprehension of cultural meanings. In T. Schwartz, G. M. White, & C. A. Lutz (Eds.), *New directions in psychological anthropology* (pp. 83–101). Cambridge: Cambridge University Press.

Morelli, G. A., Rogoff, B., Oppenheim, D., & Goldsmith, D. (1992). Cultural variation in infants' sleeping arrangements: Questions of independence. *Developmental psychology, 28*(4), 604–613.

Ochs, E., & Schieffelin, B. (1984). Language acquisition and socialization: Three developmental stories and their implications. In R. A. Shweder & R. A. LeVine (Eds.), *Culture theory: Essays on mind, self, and emotion* (pp. 276–322). Cambridge: Cambridge University Press.

Quinn, N., & Holland, D. (1987). Culture and cognition. In D. Holland & N. Quinn (Eds.), *Cultural models in language and thought* (pp. 3–42). Cambridge: Cambridge University Press.

Raghavan, C. (1993). *Cultural models of female children in Indian and American families.* Unpublished doctoral dissertation, The Pennsylvania State University.

Rogoff, G., Baker-Sennett, J., Lacasa, P., & Goldsmith, D. (1995). Development through participation in sociocultural activity. In J. J. Goodnow, P. J. Miller, & F. Kessel (Eds.), *Cultural practices as contexts for development.* New Directions for Child Development, Vol. 67. San Francisco: Jossey-Bass.

Shweder, R. A., Jensen, L. A., & Goldstein, W. M. (1995). Who sleeps by whom revisited: A method for extracting the moral goods implicit in practice. In J. J. Goodnow, P. J. Miller, & F. Kessel (Eds.), *Cultural practices as contexts for development* (pp. 21–39). New Directions for Child Development. Vol. 67. San Francisco: Jossey-Bass.

Sigel, I. E., McGillicuddy-DeLisi, A.V., & Goodnow, J. J. (1992). *Parental belief systems: The psychological consequences for children.* New Directions in Child Development. San Francisco, CA: Jossey-Bass.

Smetana, J. G. (1995). *Beliefs about parenting: Origins and development implications.* New Directions in Child Development. San Francisco, CA: Jossey-Bass.

Super, C. M., & Harkness, S. (1986). The developmental niche: A conceptualization at the interface of child and culture. *International Journal of Behavioral Development, 9,* 545–569.

Super, C. M., Harkness, S., van Tijen, N., van der Vlugt, E., Dykstra, J., & Fintelman, M. (1996). The three R's of Dutch child rearing and the socialization of infant arousal. In S. Harkness & C. M. Super (Eds.), *Parents' cultural belief systems: Their origins, expressions, and consequences.* (pp. 447–466). New York: Guilford Press.

Wallace, A. F. C. (1961). *Culture and personality.* New York: Random House.

Weisner, T. S., Gallimore, R., & Jordan, C. (1988). Unpackaging cultural effects on classroom learning: Native Hawaiian peer assistance and child-generated activity. *Anthropology and Education Quarterly, 19,* 327–351.

Weisner, T. (1996). Why ethnography should be the most important method in the study of human development. In A. Colby, R. Jessor, & R. Shweder (Eds.), *Ethnography and human development: Context and meaning in social inquiry* (pp. 305–324). Chicago: University of Chicago Press.

Whiting, B. B. (1980). Culture and social behavior: A model for the development of social behavior. *Ethos, 8,* 95–116.

Whiting, B. B., & Whiting, J. W. M. (1975). *The children of six cultures: A psychocultural analysis.* Cambridge, MA: Harvard University Press.

Whiting, J. W. M., & Whiting, B. B. (1960). Contributions of anthropology to the methods of studying child rearing. In P. H. Mussen (Ed.), *Handbook of research methods in child development* (pp. 918–944). New York: Wiley.

Context and Cognition in Early Childhood Education
Evelyn Jacob and *Patricia A. Phipps*

Early childhood education today faces its perennial challenge of providing quality teaching and learning. Many scholars and practitioners are trying to address this challenge, but past experience does not lead to optimism about current efforts. In many early childhood classrooms, quality teaching and learning are not occurring; most educational innovations have failed when used in "everyday" classrooms.

One reason for the pattern of deficiency is that context and cognition have not been considered together in developing, researching, disseminating, or using educational practices or innovations. Educational developers and researchers, using positivist lenses, have focused primarily on cognitive issues, what Erickson (1982) has termed "taught cognitive learning," and have largely ignored context. They have had cognition without context. Educational anthropologists, using interpretivist lenses and generally operating outside the mainstream, have focused primarily on the contexts of education, and usually have not addressed "taught cognitive learning."[1] They have had context without cognition. This historical separation of context and cognition has been a contributing factor to the current dominance of less than successful educational practice and innovations.

Cooperative learning offers a good example of the consequences of divorcing cognition from context. Educational developers and researchers have focused primarily on the outcomes of cooperative learning (see Slavin, 1990, for a review), documenting its success in "field experiments" where they often expend great effort to assure that cooperative learning is implemented by the teachers in the way developers think it should be implemented (e.g., Cohen, 1993; Cohen, Lotan, & Catanzarite, 1990; Sharan, Kussell, Sharan, & Bejarano, 1984).[2] Context is either viewed as a hindrance or ignored. Disseminators usually take an acontextual approach, emphasizing "fidelity." Practitioners are left trying to use one or more forms of cooperative learning, adapting them to their local context, but usually not attending consciously to contextual features. A result is that cooperative learning has had mixed results when used in everyday classrooms (Castle & Arends, 1992; Cohen et al., 1990; Meloth & Deering, 1994).

The field of culture and cognition, given its interdisciplinary focus, might have been expected to provide a way to combine context and cognition. However, it is only recently that scholars in the field have linked context and cognition in a theoretically complex way and have shown that context is central to cognition.

In this chapter we discuss the development of the concept of context within the field of culture and cognition, focusing in particular on work in the cultural-historical tradition.[3] We also discuss implications of this work for practice and innovation in early childhood education.

CONTEXT IN CULTURE AND COGNITION

The earliest work in the field of culture and cognition did not explicitly address context at all; instead, researchers focused on comparing cultural groups. In the 1960s, some researchers refined the focus by examining the relationships between cognition and observable traits within cultural groups. Vygotsky and other early scholars in the cultural-historical tradition provided an integrating theory, but used a limited view of context. Recent work within the cultural-historical tradition has begun elaborating the aspects and concept of context to provide a more complex view of its relationships with cognition.

Cultural Groups

Prior to the 1960s the few psychologists who had an interest in cultural issues (usually operating within the field of cross-cultural psychology) used theories to guide their work that viewed cognitive development in terms of universal, context-free processes. Most research in cross-cultural psychology compared the performance of non-Western groups to a Western group (using tests developed for Western populations). Researchers viewed their experiments not as measuring performance in a particular context, but as measuring underlying abilities. The researchers usually viewed culture in broad terms as an independent variable and cognition as the dependent variable, with culture often being the gloss for underlying biological characteristics of a group, not their learned patterns of meanings, behavior, and social organization.

Although anthropologists of the time were concerned with culture and personality (e.g., Barnouw, 1973) and the cognitive content of culture (e.g., Tyler, 1969), few examined how culture influenced the kinds of cognitive activity examined by psychologists. Those that did (e.g., Bateson, 1958; Fortes, 1970) took a broad approach, studying at the level of general cultural group.

Observable Traits Within Cultures

In the 1960s, some cross-cultural psychological studies compared intracultural groups in an effort to identify the relationships between more specific aspects of culture and specific aspects of cognition. For example, many studies (e.g., Greenfield, Reich & Olver, 1966; Wagner, 1974) examined the impact of urbanization and formal schooling on cognitive skills such as classification and memory.

In the late 1960s and early 1970s, scholars (e.g., Cole, Gay, Glick, & Sharp, 1971; Lave, 1977; Munroe & Munroe, 1971; Nerlove, Roberts, Klein, Yarbrough, & Habicht, 1974) began conducting research that consciously drew on both psychology and anthropology. These studies usually compared groups within a culture through the use of tests or experimental tasks, but often developed the tasks and interpreted the results based on anthropological data about the culture. Some studies also made an effort to provide more detailed understandings of intracultural variation by linking a variety of data on individuals (from surveys, interviews, and nonparticipant observation data) to their performance on tests or experiments.

Although these studies still tended to view culture as an "independent variable," the researchers took a more finely grained approach to local culture, and their findings pointed to the importance of context. By comparing the same group's performance on the same or similar tasks in experimental and natural settings, researchers documented that context influences the display of skills. For example, Micronesian navigators displayed complex memory, inference, and calculation skills when traveling from island to island but performed poorly on standard tests of intellectual functioning (Gladwin, 1970).

By comparing the cognitive performance of groups that have documented differences in prior experience, researchers showed that different experiences lead to different patterns of cognitive development (Cole et al., 1971; Scribner & Cole, 1981). For example, Scribner and Cole (1981) found that among the Vai in Liberia, Vai, English, and Arabic literacies involved different literacy "practices" (i.e., different goals, technologies, and activities), and that these different practices were associated with different effects as measured on various cognitive tasks.

In spite of the contributions of this period, the cultural features the researchers examined were still "packaged," that is, they included "clusters of correlated and often ill-defined traits" (Whiting, 1976, p. 305). The studies rarely examined or reported important aspects of context such as cultural attitudes and values, social organization, or daily experiences that were related to the cultural activities under study. Moreover, the work lacked a unifying theoretical framework (Cole et al., 1971; Scribner & Cole, 1981).

An Integrating Theory

Work by Lev Vygotsky and others in the Soviet cultural-historical school provided a theoretical framework that combined context and cognition. In 1978, Vygotsky's *Mind in Society* was published in English. Subsequently, more of his work and that of the cultural-historical school has become available to English-speaking audiences.

Vygotsky focused primarily on understanding the development of "higher mental functions" (e.g., thinking, reasoning, and problem-solving), which he saw as heavily influenced by sociocultural, that is, contextual, factors. Two kinds of contextual influences have received widespread attention among English-speaking scholars—tools provided by society for cognitive activity, and face-to-face social interaction. Technical tools (e.g., pens, computers, textbooks) and psychological tools (e.g., language, writing, number systems) transform the structure and processes of the action being performed (Vygotsky, 1981). For example, revising is a different activity depending on whether one is using a word processor or a pencil. Vygotsky also asserted that higher mental functions have their origins in face-to-face interactions: "Every function in the child's cultural development appears twice: first, on the social level, and later, on the individual level" (Vygotsky, 1978, p. 57).

Vygotsky and others in the cultural-historical school provided to English-speaking researchers an integrated framework for understanding context and cognition, and an expanded view of contextual influences on cognition. To the prevalent cognitivist views that saw task structure and knowledge domains as the only relevant contexts for cognitive activity (Engestrom, 1993), the cultural-historical tradition added psychological and technical tools provided by society, and the immediate interpersonal context. Moreover, Leont'ev's (1978, 1981) work on "activity" shifted the focus from individuals to "persons in activities," and drew attention to socially constructed motives and goals in activities and their influences on cognition.

However, based on his historical review of Vygotsky's scholarship in both Russian and English, Minick (1989) pointed out that because only a few of Vygotsky's works were translated into English, English-speaking scholars had a limited view of Vygotsky's ideas about sociocultural influences on cognitive activity: "While Vygotsky was certainly concerned with the role that speech and social interaction play in human psychological development, he ultimately saw the child's inclusion in socially defined systems of activity or practice as more fundamental" (p. 163).

Developing a More Complex View of Context

Since the late 1970s, researchers in the cultural-historical tradition have worked to clarify and extend the theoretical framework of the cultural-historical school and to build a body of empirical research based on its premises. The earliest work focused on elaborating Vygotsky's ideas about tools and interpersonal processes. More recently, English-speaking scholars have been adding new contextual categories and elaborating on the concept of context itself. This recent research on context expands work within the cultural-historical tradition, bringing it closer to Vygotsky's original ideas.

Elaborating Interpersonal Processes and Psychological Tools

Working in both naturalistic and experimental settings, cultural-historical researchers in English-speaking countries in the 1970s examined interpersonal processes involving more knowledgeable persons (usually adults) and children as learners. They identified a number of interactional processes that provide important contexts for learning: scaffolding (Greenfield, 1984; Wood, Bruner, & Ross, 1976), mutual appropriation (Newman, Griffin, & Cole, 1989), apprenticeship (Rogoff, 1990), and limited peripheral participation (Lave & Wenger, 1991). Scholars also pointed out that the participants present during an activity (Gallimore & Goldenberg, 1993) and the power relationships among the participants (Goodnow, 1990; Litowitz, 1993) are important in studying cognitive processes.

Other work focused on the concept of psychological tools, which include the physical arrangement of objects, common mnemonic devices (Rogoff, 1984), and scripts for conduct (Gallimore & Goldenberg, 1993). Chang-Wells and Wells (1993) argued that it is important to examine cultural variability in task representations, problem-solving strategies, and mental models.

However, much of the early cultural-historical research conducted in English had a narrow view of context, focusing almost entirely on interpersonal contexts (Jacob, 1992; Minick, Stone, & Forman, 1993; Nicolopoulou & Cole, 1993). Other aspects of context were not explored seriously until recently. Although there is no accepted consensus about what is required for a sufficient study of context (Griffin, Belyaeva, Soldatova, & the Velikhov-Hamburg Collective, 1993), recent work has begun to elaborate on aspects of context and to develop a more complex understanding of its roles.

Elaborating Aspects of Context

Recently, cultural-historical researchers have examined features of context beyond those identified in early English translations of Vygotsky's work. This work is an explicit attempt by scholars from diverse backgrounds to link multiple aspects of context to cognition and the processes of teaching and learning. Three foci are: the goals and social meanings of activity; local culture, patterns, and institutions; and the larger culture and social institutions.

Scholars pointed out the need to examine the goals of activities (Wertsch, Minick, & Arns, 1984), and how the participants in an activity define them (Serpell, 1993). Säljö and Wyndhamn (1993) found that the same mathematics task was done differently when embedded within social studies and mathematics contexts, and argued that the differences reflect the students' understandings of what mathematics problems mean in these different contexts. Goodnow

(1993) also argued that broader meanings held by participants, such as adults' theories of intelligent behavior, are important for understanding their behavior and that of children they are trying to teach.

Another aspect of context comprises the social values associated with cognitive activities—for example, what counts as a problem or appropriate knowledge for specific groups, what are acceptable ways of learning, and which solutions are valued (Goodnow, 1990).

In examining the implementation of new programs in varied contexts, some scholars have documented culture in learning: for example, when Nicolopoulou and Cole (1993) compared the Fifth Dimension Program at two different after-school sites. The Fifth Dimension Program, a long-term project of the Laboratory of Comparative Human Cognition, was designed to provide basic computer literacy and to use computer software as a tool for the development of more general cognitive and social skills. Nicolopoulou and Cole reported that cognitive success was influenced by the strength of a culture of collaborative learning. The strength or weakness of this culture was related to the degree of affinity between the internal culture of the Fifth Dimension Program and the larger cultural environment of the host institution.

Some scholars have studied how larger cultural and social factors influence what occurs in a local context. Cobb, Wood, and Yackel (1993), in a study of their efforts to introduce inquiry mathematics, documented how larger institutional constraints (for example, the school district's required objectives for mathematics, and state-mandated accountability tests of basic mathematics skills) tended to foster the reproduction of traditional instructional practices.

While some cultural-historical researchers have examined institutional and cultural constraints on school-based learning, few have examined the influences of broader contextual features such as belief systems, child-care arrangements, and economic practices on cognition. Minick (1993), an exception to this pattern, linked the frequent occurrence of representational directives in teachers' instructional discourse to the worldview prevalent in Western society.

Although not operating within the cultural-historical approach, Eldering's (1995) culture-ecological model directs attention beyond the immediate context and offers a way to link larger contextual influences to the immediate context and cognition. Her integration of Bronfenbrenner's (1977) socioecological approach and Harkness and Super's (1993; this volume) developmental niche suggests, for example, that it would be useful to examine the influences of the larger economic system on parents' work lives and economic resources, and the influences of these on parents' availability to their children, child-care arrangements, and schooling opportunities, which in turn provide immediate contexts for children's cognitive development.

Elaborating the Concept of Context

Many scholars no longer view context as an independent variable, with all that that notion implies. Recent work views context as more complex and interdependent. This work focuses on three important features of context: the interweaving of contextual features; the ways in which context is both stable and created by participants; and the dialectic relationships between context and activity.

The original meaning of "context" was "to weave together" (Simpson & Weiner, 1989). Recently, this original meaning has been given new life as cultural-historical researchers examined the relationships between various aspects of context. Jacob's (1996; Jacob, Rottenberg, Patrick, & Wheeler, 1996) research on cooperative learning demonstrated that contextual features are interwoven in their influence on opportunities for learning. For example, while using the Teams-Games-Tournaments (TGT) approach to cooperative learning (see Slavin, 1986) for practice in a fourth-grade math class, students did not offer help or explanations to one another as often as they could have. This was influenced by the kind of problems posed on their question sheets (fill-in-the-blank and multiple choice), as well as the students' definition of the TGT practice sessions as competitive games, both features of the immediate context. The question sheets were produced by the developer of TGT and were consistent with the complex scoring system proposed for TGT. The teacher used them because they saved her time and she thought they covered mathematics topics required by the school district's mathematics program. The students' definition of the practice sessions as competitive games was influenced by the competition in the tournament component of TGT and the generally competitive spirit of U.S. public schools, which reflects a cultural value in the larger society. Although the teacher had some misgivings about the competition within TGT, she did not actively work to discourage the students' competitive approach in practice sessions because she thought their definition of it as a game helped to motivate them. The students' math performance was particularly important to the teacher because the class was the "high math" group, and the school valued its track record of high scores on standardized math tests. Thus, students' interactions and the opportunities for learning they provided were influenced by contextual features interwoven at several levels.

In viewing context or culture as an independent variable, earlier work tended to view culture and context as static and given. Lave and her colleagues (Lave, 1988; Lave, Murtaugh, & de la Rocha, 1984) explicated a more complex view in which context is both long-term and changing. They (Lave et al., 1984) argued that: "on the one hand, context connotes an identifiable, durable framework for the activity, with properties that transcend the experience of individuals, exist prior to them, and are entirely beyond their control. On the other hand, context is experienced differently by different individuals" (p. 71).

This approach to context is consistent with current views of individuals as active agents in culture and learning. Thus, social meanings and goals can be viewed as both stable and emergent, with the stable aspect being what a group recognizes as the prevailing meaning, and the emergent aspect being what is created between individuals during their interactions.

Lave (1988; Lave et al., 1984) also elaborated a view of the relationship between activity and context. Based on their study of grocery shopping, Lave et al. (1984) asserted that activity is dialectically constituted in relation to the personally-defined context: "For example, suppose a shopper pauses for the first time in front of the generic products section of the market, noting both the peculiarly plain appearance of the products, divested of brand names and other information to which the shopper is accustomed, and the relatively low prices of these products. This information provides a potential new category of money-saving strategies, which may be added to an existing repertoire of such strategies. This in turn leads the shopper to attend to the generic products on subsequent shopping trips. The setting for these future trips, within the supermarket as arena, is thereby transformed" (pp. 73–74).

Current Status

Approaches to context within the field of culture and cognition have developed dramatically over the past thirty years. The field has moved from viewing culture in the broadest terms to focusing on context and elaborating how context influences cognition.

Moreover, this approach is becoming institutionalized within the educational community. Scholars have developed educational practices and models based on cultural-historical theory. Palincsar and Brown (1984), for example, developed "reciprocal teaching," an effective instructional method for reading. Brown and Ferrara (1985) developed "dynamic assessment methods" that offer graduated assistance to children so that the tester is able to evaluate how much a child is able to improve after his or her initial performance. Taking a broader perspective, Collins, Brown, and Newman (1989) argued for a cognitive apprenticeship model of teaching, which focuses on helping students to acquire the cognitive and metacognitive strategies needed for expert skill in reading, writing, and mathematics.

APPLICATION TO EARLY CHILDHOOD EDUCATION

An increased understanding of the relationships between context and cognition and the institutionalization of the cultural-historical approach offers a rich base for the improvement of early childhood education practice and innovations. As discussed above, work on context and cognition can offer a base for the development of specific innovations and approaches to practice as well as for research. However, we think it can also make a broader contribution. By consciously attending to contextual features and influences, scholars and practitioners can increase the effectiveness of the range of early childhood education practices and innovations.

Mismatch of Cultural Interaction Styles

A number of research studies in the United States and its territories have documented the importance of context in early childhood education. In a study of Native-American children on the Warm Springs Indian Reservation in Oregon, Philips (1972) observed Athabaskan children in classrooms with Anglo-American teachers. She noted that the children were reluctant to participate in group lessons directed by the teachers. Yet when engaged with their peers, these children were exceedingly verbal. Based on that research, Erickson & Mohatt (1981, 1982) examined the teaching styles of a Native Athabaskan and an Anglo-Canadian teacher with Odawa and Objibwa students. Their results were congruent with Philip's findings: the Anglo-Canadian teacher taught in ways that were compatible with how the Anglo-Canadian children were accustomed to learning, but were not compatible with the ways in which the Odawa and Objibwa children learned. In a later investigation of Athabaskan children, Barnhardt (1982) discovered that students who received culturally congruent instruction achieved at higher levels than those who did not.

Comparisons between communication patterns inside and outside the classroom also show the strong effect of context on student performance. Michaels (1981) found that the narratives of first-grade African-American children during "sharing time" took the form of "topic-chaining" and were not valued by the Anglo teacher, who expected "topic-centered" or theme-related narratives typical of what was produced by the Anglo students. The African-American children in this study did not demonstrate school competency because their "topic-chaining" approach was not one the teacher could understand and respond to appropriately. Consequently, the African-American students did not receive validation and ongoing interaction with the teacher the way the Anglo students did. The African-American children's power was cut off and their development circumscribed. The outcome—underachievement—was a product of the teacher-student interactions (Phillips, 1994).

Similarly, in an examination of the role of questioning in language and socialization in classrooms with African-American children in a working-class community in the Southeast, Shirley Brice Heath (1982) documented why the students appeared to be unresponsive to questions by their Anglo teachers. She noted that the teachers were asking the children questions that the children considered silly because they believed the teachers already knew the answers. Therefore, the students saw no need to respond. Through her five-year ethnographic study, Heath chronicled the different ways in which questions were used within the home and the schools, in addition to identifying cultural and contextual factors that influenced how the children communicated with others. Heath also described the many ways in which teachers learned to "build bridges" and support the children's success in school by making accommodations to the local context in their classroom practices.

McCollum (1991) also documented the importance of student-teacher social interactions as context in a cross-cultural comparison of a Chicago classroom with an English-speaking teacher and students, and a Puerto Rican class with a Spanish-speaking teacher and students in Rio Piedras, Puerto Rico. McCollum found that the greatest difference in the context of the two classes was in the social relations between the teacher and the students. In the Chicago classroom, the teacher initiated almost all interactions and used controlling strategies to elicit student responses during lessons. In addition, the teacher usually responded to students' comments during lessons by ignoring them, and she rarely incorporated the students' comments into lessons. In contrast, the Puerto Rican students interacted with the teacher as conversational partners who were free to explore topics of mutual interest with the teacher. With this equalization of speaking rights, the students became active participants in lessons even though they might not have possessed specific academic information. The students' participation was valued and they were reinforced for cultural information in addition to the school's curriculum.

In an ethnographic study of Hispanic, Hmong, Laotian, Vietnamese, and Sudanese students across school and home settings in the United States, Trueba (1988) found that cultural conflict was a major explanatory determinant for the lack of school achievement among these recently immigrated students. He determined that classroom activities did not take the students' cultural knowledge and values into consideration, thereby disabling learning.

Tharp (1989) acknowledged that many have studied the unique culturally-based interactional styles or discourse patterns of various groups and attempted to relate them to academic outcomes as a function of real or hypothesized mismatches. Differences in learning-task environments for students can affect their ability to learn or to display knowledge. Equally important is the consideration that, when patterns of social interaction are altered from customary patterns, children's usual ways of thinking and interacting are also altered, which could affect academic performance (McCollum, 1991).

Cultural Compatibility in Teaching and Learning

Although most studies, like those discussed above, have documented the importance of context "after the fact," a few projects show that taking context into account during the development and dissemination of practice in early childhood can contribute to its effectiveness. The following are examples of "cultural compatibility" in education. Cultural compatibility might be thought of as one aspect of context within the broader area of context and cognition.

Probably the best documented example of a systematic attempt to accommodate cultural learning patterns or cultural compatibility is the Kamehameha Early Education Project (KEEP) (Au, 1980; Vogt,

Jordan, & Tharp 1993), a collaborative endeavor between teachers and an interdisciplinary team of researchers combining attention to context and cognition in its efforts to develop and study a successful K–3 language arts program for at-risk Hawaiian children. Initially developed in a lab school setting, the KEEP program was also effective in a small-scale dissemination to some public schools. The developers attribute their success to changes in the following contextual features: instructional practice, classroom social organization, and motivation management (Vogt et al., 1993).

However, in examining the cultural compatibility of task and talk structures for particular groups of students, Hiebert and Fisher (1991) found that although it might be desirable to have culturally compatible task and talk structures operating in the classroom as often as possible, what constitutes cultural compatibility in one context may be rendered unauthentic by marginal changes in the context. In other words, cultural compatibility pertains not to the task itself but to an interaction between task and context. This interaction effect was dramatically illustrated in the attempt to extrapolate the KEEP model to Navajo children in the Southwestern United States (Vogt et al., 1993). The talk structures that had worked with native Hawaiian children did not work with Navajo children. Both talk structures and forms of tasks needed to be changed, especially for contexts involving group cooperation. Classroom practices were then restructured to be contextually congruent for the Navajo students.

The Funds of Knowledge Teaching Project, another approach to cultural compatibility, has engendered transformative consequences for teachers, parents, students, and researchers (Gonzalez et al., 1993). Because educational institutions and practitioners often view working-class minority students as emerging from households that are not rich in social and intellectual resources, they have low academic expectations and inaccurate portrayals of these children and their families. Gonzalez et al. (1993) found that when teachers engage in research visits to students' homes for the purpose of identifying and documenting knowledge that exists in their homes and participating in reflective study groups, teachers have a new appreciation of the community's resources. Subsequently, they can plan and implement educational experiences that tap into the household funds of knowledge. Inclusion of parents in this process validates students' household knowledge as worthy of pedagogical notice.

Maria Hensley (1995), one of the teachers in the Funds of Knowledge Teaching Project, asserted that teachers and administrators who see parents as lacking in parenting skills, education, and knowledge have failed to take the time to get to know the parents, to delve into their world, and to discover their true "funds of knowledge." Hensley described how finding the families' funds of knowledge benefitted her students. For example, when she interviewed Mr. Jarman, the father of one of her kindergarten students, she found out that he cared for plants in his job as a groundskeeper. She realized that this would be a wonderful way to get expert advice on starting a garden with her class. Mr. Jarman helped the class to prepare and plant a vegetable and flower garden. Even though she had tapped into a fund of knowledge and the project was a success, had she not engaged in future interviews with Mr. Jarman, she would not have discovered that he also had musical talents. By having Mr. Jarman come to class and play for the children, the relationship expanded to one in which he wrote children's songs and created a musical based on the familiar children's story, *The Little Red Hen*, which combined his expertise in music and gardening. Mr. Jarman continued to write songs for the class, which sparked an entire thematic unit on music and sound, which in turn led to spin-off projects. One of the projects involved the teaching assistant's *nana* (grandmother) and *tía* (aunt) (101 and 102 years old, respectively) coming to class to help the children make tortillas, and another engaged the students in preparing fry bread, which was guided by a Navajo parent. Hensley concluded that she would not have thought to have these experts come to her class had it not been for the Funds of Knowledge Teaching Project. Gonzalez (1995) cautioned that the curricula developed based on household knowledge must be designed to enhance traditional curricula, not to replace them. Framing the curricula and pedagogy with familiar contextual cues is key to improving students' engagement in learning.

Further discussion of cultural compatibility as an aspect of context within the broader area of context and cognition can be exemplified also through projects done in non-Western societies. Holmes (1992), investigating Australian Aboriginal language early childhood programs, reported that the independent Aboriginal schools have challenged the dominant culture to deliver culturally appropriate educational programs to meet the needs of indigenous children. Holmes further asserted that the dominant Anglo education system has alienated Aboriginal children from their families and community, and has been responsible for

Aborigines rejecting their traditional values and way of life. Increasingly, Aborigines are rejecting this ethnocentric education system and want a curriculum to meet their needs.

Holmes (1992) concluded that there are many difficulties in implementing culturally compatible early childhood programs for Aboriginal peoples. Examples of these contextual factors include the small size of many of the Aboriginal language groups, the choice of language and its orthography, inadequate teacher-education resources, an inadequate number of trained Aboriginal teachers, limited print resources, lack of parent and/or community support, and continuing resistance from policymakers, politicians, and the public.

Two cases that are examples of the success of minority-directed programs are reported by Harrison (1993). In both cases, this success can be attributed to the empowerment of the local native communities in the decision-making process. In the Alaska Native Programs, schools went through a lengthy transition from being administered by Alaska's state-operated school system to becoming "contract" schools that were controlled by the local villages. During this period, over 100 Alaska Natives were certified as classroom teachers statewide. The overall effect of these structural changes provided an opportunity for parents and other local community members to participate in the direction of their village schools at both the elementary and secondary levels.

Restructuring of the New Zealand Maori Programs (Harrison, 1993) is also key to their ongoing success. The establishment of the early childhood "language nests" (Maori language immersion preschool programs for infants from birth to five years of age) was a response to the realization that the Maori language was disappearing and an attempt to place both the authority and the responsibility for the preschools under local control. Harrison concluded that the difference between success or failure may hinge on whether or not parents have the power to make choices about appropriate education for their children, rather than on specific instructional techniques.

In a study that involved the assessment of preschools in South Africa, Whisson and Manona (1991) described a South African project in which student achievement is successful when culture is taken into account and the local communities are empowered to establish their own early childhood programs. Whisson and Manona stated that even though the preschool ideal may be to develop an active, questioning, creative child ready to seize every educational opportunity, when faced by 80 children in a packed classroom, a teacher may well prefer a child who sits still for as long as needed, asks no questions, and does what he or she is told. Parents want their children to learn, so the children will be able to compete in the world of limited employment and higher educational opportunities. For this, many will make great sacrifices. What they do not want is their children to lose respect either for them as parents or for their customs. These realities are a part of the South African preschool environment, and the teacher is a part of this environment and culture.

In South Africa, the culture's values and the ambivalences between preschool educational and local ideals manifest themselves in what the teachers, students, and parents do. Rather than impose given ways of doing things, the management, the Border Early Learning Centre (BELC), promotes learning through experience and experimentation so that trainers, teachers, and students alike learn what actually works for them. The BELC accomplishes this by providing teacher training and support and guidance for communities, and by encouraging further parental and community involvement. The minimal guidance they impose is largely aimed at protecting the facilities, personnel, and children from coming to serious harm. Everything else is communicated through encouragement, collaboration, action, and assessment. As a result, subcultural clashes are minimized, and even when the management cannot fully comprehend the complex contextual forces working in a particular environment, tolerance compensates for any lack of understanding. Goodwill is assumed until it is positively disproved.

IMPLICATIONS FOR EDUCATIONAL PROGRAMS

This discussion has shown that a number of factors must be considered when planning and implementing educational innovations and instructional contexts for students. The contextual variability of student output, especially the heightened levels of engagement in classroom activities and performance outcomes, are optimized when these factors are given attention.

Contextual features and what they mean to teachers and students can change. A classroom that is responsive to contextual changes and to children's needs and capacities as they change over time is one in which teachers make adjustments throughout the year, add new materials and activities, adjust the schedule, build on the interests and questions of the children, and involve them in decision-making about group activities and problems.

An important feature of contextualized teaching and learning is that they have elements that are nonlinear and recursive. That is, context-based education provides opportunities for teachers and learners to pause and reflect, to think back to previous ideas, and to compare new and old information, as well as to anticipate what is to come. Teachers can create such contexts if they are open to new ideas and continuously refine their practices. Strategies that can help teachers achieve this goal include:

- Consider the role of their own cultural background, biases, values, and personal experiences when preparing and implementing activities for young children.

- Analyze the needs of students in relation to both the circumstances of the moment and long-term objectives. Evaluate the relative merits of teaching practices considered exemplary and judge their appropriateness for their own particular circumstances.

- Use every class and every activity as an opportunity to reflect and improve.

- Analyze input received from parent-child-teacher conferences, parent-teacher conferences, and informal conversations with family members.

- Become familiar with each family's specific child-rearing practices. Determine what role their culture plays in their overall ideas about child rearing, health care, and education.

- Learn about the community in which each family lives, and gather information regarding different cultures within that community.

- Seek knowledge and advice from colleagues through discussions and from personal observations of other teachers' practices as well as their own in-class observations.

- Conduct action research in their classroom or collaborate with educational researchers to examine their practice critically.

• Expand their repertoire of teaching methods and deepen their knowledge base.

All young children deserve an early childhood education that is responsive to the context of their families, communities, and cultural backgrounds. If teachers are to maximize cognitive learning in young children, in addition to the other developmental domains, they must bridge what is known about each child's family, culture, and community to the classroom.

NOTES

1. Exceptions include Erickson (1982) and Wolcott (1982).

2. A few educational researchers have also examined correlations between interactional features and outcomes in some kinds of cooperative learning groups (see Webb, 1989, for a review).

3. Scholars not explicitly operating within the cultural-historical tradition (e.g., Light & Butterworth, 1993; Sternberg & Wagner, 1994) have also begun developing ideas about context and cognition. Some early attempts (Feldman, 1980, and Fischer, 1980, as cited in Rogoff, 1984) limited their discussion to the features of the task or domain of knowledge. More recently, scholars (e.g., Eckensberger, 1990) are attempting to develop theories that encompass cognition and multiple levels of context.

REFERENCES

Au, K. (1980). Participation structures in a reading lesson with Hawaiian children: Analysis of a culturally appropriate instructional event. *Anthropology and Education Quarterly, 11*(2), 91–115.

Barnhardt, C. (1982). Tuning-in: Athabaskan teachers and Athabaskan students. In R. Barnhardt (Ed.), *Cross-cultural issues in Alaskan education* (Vol. 2, pp. 144–164). Fairbanks: University of Alaska, Center for Cross-Cultural Studies.

Barnouw, V. (1973). *Culture and personality* (Rev. ed.). Homewood, IL: Dorsey Press.

Bateson, G. (1958). *Naven: A survey of the problems suggested by a composite picture of the culture of a New Guinea tribe drawn from three points of view* (2nd ed.). Stanford, CA: Stanford University Press.

Bronfenbrenner, U. (1977). Toward an experimental ecology of human development. *American Psychologist*, July, 513–531.

Brown, A. L., & Ferrara, R. A. (1985). Diagnosing zones of proximal development. In J. V. Wertsch (Ed.), *Culture, communication and cognition: Vygotskian perspectives* (pp. 273–305). Cambridge, MA: Harvard University Press.

Castle, S., & Arends, R. (1992). *The practice of teaching: Cooperative learning.* Paper presented at the annual meetings of the American Educational Research Association, Boston, MA.

Chang-Wells, G. L., & Wells, G. (1993). Dynamics of discourse: Literacy and the construction of knowledge. In E. A. Forman, N. Minick, & C. A. Stone (Eds.), *Contexts for learning: Sociocultural dynamics in children's development* (pp. 58–90). New York: Oxford University Press.

Cobb, P., Wood, T., & Yackel, E. (1993). Discourse, mathematical thinking, and classroom practice. In E. A. Forman, N. Minick, & C. A. Stone (Eds.), *Contexts for learning: Sociocultural dynamics in children's development* (pp. 91–119). New York: Oxford University Press.

Cohen, E. (1993). From theory to practice: The development of an applied research program. In J. Berger & M. Zelditch, Jr. (Eds.), *Theoretical research programs: Studies in the growth of theory* (pp. 385–415). Stanford, CA: Stanford University Press.

Cohen, E., Lotan, R., & Catanzarite, L. (1990). Treating status problems in the cooperative classroom. In S. Sharan (Ed.), *Cooperative learning: Theory and research* (pp. 203–229). New York: Praeger.

Cole, M., Gay, J., Glick, J., & Sharp, D. (1971). *The cultural context of learning and thinking: An exploration in experimental anthropology.* New York: Basic Books.

Collins, A., Brown, J. S., & Newman, S. E. (1989). Cognitive apprenticeship: Teaching the crafts of reading, writing, and mathematics. In L. Resnick (Ed.), *Knowing, learning, and instruction: Essays in honor of Robert Glaser* (pp. 453–494). Hillsdale, NJ: Erlbaum.

Eckensberger, L. H. (1990). From cross-cultural psychology to cultural psychology. *The Quarterly Newsletter of the Laboratory of Comparative Human Cognition, 12*(1), 37–52.

Eldering, L. (1995). Child-rearing in bi-cultural settings: A culture-ecological approach. *Psychology and Developing Societies, 7*(2), 133–153.

Engestrom, Y. (1993). Developmental studies of work as a testbench of activity theory: The case of primary care medical practice. In S. Chaiklin & J. Lave (Eds.), *Understanding practice: Perspectives on activity and context* (pp. 64–103). New York: Cambridge University Press.

Erickson, F. (1982). Taught cognitive learning in its immediate environments: A neglected topic in the anthropology of education. *Anthropology & Education Quarterly, 13,* 149–180.

Erickson, F., & Mohatt, G. (1981). Cultural differences in teaching styles in an Odawa school: A sociolinguistic approach. In H. T. Trueba, G. P. Gutherie, & K. H. Au (Eds.), *Culture in the bilingual classroom: Studies in classroom ethnography* (pp. 105–119). Rowley, MA: Newbury House.

Erickson, F., & Mohatt, G. (1982). Cultural organization of participant structures in two classrooms of Indian students. In G. D. Spindler (Ed.), *Doing the ethnography of schooling: Educational anthropology in action* (pp. 132–174). New York: Holt, Rinehart & Winston.

Fortes, M. (1970). Social and psychological aspects of education in Taleland. In J. Middleton (Ed.), *From child to adult: Studies in the anthropology of education* (pp. 14–74). Garden City, NY: Natural History Press. (Reprinted from *Africa*, 1938, 11(4).)

Gallimore, R., & Goldenberg, C. (1993). Activity settings of early literacy: Home and school factors in children's emergent literacy. In E. A. Forman, N. Minick, & C. A. Stone (Eds.), *Contexts for learning: Sociocultural dynamics in children's development* (pp. 315–335). New York: Oxford University Press.

Gladwin, T. (1970). *East is a big bird: Navigation and logic on a Puluwat atoll.* Cambridge, MA: Harvard University Press.

Gonzalez, N. (1995). The funds of knowledge teaching project. *Practicing Anthropology, 17*(3), 3–6.

Gonzalez, N., Moll, L., Floyd-Tenery, M., Rivera, A., Rendon, P., Gonzales, R., & Amanti, C. (1993). *Teacher research on funds of knowledge: Learning from households* (Educational Practice Report No. 6). Washington, DC: National Center for Research on Cultural Diversity and Second Language Learning.

Goodnow, J. J. (1990). The socialization of cognition: What's involved? In J. W. Stigler, R. A. Shweder, & G. Herdt (Eds.), *Cultural psychology: Essays on comparative human development* (pp. 259–286). Cambridge: Cambridge University Press.

Goodnow, J. J. (1993). Direction of post-Vygotskian research. In E. A. Forman, N. Minick, & C. A. Stone (Eds.), *Contexts for learning: Sociocultural dynamics in children's development* (pp. 369–381). New York: Oxford University Press.

Greenfield, P. (1984). A theory of the teacher in the learning activities of everyday life. In B. Rogoff & J. Lave (Eds.), *Everyday cognition: Its development in social context* (pp. 117–138). Cambridge, MA: Harvard University Press.

Greenfield, P., Reich, L., & Olver, R. (1966). On culture and equivalence: II. In J. Bruner, R. Olver, & P. Greenfield (Eds.), *Studies in cognitive growth* (pp. 270–318). New York: Wiley.

Griffin, P., Belyaeva, A., Soldatova, G., & the Velikhov-Hamburg Collective. (1993). Creating and reconstituting contexts for educational interactions, including a computer program. In E. A. Forman, N. Minick, & C. A. Stone (Eds.), *Contexts for learning: Sociocultural dynamics in children's development* (pp. 120–152). New York: Oxford University Press.

Harkness, S., & Super, C. (1993) The developmental niche: Implications for children's literacy development. In L. Eldering & P. Leseman (Eds.), *Early intervention and culture: Preparation for literacy. The interface between theory and practice* (pp. 115–132). Paris: UNESCO.

Harrison, B. (1993). Building our house from the rubbish tree: Minority-directed education. In E. Jacob & C. Jordan (Eds.), *Minority education: Anthropological perspectives* (pp. 147–164). Norwood, NJ: Ablex.

Heath, S. B. (1982). Questioning at home and at school: A comparative study, doing the ethnography of schooling. In G. Spindler (Ed.), *Educational anthropology in action* (pp. 102–131). New York: Holt, Rinehart & Winston.

Hensley, M. (1995). From untapped potential to creative realization: Empowering parents. *Practicing Anthropology, 17*(1), 13–16.

Hiebert, E., & Fisher, C. (1991). Task and talk structures that foster literacy. In E. H. Hiebert (Ed.), *Literacy for a diverse society: Perspectives, practices, and policies* (pp. 141–156). New York: Teachers College Press.

Holmes, T. (1992). *Australian Aboriginal language early childhood education programmes* (Report No. PS 020889). Aotearoa/New Zealand: Australia-New Zealand Foundation. (ERIC Document Reproduction Service No. ED 351 134)

Jacob, E. (1992). Culture, context, and cognition. In M. LeCompte, W. Millroy, & J. Preissle (Eds.), *The handbook of qualitative research in education* (pp. 293–335). San Diego, CA: Academic Press.

Jacob, E. (1996). *Cooperative learning in context.* Unpublished Manuscript.

Jacob, E., Rottenberg, L., Patrick, S., & Wheeler, E. (1996). Cooperative learning: Context and opportunities for acquiring academic English. *TESOL Quarterly, 30*(2), 253–280.

Lave, J. (1977). Cognitive consequences of traditional apprenticeship training in West Africa. *Anthropology & Education Quarterly, 8*, 177–180.

Lave, J. (1988). *Cognition in practice: Mind, mathematics and culture in everyday life*. New York: Cambridge University Press.

Lave, J., Murtaugh, M., & de la Rocha, O. (1984). The dialectic of arithmetic in grocery shopping. In B. Rogoff & J. Lave (Eds.). *Everyday cognition: Its development in social context* (pp. 67–94). Cambridge, MA: Harvard University Press.

Lave, J., & Wenger, E. (1991). *Situated learning: Legitimate peripheral participation*. New York: Cambridge University Press.

Leont'ev, A. N. (1978). *Activity, consciousness, and personality*. Englewood Cliffs, NJ: Prentice Hall.

Leont'ev, A. N. (1981). *Problems in the development of mind*. Moscow: Progress Publishers.

Light, P., & Butterworth, G. (Eds.). (1993). *Context and cognition: Ways of learning and knowing*. Hillsdale, NJ: Erlbaum.

Litowitz, B. (1993). Deconstruction in the zone of proximal development. In E. Forman, N. Minick, & C. A. Stone (Eds.), *Contexts for learning: Sociocultural dynamics in children's development* (pp. 184–196). New York: Oxford University Press.

McCollum, P. (1991). Cross-cultural perspectives on classroom discourse and literacy. In E. Hiebert (Ed.), *Literacy for a diverse society: Perspectives, practices, and policies* (pp. 108–121). New York: Teachers College Press.

Meloth, M., & Deering, P. (1994). Task talk and task awareness under different cooperative learning conditions. *American Educational Research Journal, 31*(1): 138–165.

Michaels, S. (1981). "Sharing time": Children's narrative styles and differential access to literacy. *Language in Society, 10*, 423–442.

Minick, N. (1989). Mind and activity in Vygotsky's work: An expanded frame of reference. *Cultural Dynamics, 2*, 162–187.

Minick, N. (1993). Teacher's directives: The social construction of "literal meanings" and "real worlds" in classroom discourse. In S. Chaiklin & J. Lave (Eds.), *Understanding practice: Perspectives on activity and context* (pp. 343–375). New York: Cambridge University Press.

Minick, N., Stone, C. A., & Forman, E. A. (1993). Introduction: Integration of individual, social, and institutional processes in accounts of children's learning and development. In E. A. Forman, N. Minick, & C. A. Stone (Eds.), *Contexts for learning: Sociocultural dynamics in children's development* (pp. 3–16). New York: Oxford University Press.

Munroe, R. L., & Munroe, R. H. (1971). Effects of environmental experience on spatial ability in an East African society. *Journal of Social Psychology, 83*, 15–22.

Nerlove, S. B., Roberts, J. M., Klein, R. E., Yarbrough, C., & Habicht, J.-P. (1974). Natural indicators of cognitive development: An observational study of rural Guatemalan children. *Ethos, 2,* 265–295.

Newman, D., Griffin, P., & Cole, M. (1989). *The construction zone: Working for cognitive change in school.* Cambridge: Cambridge University Press.

Nicolopoulou, A., & Cole, M. (1993). Generation and transmission of shared knowledge in the culture of collaborative learning: The Fifth Dimension, its play-world, and its institutional contexts. In E. A. Forman, N. Minick, & C. A. Stone (Eds.), *Contexts for learning: Sociocultural dynamics in children's development* (pp. 283–314). New York: Oxford University Press.

Palincsar, A. S., & Brown, A. L. (1984). Reciprocal teaching of comprehension-fostering and monitoring activities. *Cognition and Instruction, 1,* 117–175.

Philips, S. (1972). Participant structures and communicative competence: Warm Springs children in community and classroom. In C. Cazden, V. John, & D. Hymes (Eds.), *Functions of language in the classroom* (pp. 370–394). Prospect Heights, IL: Waveland Press.

Phillips, C. (1994). The movement of African-American children through sociocultural contexts: A case of conflict resolution. In B. Mallory & R. New (Eds.), *Diversity and developmentally appropriate practices: Challenges for early childhood education* (pp. 137–154). New York: Teachers College Press.

Rogoff, B. (1984). Introduction: Thinking and learning in social context. In B. Rogoff & J. Lave (Eds.), *Everyday cognition: Its development in social context* (pp. 1–8). Cambridge, MA: Harvard University Press.

Rogoff, B. (1990). *Apprenticeship in thinking: Cognitive development in social context.* New York: Oxford University Press.

Säljö, R., & Wyndhamn, J. (1993). Solving everyday problems in the formal setting: An empirical study of the school as context for thought. In S. Chaiklin & J. Lave (Eds.), *Understanding practice: Perspectives on activity and context* (pp. 327–342). New York: Cambridge University Press.

Scribner, S., & Cole, M. (1981). *The psychology of literacy.* Cambridge, MA: Harvard University Press.

Serpell, R. (1993). Interface between sociocultural and psychological aspects of cognition. In E. A. Forman, N. Minick, & C. A. Stone (Eds.), *Contexts for learning: Sociocultural dynamics in children's development* (pp. 357–368). New York: Oxford University Press.

Sharan, S., Kussell, P., Sharan, Y., & Bejarano, Y. (1984). Cooperative learning: Background and implementation of this study. In S. Sharan, P. Kussell, R. Hertz-Lazarowitz, Y. Bejarano, S. Raviv, & Y. Sharan (Eds.), *Cooperative learning in the classroom: Research in desegregated schools* (pp. 1–45). Hillsdale, NJ: Erlbaum.

Simpson, J., & Weiner, E., (Eds.). (1989). *The Oxford English dictionary* (2nd ed.). Oxford: Clarendon Press.

Slavin, R. (1986). *Using student team learning* (3rd ed.). Baltimore, MD: Johns Hopkins University, The Johns Hopkins Team Learning Project.

Slavin, R. (1990). *Cooperative learning: Theory, research, and practice.* Englewood Cliffs, NJ: Prentice Hall.

Sternberg, R. J., & Wagner, (Eds.). (1994). *Mind in context: Interactionist perspectives on human intelligence.* Cambridge: Cambridge University Press.

Tharp, R. (1989). Psychocultural variables and constants: Effects on teaching and learning in schools. *American Psychologist, 44*(2), 349–359.

Trueba, H. (1988). English literacy acquisition: From cultural trauma to learning disabilities in minority students. *Linguistics and Education, 1,* 125–152.

Tyler, S. (Ed.). (1969). *Cognitive anthropology.* New York: Holt, Rinehart, & Winston.

Vogt, L., Jordan, C., & Tharp, R. (1993). Explaining school failure, producing school success: Two cases. In E. Jacob & C. Jordan, (Eds.), *Minority education: Anthropological perspectives* (pp. 53–65). Norwood, NJ: Ablex.

Vygotsky, L. S. (1978). *Mind in society: The development of higher psychological processes.* Cambridge, MA: Harvard University Press.

Vygotsky, L. S. (1981). The genesis of the higher mental function. In J. V. Wertsch (Ed.), *The concept of activity in Soviet Psychology* (pp. 144–188). Armonk, NY: Sharpe.

Wagner, D. (1974). The development of short-term and incidental memory: A cross-cultural study. *Child Development, 45,* 389–396.

Webb, N. (1989). Peer interaction and learning in small groups. *International Journal of Educational Research, 13,* 21–39.

Wertsch, J. V., Minick, N., & Arns, F. (1984). The creation of context in joint problem-solving. In B. Rogoff & J. Lave (Eds.), *Everyday cognition: Its development in social context* (pp. 151–171). Cambridge, MA: Harvard University Press.

Whisson, M., & Manona C. (1991). *Assessing pre-schools: An ethnographic approach* (Report No. PS 019961). The Hague, the Netherlands: Bernard van Leer Foundation. (ERIC Document Reproduction Service No. ED 338 384)

Whiting, B. (1976). The problem of the packaged variable. In K. F. Riegel & S. A Meacham (Eds.), *The developing individual in a changing world* (Vol. 1, pp. 303–309). The Hague, the Netherlands: Mouton.

Wolcott, H. (1982). The anthropology of learning. *Anthropology and Education Quarterly, 13*, 83–108.

Wood, D., Bruner, J., & Ross, G. (1976). The role of tutoring in problem solving. *Journal of Child Psychology and Psychiatry, 17*, 89–100.

CHAPTER SIX

Modifiability of Cognitive Components

Fons Van de Vijver

INTELLIGENCE AND INTERVENTION STUDIES

There is a long history of debate on the success of cognitive enrichment programs (for recent updates, see Locurto, 1991, and Brand, 1996). The leading question debated is simple: Can interventions permanently change intelligence? The answer has turned out to be far from straightforward. A particularly heated debate was triggered by Jensen's (1969) review of the findings of the early Head Start programs. According to him, these "produced only modest gains of 10 IQ points—little more than is expected from the practice effect conferred by a first occasion of being tested; and even these gains were lost within two years" (Jensen quoted in Brand, 1996, p. 129). I do not intend to discuss the validity of Jensen's claim and thereby join in the debate with its strong political overtones. Rather, I will argue that the debate has been hampered by the way in which intelligence has been conceptualized. I contend that instead of conceptualizing intelligence as a general intellectual ability that is measured by omnibus tests and expressed in IQ, evaluations of intervention studies would benefit more from a componential view of intelligence (e.g., Embretson, 1984, 1985; Sternberg, 1977, 1985; Van de Vijver, 1991), which would allow the components of the cognitive system that are affected by intervention to be more precisely identified. To this end, various issues related to the modifiability of the cognitive system of the child will be discussed in the present chapter from a componential perspective. In the next section, current views on intelligence are described, followed by the presentation of a componential model of intelligence in the third section. The fourth section will address the modifiability of each component. The introduction of a componential model enables us to discuss a pivotal question of intervention programs. To what extent will the cognitive training effects generalize to other contexts? Many intervention programs involve preschool children. Implications for intervention studies will be discussed in the final section.

CURRENT VIEWS ON INTELLIGENCE

Lumpers and Splitters

The question of how intelligence is composed has been discussed at length in the literature. In essence, two camps can be discerned: lumpers and splitters (Mayr, 1982; Weinberg, 1989). Lumpers such as Spearman (1923; Brand, 1996; Jensen, 1980) consider intelligence "as a general, unified capacity for acquiring knowledge, reasoning and solving problems that is demonstrated in different ways (navigating a course without a compass, memorizing the Koran, or programming a computer)" (Weinberg, 1989, p. 98). Empirical evidence for the lumpers' view is commonly derived from factor analysis studies of intellectual tasks. Cognitive tasks tend to show positive intercorrelations. This so-called "positive manifold" will give rise to a strong first factor, labeled "g" (for general intelligence).

Spearman also put forward some ideas about the principles underlying g, namely "abstractness" and "noegenesis" (Spearman & Jones, 1950, quoted in Jensen, 1980, p. 29). Abstractness refers to phenomena that are not perceivable by the senses. The noegenetic principles refer to the transformations of abstract material that are characteristic of intellectual functioning. One such transformation is the eduction of relations, according to which the perception of two stimuli (for example, *day* and *night*) "tends to evoke immediately a knowing of relation between them." (Spearman, 1923, quoted in Radford & Burton, 1974, p. 125). So, in Spearman's view, the characteristic elements of g are stimulus transformations that are commonly found in tests of reasoning and abstract thinking.

Since the 1920s, the question of the psychological nature of g has received little attention. Only fairly recently has it regained prominence. For instance, there have been several studies aiming to break down intelligence into elementary cognitive operations (Vernon, 1987). It was question red whether or not it was possible to devise tests that show a high correlation with *g* and that require stimulus transformations that are as simple as possible. A good example of this paradigm is constituted by the study of inspection times (Brand & Deary, 1982; Nettelbeck, 1987). In these studies, slides showing two vertical lines of unequal length were very briefly projected on to a screen. The subjects had to indicate whether the longer line was on the left or on the right. Inspection time is defined as the time taken by the subject to identify correctly the location of the longer line at a given accuracy rate (usually 97.5 percent). Inspection time was found to be significantly correlated with intelligence; individuals with a high IQ tended to require shorter inspection times. This line of research suggests that *g* is associated with rapid extraction of information— much more than with rapid execution of responses (Brand, 1996, p. 78); thus, individual differences in *g* are essentially differences in "extraction speed."

Splitters such as Thurstone "hold that intelligence is composed of many separate mental abilities that operate more or less independently" (Weinberg, 1989, p. 99). Like Spearman, Thurstone (1938) used factor analysis to identify these mental abilities. He called these the Primary Mental Abilities: verbal comprehension, memory, perceptual speed, space, verbal fluency, and reasoning, the latter which he labelled a combination of induction and deduction. The factor analytical tools developed by Spearman and Thurstone and refined by others triggered an impressive number of studies. See Carroll (1993) for a recent, comprehensive review of studies of this paradigm that has been steadily declining in popularity in the last few decades.

RAPPROCHEMENTS

Despite the vast amount of effort and publications devoted to the factorial structure of intelligence, there is no clear winner of the lumper-splitter debate. Rather, two kinds of syntheses of the lumper and splitter perspectives have been proposed, both of which employ more recent statistical techniques to address the structure underlying a correlation matrix. First, in a study of 1,254 Swedish sixth graders, Gustafsson (1984) used confirmatory factor analysis to show that hierarchical models are compatible with both lumper and splitter models. The top of the structure of intellectual abilities is formed by *g*. This (Spearmanian) general intelligence can be taken to consist of two broad factors, namely, the ability to deal with both verbal and figural information. The third and lowest level contains the Thurstonian primary mental abilities. The lumper and splitter perspectives are reconciled here by introducing a layered view of intellectual functioning. Gustafsson's work is a continuation of the tradition of factor analysts such as Burt, Cattell, Horn, and Vernon. In his extensive review of factor analysis studies, Carroll (1993) also concluded that a hierarchical model of intelligence is the best synthesis of the available evidence. In his model, intelligence has three strata, with g being the bottom stratum. The middle stratum consists of broad ability factors such as fluid intelligence (i.e., reasoning skills) and general memory ability. The top stratum has specific abilities that are specific realizations of middle stratum factors. For instance, quantitative reasoning and induction are aspects of fluid intelligence.

The second synthesis is based on multidimensional scaling; an example can be found in the work of R. E. Snow (e.g., Marshalek, Lohman, & Snow, 1983; Snow, 1980; Snow, Kyllonen, & Marshalek, 1984). A two-dimensional solution tends to give a good approximation of a correlation matrix of intellectual tasks. In a reanalysis, Snow et al., (1984) found a reasonable fit for two-dimensional solutions for a variety of data, even for the 1938 and 1941 data matrices of Thurstone, which were used to illustrate Multiple Factor Theory. In each of these analyses, Snow and his colleagues found approximately the same structure, tests which presumably measure g-like aspects were located in or near the "bull's eye," while psychologically less complex tasks were located more peripherally.

It can be concluded that upon closer scrutiny, the old problem of the inequivalence of solutions based on different factor analysis models has lost much of its meaning and actuality; with more recent statistical techniques such as structural equation modeling (confirmatory factor analysis) and multidimensional scaling, a large congruence in solutions can be obtained.

Evaluation

The lumper perspective was fruitful for the study of intelligence; Spearman's g gave rise to various new theories, instruments, and even new statistical methods (rotation methods and new models in factor analysis, (cf., Van de Vijver, 1993). However, the concept of general intelligence is counterproductive for intervention studies. First, because of the concept's high aggregation level, or abstractness, it is difficult to pinpoint loci of changes after intervention. What does it mean that a child shows an IQ gain of 10 points after training? Does the gain refer to an increased reasoning capacity, to mere test wiseness, or to a training-induced increment of knowledge in areas tapped by the test? Lumper models do not provide us with hints as to how to enhance the development of reasoning by training. Second, the concept of general intelligence is unlikely to generate accurate insight into transfer, a vital issue in enrichment programs.

Although both lumper and splitter models provide structural descriptions of intelligence, they do not address the question of how the structural aspects are functionally interrelated in practical problem-solving. None of these structural models addresses the actual solution process (cf., Messick, 1972). It is not surprising that after decades of emphasis on the structure of intelligence, more recent models, called componential models, focus instead on functional and process aspects (e.g., Embretson, 1984, 1985; Sternberg, 1977, 1985). Even though the scope of these models is broader, their primary domain of application has been the study of reasoning, mainly involving analogy tasks. Componential models turned out to be attempts to develop process descriptions of Spearman's *g* and Thurstone's reasoning factor. Compared to these structural models of intelligence, componential models offer more scope for designing and implementing educational programs. Therefore, two of these models will be described in the next section.

A COMPONENTIAL VIEW OF INTELLIGENCE

Probably the best known componential model is the one developed by Sternberg (1977). He argued that in the solution process of an analogical reasoning item of the form $a : b = c : d$ the following component processes are present: (1) an encoding phase, in which the subject identifies the attributes and values of each term of the problem; (2) an inference phase, in which the subject tries to discover the relationship between a and b; (3) a mapping phase, in which the subject tries to determine the relationship between a and c; (4) an application phase, in which the subject applies a relation found in the inference phase to c and an imaginary ideal response d'; and (5) an optional justification phase, which will occur in a multiple choice format when the subject is unable to find a d that is identical to d'. In such a case, the subject is assumed to choose the next best alternative.

Another, closely related model has been proposed by Embretson (1984, 1985). She developed a family of statistical models based on item response theory (Hambleton, Swaminathan, & Rogers, 1991; Molenaar & Fischer, 1995), in which the difficulty of an item is broken down into a number of components. The solution process of verbal analogies of the form $a : b = c : (x_1, x_2, x_3, x_4, x_5)$ is assumed to consist of three phases. The first is rule construction; in this phase the subject generates the rule that applies to the item. On the basis of this rule, the subject will select the corresponding alternative x_1 to x_5; this is called response evaluation. Only when the rule generated does not lead to a satisfactory answer will the subject need an additional phase, called rule recovery. A new rule is then generated to select from among the available alternatives. In both Sternberg's and Embretson's models, component processes are conceived of as building blocks that are needed during the solution process. Component processes are the basic units of cognitive functioning; abilities are concatenated components.

A fundamental weakness of these models is that little attention is paid to the knowledge structures involved in intellectual processes. This seems to be a serious omission, especially with respect to educational programs. Therefore, a componential model of intellectual functioning is presented that encompasses both the knowledge and its transformations in problem-solving being proposed (Van de Vijver, 1991; Van de Vijver & Willemsen, 1993). The model is closely related to Sternberg's and Embretson's models. It has four components: pragmatic knowledge, reasoning schemes, metacognitive knowledge, and execution. These elements are discussed in the following subsections.

Pragmatic Knowledge

People acquire a massive amount of factual information about themselves and their environment during their lives. Some of the knowledge may be derived from formal scientific theories, but most of it comes from daily experience. Examples of the latter are the knowledge that a ball can roll, that the sun generates heat, that there is a drink in the refrigerator. An example of the former is that the outcome of 1,000 times 1,000 is called a million, etc. Some of the knowledge can be made explicit (e.g., Homer was a Greek poet), but some knowledge is based on implicit inferences (e.g., children may be able to tell relatives from nonrelatives long before they can adequately describe the concept of "relatives"). Pragmatic knowledge is a summary label for all these facts and theories. Its role in intelligence is vital; it is involved in all intellectual abilities. Pragmatic knowledge is the content to which the reasoning is applied.

It should be acknowledged that terms such as facts and theories could easily convey the incorrect impression that this knowledge is invariably accurate; pragmatic knowledge may be inaccurate, incomplete, or even incorrect.

Reasoning Schemes

The availability of pragmatic knowledge is necessary though insufficient for attaining correct solutions to problems. Stimulus transformations of pragmatic knowledge are also needed. For example, when a child learns to speak, he or she has to master subtle generalizations and discriminations, such as in learning the difference between the concepts of "mother" and "woman." The pragmatic knowledge of the words has to be refined by stimulus transformations (generalization and discrimination). Reasoning schemes, the second aspect of intellectual reasoning, refer to these stimulus transformation rules. They are comparable to Piaget's notion of schema, which is defined as a cognitive structure "that is a more or less fluid form or plastic organization to which actions and objects are assimilated during cognitive functioning" (Flavell, 1963, p. 55).

Theories of intellectual functioning tend to emphasize the role of stimulus transformation rules; reasoning schemes are often considered the core of intelligence. Spearman's (1923) theory of the psychological meaning of g focuses on stimulus transformation rules such as the recognition of a relation between stimulus elements that are presented together (e.g., recognizing the opposition in the stimulus pair "father—mother"). Piaget's theory of cognitive development provides a second example; the theory essentially amounts to a hierarchy of reasoning schemes mastered successively by the developing child. In my view, the role of reasoning schemes in intelligence should not be overestimated. Stimulus transformations play an important role in the daily functioning of both children and adults but form merely one aspect of intellectual functioning. A child may have mastered the scheme required for conservation, that is to say, he or she is aware of the invariance of certain physical properties after transformation. But the child should know some elementary concepts of physics such as volume or weight before the scheme can be applied. Failure to show conservation behavior in a testing situation does not preclude a successful mastery of conservation in stimulus domains more familiar to the child (Dasen, 1977).

The separation of pragmatic knowledge and reasoning schemes can be superficial, particularly when it is applied to the behavior of young children; knowledge and transformation rules often do not refer to temporally separable processes or entities. This is best illustrated with an example. It is not uncommon to observe a close link between skill and domain of application in young children. Small changes to the initial problem (e.g., a slight rephrasing) may lead to major changes in the speed or the accuracy of the solution obtained. Reasoning schemes are often intrinsically linked to the problem-solving behavior in which they are applied (Dasen, 1977).

Metacognitive Knowledge

The third component of intelligence refers to the establishment of the link between pragmatic knowledge and one or more reasoning schemes. The child should realize that the solution of a problem requires a particular cognitive transformation. In order to find an adequate way to solve the problem, the child should be able to link pragmatic knowledge and reasoning schemes successfully. Metacognition involves the processes that control the monitoring of the solution (Sternberg, 1985). Examples of metacognitive components are the recognition and the choice of the relevant pragmatic knowledge, the choice of solution strategy, the monitoring of the solution process, and the change of solution strategy if the solution process does not lead to an outcome that has been envisaged.

Metacognitive knowledge is closely related to transfer and generalization. Transfer training usually amounts to learning to apply previously acquired schemes to new problems. As argued, work in the tradition of Piaget shows the inadequacy of the assumption of the intertask stability of reasoning schemes. Therefore, one of the targets of training programs should be a change in metacognitive knowledge.

Execution

The execution of the process refers to the final element of intellectual functioning. It involves the combination of the previous three elements in actual practice. The implications of the current model of intellectual functioning can be illustrated by a thought experiment in which a Piagetian conservation task is administered to a child that has never been exposed to a psychological task. The child is shown three transparent beakers of the same volume, two of which are identical— tall and thin—while the third is short and fat. The two tall beakers contain the same amount of colored liquid. The contents of one of the tall beakers is poured into the short beaker. The child is then asked to compare the amounts of liquid in the two beakers. The problem presupposes a fair amount of pragmatic knowledge, varying from the physical concept of quantity, to more mundane concepts and objects such as liquid fluid and transparent beakers. The reasoning scheme, the conservation of the amount of liquid, is the actual target of study. Metacognitive knowledge is involved in the recognition that the physical concepts mentioned are required, and also in the ability to express the ideas verbally. Moreover, the experimental situation presupposes knowledge about what kind of behavior is expected in question-and-answer games such as a testing situation (Serpell, 1979).

The actual behavior (the execution component) is the outcome of this complex combination of pragmatic knowledge, reasoning scheme, and metacognitive knowledge. Suppose that the child's verbal answer fails to demonstrate that it understands the principle of the conservation of an amount of liquid. This raises the question of how the failure should be explained. Perhaps the child has indeed not mastered the reasoning scheme yet, as the failure suggests. However, there may be other explanations connected to the other cognitive components. For instance, the child may be unable to give an adequate verbal account of his or her ideas (but may still accurately predict the level of liquid that will be attained by the water in a beaker of a model not yet used). Also, the child may not be used to working with transparent beakers. If the stimulus material is unfamiliar to the child, there is an increased likelihood that the child will be unable to link its knowledge to a relevant problem solution. Finally, the child may be confused about the testing situation, and be unable to execute the appropriate behavior. In sum, an adequate final product is conditional on the availability (or successful application) of each of the four elements.

The differences between the four components presented here, and between Sternberg's and Embretson's models, are smaller than a cursory reading might suggest. Sternberg and Embretson attempted to break down the process of solving an analogy item into components. A model of analogical reasoning is adequate if the time required to solve an item is the sum of the times required to go through the separate stages. The models pay less attention to the prerequisites for solving the items: What kind of knowledge is needed to detect the relationship between the first two elements of an analogy? What kind of knowledge is needed to recognize that the relationship between the first two elements should also be applied to the second pair? The model presented here pays attention to these questions. The two kinds of models have a different focus; whereas Sternberg and Embretson focus more on the modeling of a process, the present model pays more attention to the functional prerequisites.

The componential model is more fruitful from the perspective of training and intervention programs. It leaves more scope for a delineation of the modifiability of the components. It is easier to address the modifiability of, say, pragmatic knowledge and metacognitive knowledge than the modifiability of encoding and mapping.

MODIFIABILITY OF COGNITIVE COMPONENTS

Educational enrichment programs often involve massive investments of human effort and money. In order to avoid wasting energy and money on interventions with a low probability of success, an accurate assessment of the modifiability of each component is called for. The need for such an analysis is particularly evident from the debate on the modifiability of intelligence; in Weinberg's (1989) words: "The accumulating evidence suggests that the substandard intellectual skills and 'thinking' capacities of mildly mentally retarded populations, most of whom manifest no particular organic or central nervous system pathology (cultural-familial retardation), cannot be substantially or permanently raised by special training. But there is good reason to believe that interventions can enhance the functional abilities, learning strategies, adaptive skills, and social competencies of children whose measured IQ is low" (p. 103).

There is little reason to assume that Weinberg's conclusion is restricted to retarded populations. Moreover, the conclusion is interesting because of the distinction between broad cognitive aptitudes and specific functional abilities and the acknowledged differential modifiability of cognitive components. In my view, all four components are in principle modifiable through intervention, but the components strongly differ in the energy required to engender substantial changes through training. In order to arrive at adequate programs and realistic expectations of the size and duration of the training effects, designers of intervention programs should take differential modifiability into account.

Modifiability of Pragmatic Knowledge

Pragmatic knowledge is easily modifiable. Scholastic information is a good example of a type of pragmatic knowledge that is expanded over a long period. The training tasks of preschool programs will often contain pragmatic knowledge aimed at preparing the child for formal education, such as the teaching of letters and digits. Pragmatic knowledge will frequently be included in enrichment programs for at least two reasons. First, the child will master knowledge that can be used directly in the regular curriculum (e.g., the recognition of letters and digits, as mentioned previously). Second, much scholastic knowledge is cumulative; one concept is presupposed in the understanding of another. Hence, having mastered one concept will facilitate the comprehension of another one.

There is no critical period in life after which individuals cannot amass new pragmatic knowledge (without organic damage). There is abundant evidence for the modifiability of pragmatic knowledge in old age (e.g., Baltes & Schaie, 1976).

Modifiability of Reasoning Schemes

Cross-cultural research constitutes an interesting domain in which to study the modifiability of reasoning schemes. Two basic views on the modifiability can be found in the cross-cultural literature. The first view holds that formal education (or enrichment programs, for that matter) can have a formative influence on reasoning schemes. This view is most clearly represented in the work of Vygotsky (1978) and, more recently, Tulviste (1991). Although these authors were primarily interested in the psychological consequences of schooling and literacy programs among adults, their argument can be readily generalized to preschoolers. In this view, training could lead to substantial cognitive changes. Vygotsky's theory gave rise to interesting empirical studies of "unschooled literacy" (i.e., literacy that is not taught in a formal school setting). However, Berry and Bennett (1991) found that, in contrast to what could be expected from a Vygotskian perspective, unschooled literates and unschooled illiterates showed similar performances with regard to cognitive tasks. A lack of empirical corroboration has also been reported by Scribner and Cole (1981). So, the view that training will have a formative influence on reasoning schemes is seriously challenged by empirical findings.

The second view is more in line with Berry and Bennett's findings. It holds that reasoning schemes are not imparted well by training. This view is expressed by Cole (1990), who wrote in relation to concrete operational thinking that "Although there is room for disagreement, I believe that it is sensible to conclude that concrete operational thinking is not influenced by schooling; what is influenced is subjects' ability to understand the language of testing and the presuppositions of the testing situation itself" (p. 99).

I concur with this view. It is unlikely that children will acquire reasoning schemes through training; the teaching of thinking will rarely result in the acquisition of new reasoning schemes. Rather, training will broaden the domain of application of reasoning schemes, and hence promote other aspects of intellectual functioning such as metacognitive skills. Recognizing which skills can be applied to solve a particular problem, and successfully applying these skills, may be more important in the teaching of thinking than the mastery of new reasoning schemes.

The poor trainability of reasoning schemes via training can easily be misconstrued. It does not imply that the impact of intervention programs is necessarily superficial and short-lasting, because reasoning schemes, incorrectly considered to constitute the core of intellectual functioning, are hardly susceptible to training influences. Rather, there will be no need to teach reasoning skills, because regardless of their socioeconomic and cultural circumstances, the children will already have mastered the schemes; what is lacking is the ability to use the schemes in testing situations, and this is mostly because of a lack of pragmatic and metacognitive knowledge. This view is in line with Case (1992), who contends that the cognitive system is characterized by "conceptual structures" (comparable to our reasoning schemes) which are not applicable to the entire range of the children's experience, but merely to experience within some particular domain (p. 62). Goossens (1992) even refers to "local structures" to emphasize the domain specificity of newly mastered cognitive skills.

Modifiability of Metacognitive Knowledge

In recent decades, there have been various studies on the training of metacognitive knowledge and skills, particularly the skills of reasoning (e.g., Crisafi & Brown, 1986; Holyoak, Junn, & Billman, 1984), memory (e.g., Cox, 1994; Jackson & Gildemeister, 1991; Lucangeli, Galderisi, & Cornoldi, 1995), and reading (e.g., Paris & Oka, 1986; Wright & Cashdan, 1991). Some tentative conclusions can be drawn from studies of the training of metacognition. First, metacognitive knowledge is modifiable through training. This has been demonstrated by various studies. Second, a successful intervention can lead to both narrow and broad effects on metacognition. The former refers to test-wiseness, that is, test-specific or assessment-specific skills that lead to higher scores. Test-wiseness can create a threat to the assessment of preschool training by inflating true intervention effects. Moreover, as Spitz (1991) argues, it is questionable whether test-wiseness can be circumvented: "It is just about impossible for intervention programs not to 'teach the test' or to the experimental learning and performance tasks, because there are limited kinds of materials and mental and physical challenges that are testable at early ages" (p. 332).

The second kind of effect is much broader and involves metacognitive knowledge that is not restricted to the training or assessment procedures but refers to the establishment and successful application of a cognitive plan of action to solve a problem. Training can have a pervasive effect on various aspects of metacognitive knowledge, such as the selection of stimuli to be acted upon, the activation of retrieval systems, and the monitoring of the solution (Rand & Kaniel, 1987). It is easy to underrate the role of metacognition in intervention studies. Indeed, it can be argued that the crucial link between problem characteristics and effective solution strategies is the recognition of which solution strategy should be used. Effective training *both* imparts skills *and* helps to delineate conditions in which these skills can be applied. The effectiveness of a metacognitive training, or of metacognitive aspects of a more general-purpose training, will largely determine the extent of the transfer that can be expected.

Modifiability of Execution

In problem-solving, the three previous components—pragmatic knowledge, reasoning schemes and metacognitive knowledge—are combined in a single action. The whole set can be considered as a skill (Fischer, 1980). Skills need training to be developed, but their execution as such will not change fundamentally after training. Increased efficiency after repeated exposure to a task is unlikely to be largely induced by mere execution. Rather, the improved performance is more likely to affect metacognitive knowledge. However, repeated exposure will often increase the degree of automatization of subprocesses in the execution and lead to an increased efficiency of metacognitive knowledge (e.g., an increased ability to eliminate irrelevant task features, and a reduced need to ponder which course of action to take).

There is evidence that the repeated execution of a task can affect the psychological structure of the skill involved. Several descriptions of this process have been given, following Fleishman and Hempel's (1954, 1955) seminal work. They found that intellectual components showed a stronger relationship with psychomotor performance in initial stages of skill learning, while motor performance became more prominent after prolonged training. More recently, Ackerman (1989) proposed a three-phase model of the learning of simple psychomotor skills; in the first phase, declarative knowledge is the most important source of individual differences, while perceptual processes (particularly perceptual speed) become more salient in a later stage. Longer training will lead to automatized routines of the use of pragmatic and metacognitive knowledge, and at the same time restore procedural knowledge (e.g., psychomotor skill, perceptual skill) as the most important source of individual differences. The models by Fleishman and Hempel and by Ackerman were developed to describe the learning process of psychomotor skills; they are not intended to account for the learning of skills with a larger cognitive complexity. Yet the basic idea that repeated solution of cognitive problems is characterized by a change in the underlying psychological composition of the skill is assumed to be valid across a wide range of skills.

Transfer

An essential question in the design, implementation, and evaluation of early educational intervention programs has to do with transfer of training effects: To what extent are the knowledge and skills acquired in the intervention available beyond the training sessions? Can they be transferred to school and daily life? The need to deal with transfer is illustrated in the literature on what are called problem isomorphs, (i.e., structurally similar problems dealing with different stimulus contents. An example of two problem isomorphs would be "What is 2 + 2?" and "There are two sons and two daughters in the Johnson family. How many children are there in the Johnson family?" (cf., Van de Vijver, 1991). Young children often experience difficulty in recognizing the structural similarity of problems—hence the applicability of mastered solution strategies. Children should therefore be taught how previously mastered solution strategies can be applied, in the original or adapted form, to new problem situations.

Transfer is an elusive concept. The literature on transfer does not yield clear answers about which conditions and tasks will make its appearance more likely. Reviewing the evidence, Holyoak and Spellman (1993) concluded that "the extent of transfer varies enormously as a function of the content and context of learning" (p. 300). Yet it is clear that humans, especially young children, are not very good at detecting structural similarities of problems. We often tend to be distracted by the framing of a problem, and we often fail to recognize the underlying structure. Training in one ability is not very likely to result in changes in related abilities. In Horn and Hofer's (1992) words, "The evidence of several decades of research (Ackerman, 1989) indicates that transfer is largely a function of similarity: the more similar the trained ability is to another ability, the more transfer there will be to that other ability. This evidence also indicates that the amount of transfer is often depressingly small, even when there appears to be considerable similarity" (p. 89).

Extensive research on the arithmetic behavior of children in school and in daily life (e.g., among street children in Brazil who sell sweets) has shown that the strategies taught in school are rarely applied in daily life (Lave, 1988). Various strategies used by street vendors are their own inventions, highly applicable in that context but probably less so in others. School math and street math frequently involve different solution strategies.

Intervention programs may suffer from similar problems: skills trained in these programs may remain resources that are not exploited when needed elsewhere. Various measures can be taken to maximize the probability of successful transfer from tasks trained in the intervention program to other contexts, such as home and school. First, because transfer is mainly determined by similarity between the context of learning and the context of application, the distance between these contexts should be minimized as much as possible. The design of educational programs may profit considerably from a good insight into the cognitive demands that are imposed upon children in school and in daily life. Such an analysis is likely to show that the cognitive transformations used at home and in school will not differ appreciably, but that the domain of application of the stimulus transformations is vastly different. Closing the gap between school and home could then start from the question of what kind of stimulus transformations are required (e.g., in reading) and which daily activities require similar transformations. Unfortunately, the design of preschool programs is thwarted by a lack of such knowledge. I agree with Case (1992), who has pointed out that school curricula have hardly been analyzed from the viewpoint of their central conceptual structure; we do not know very much about the reasoning schemes required in formal education (cf., however, Snow, this volume). Case's view also holds for the daily activities of children. As a consequence, it is easier to devise an intervention program in which scholastic or related knowledge is transmitted (cf., Slavin & Madden, this volume), than to devise one that attempts to modify the cognitive transformations that are required in school.

Second, the use of strategies as such can be imparted by training. It has repeatedly been pointed out that transfer of knowledge and strategies is an important aspect of schooling; the use of generalized solution strategies has indeed been put forward as a distinctive feature of schooled subjects as compared to unschooled subjects (cf., Rogoff, 1981). Spontaneous use of strategies such as clustered recall in memory tasks can be assumed to be strongly influenced by schooling (cf., Wagner, 1981). The recognition of the relevance of strategies and the ability to use these in problem-solving is probably one of the most characteristic aspects of what has been referred to as the "hidden curriculum" of formal education (i.e., the curriculum that is informally rather than formally transmitted).

Third, procedures proposed in educational psychology to foster transfer could be implemented in intervention studies. Examples of relevant aspects that could be addressed in metacognitive training are the recognition of problem similarity and isomorphism (Does the problem look like one that I have solved before?), and the adoption of general solution strategies (Can I split the problem into smaller parts that are easier to solve?). The training of metacognition is probably only successful when general rules are outlined, such as "think about the problem before you act," and "try to think of other solutions." These strategies have the advantage of a high generalizability across problem domains; however, because of their context aspecificity, they do not offer much help in generating domain-dependent solution strategies (see Sternberg, 1987, for an application of these principles to a thinking training program for secondary and college students, Feuerstein, 1980, for an application to mental retardates, and Klein and Alony, 1993, for an application to young children).

Fourth, reducing the disparities in cognitive functioning of the child across various domains should be an important aim of intervention studies. This aim is not accomplished by teaching reasoning schemes, but by broadening the domain of application of mastered reasoning schemes. A lack of correspondence of the tasks in the intervention study training and in daily activities at home or in school can seriously impede the transfer and maintenance of skills acquired in the training. Young children will find it especially difficult to recognize structural similarities between different tasks. They will have to be trained to check routinely whether skills they have already mastered apply to the solution of a novel task.

CONCLUSION

At present, intervention programs are numerous; in the United States, there are more than 100 in the area of thinking alone (Coles, 1993). Obviously, there is a problem of choice. It may be impossible to find "the best" among all these programs; what will be the most appropriate program will depend on aspects such as subjects' age, their cultural and socioeconomic background, the cognitive functions to be stimulated or remediated, and the resources available. A componential view of intelligence is effective, as it will enhance the composition of a targeted and efficient intervention program. Pragmatic knowledge is relatively easily modifiable, but its effect will be local (i.e., will not influence nontrained skills); metacognitive knowledge is more difficult to impart by training, but its effect will be broader. Reasoning schemes will hardly ever require to be imparted by training. Finally, execution is easily trainable through repeated exposure.

The modifiability of the various components and the need or desirability to change these should be taken into account in the design of an intervention program. It is usually necessary to train subjects in metacognitive knowledge, and there is usually no reason to assume the absence of reasoning schemes. The generalization of the domain of application of previously mastered skills to new areas can hardly be overestimated in intervention studies; transfer and generalization are essential concepts in the design, implementation, and evaluation of training programs.

The size of effects that can be expected after training depends on the cognitive component involved. Training of pragmatic knowledge (such as letter recognition) will often yield a considerable change in scores after training, but the transfer to untrained tasks will be limited; metacognitive training, often geared to the domain broadening of a previously mastered skill, can be expected to lead to less dramatic though more broadly generalizing score increments.

By focusing on cognitive components and their modifiability, important features of intervention have been neglected, such as the role played by noncognitive factors and by the environment, including the caretakers of the child. There are strong indications that, particularly in effective programs with long-lived effects such as described by Kağıtçıbaşı (1994, this volume) and Reynolds (1994), noncognitive factors such as the enthusiasm of the mothers and attitude changes in the mothers that result in more attention to the formal and informal learning process of the child are also involved. Such an intervention program will have initiated a chain of lasting effects in mother and child.

REFERENCES

Ackerman, P. L. (1989). Individual differences and skill acquisition. In P. L. Ackerman, R. J. Sternberg, & R. Glaser (Eds.), *Learning and individual differences: Advances in theory and research* (pp. 164–217). New York: Freeman.

Baltes, P. B., & Schaie, K. W. (1976). On the plasticity of intelligence in adulthood and old age: Where Horn and Donaldson fail. *American Psychologist, 31,* 720–725.

Berry, J. W., & Bennett, J. A. (1991). Cree literacy: Cultural context and psychological consequences. In F. J. R. Van de Vijver & Y. H. Poortinga (Eds.), *Cross-cultural Psychology Monographs, no. 1.* Tilburg, the Netherlands: Tilburg University Press.

Brand, C. (1996). *The g factor. General intelligence and its implications*. New York: Wiley.

Brand, C., & Deary, I. J. (1982). Intelligence and "inspection time." In H. J. Eysenck (Ed.), *A model for intelligence* (pp. 133–150). New York: Springer.

Carroll, J. B. (1993). *Human cognitive abilities: A survey of factor-analytic studies.* Cambridge: Cambridge University Press.

Case, R. (1992). The role of conceptual structures in the development of children's scientific and mathematical thought. In A. Demetriou, M. Shayer, & A. Efklides (Eds.), *Neo-Piagetian theories of cognitive development.* London: Routledge.

Cole, M. (1990). Cognitive development and formal schooling. In L. C. Moll (Ed.), *Vygotsky and education* (pp. 89–110). Cambridge: Cambridge University Press.

Coles, M. J. (1993). Teaching thinking: Principles, problems and programmes. *Educational Psychology, 13,* 333–344.

Cox, B. D. (1994). Children's use of mnemonic strategies: Variability in response to metamemory training. *Journal of Genetic Psychology, 155,* 423–442.

Crisafi, M. A., & Brown, A. L. (1986). Analogical transfer of very young children: Combining two separately learned solutions to reach a goal. *Child Development, 57,* 953–968.

Dasen, P. R. (Ed.). (1977). *Piagetian psychology: Cross-cultural contributions.* New York: Gardner.

Embretson, S. E. (1984). A general latent trait model for response processes. *Psychometrika, 49,* 175–186.

Embretson, S. E. (1985). Multicomponent latent trait models for test design. In S. E. Embretson (Ed.), *Test design* (195–218). New York: Academic Press.

Feuerstein, R. (1980). *Instrumental enrichment: An intervention program for cognitive modifiability.* Baltimore, MD: University Park Press.

Fischer, K. W. (1980). A theory of cognitive development: The control and construction of hierarchies of skills. *Psychological Review, 57,* 477–531.

Flavell, J. H. (1963). *The developmental psychology of Jean Piaget.* New York: Van Nostrand Reinhold.

Fleishman, E. A., & Hempel, W. E. (1954). Change in factor structure of a complex psychomotor test as a function of practice. *Psychometrika, 19,* 239–252.

Fleishman, E. A., & Hempel, W. E. (1955). The relation between abilities and improvement with practice in a visual discrimination task. *Journal of Experimental Psychology, 49,* 301–310.

Goossens, L. (1992). Training scientific reasoning in children and adolescents. In A. Demetriou, M. Shayer, & A. Efklides (Eds.), *Neo-Piagetian theories of cognitive development*. London: Routledge.

Gustafsson, J-E. (1984). A unifying model for the structure of intellectual abilities. *Intelligence, 8,* 179–203.

Hambleton, R. K., Swaminathan, H., & Rogers, H. J. (1991). *Fundamentals of item response theory*. Newbury Park, CA: Sage.

Holyoak, K. J., Junn, E. N., & Billman, D. O. (1984). Development of analogical problem-solving skill. *Child Development, 55,* 2042–2055.

Holyoak, K. J., & Spellman, B. A. (1993). Thinking. *Annual Review of Psychology, 44,* 265–315.

Horn, J. L., & Hofer, S. M. (1992). Major abilities and development in the adult period. In R. J. Sternberg & C. A. Berg (Eds.), *Intellectual development*. Cambridge: Cambridge University Press.

Jackson, J. V., & Gildemeister, J. (1991). Effects of strategy training on black children's free recall, strategy maintenance, and transfer. *Contemporary Educational Psychology, 16,* 183–191.

Jensen, A. R. (1969). How much can we boost IQ and scholastic achievement? *Harvard Educational Review, 39,* 1–123.

Jensen, A. R. (1980). *Bias in mental testing*. New York: Free Press.

Kağıtçıbaşı, Ç. (1994). Human development and societal development: Linking theory and application. In A. Bouvy, F. J. R. Van de Vijver, P. Boski, & P. Schmitz, (Eds.), *Journeys into cross-cultural psychology* (pp. 7–27). Lisse, the Netherlands: Swets & Zeitlinger.

Klein, P. S., & Alony, S. (1993). Immediate and sustained effects of maternal mediating behaviors on young children. *Journal of Early Intervention, 17,* 177–193.

Lave, J. (1988). *Cognition in practice: Mind, mathematics and culture in everyday life*. Cambridge: Cambridge University Press.

Locurto, C. (1991). Beyond IQ in preschool programs? *Intelligence, 15,* 295–312.

Lucangeli, D., Galderisi, D., & Cornoldi, C. (1995). Specific and general transfer effects following metamemory training. *Learning Disabilities Research and Practice, 10,* 11–21.

Marshalek, B., Lohman, D. F., & Snow, R. E. (1983). The complexity continuum in the Radex and Hierarchical Models of intelligence. *Intelligence, 7,* 107–127.

Mayr, E. (1982). *The growth of biological thought*. Cambridge, MA: Belknap.

Messick, S. (1972). Beyond structure: In search of functional models of psychological processes. *Psychometrika, 37,* 357–375.

Molenaar, I. W., & Fischer, G. H. (Eds.). (1995). *Rasch models: Foundations, recent developments, and applications.* New York: Springer.

Nettelbeck, T. (1987). Inspection time and intelligence. In P. A. Vernon (Ed.), *Speed of information processing and intelligence.* Norwood, NJ: Ablex.

Paris, S. G., & Oka, E. R. (1986). Children's reading strategies, metacognition, and motivation. *Developmental Review, 6,* 25–56.

Radford, J., & Burton, A. (1974). *Thinking: Its nature and development.* New York: Wiley.

Rand, Y., & Kaniel, S. (1987). Group administration of the LPAD. In C. S. Lidz (Ed.), *Dynamic assessment* (pp. 196–214). New York: Guilford Press.

Reynolds, A. J. (1994). Effects of a preschool plus follow-on intervention for children at risk. *Developmental Psychology, 30,* 787–804.

Rogoff, B. (1981). Schooling and the development of cognitive skills. In H. C. Triandis & A. Heron (Eds.), *Handbook of cross-cultural psychology* (Vol. 4, pp. 233–294). Boston: Allyn & Bacon.

Scribner, S., & Cole, M. (1981). *The psychology of literacy.* Cambridge, MA: Harvard University Press.

Serpell, R. (1979). How specific are perceptual skills? A cross-cultural study of pattern reproduction. *British Journal of Psychology, 70,* 365–380.

Snow, R. E. (1980). Aptitude processes. In R. E. Snow, P-A. Federico & W. E. Montague (Eds.), *Aptitude, learning, and instruction* (Vol. 1, pp. 27–64). Hillsdale, NJ: Erlbaum.

Snow, R. E., Kyllonen, P. C., & Marshalek, B. (1984). The topography of ability and learning correlations. In R. J. Sternberg (Ed.), *Advances in the psychology of human intelligence* (pp. 47–103). Hillsdale, NJ: Erlbaum.

Spearman, C. (1923). *The abilities of man.* New York: Macmillan.

Spitz, H. (1991). Commentary on Locurto's "Beyond IQ in preschool programs?". *Intelligence, 15,* 327–333.

Sternberg, R. J. (1977). *Intelligence, information processing, and analogical reasoning: The componential analysis of human abilities.* New York: Wiley.

Sternberg, R. J. (1985). *Beyond IQ. A triarchic theory of intelligence.* Cambridge: Cambridge University Press.

Sternberg, R. J. (1987). Teaching intelligence: The application of cognitive psychology to the improvement of intellectual skills. In J. B. Baron & R. J. Sternberg (Eds.), *Teaching thinking skills: Theory and practice* (pp. 182–218). New York: Freeman.

Thurstone, L. L. (1938). *Primary mental abilities.* Psychometric Monographs 1. Chicago: University of Chicago Press.

Tulviste, P. (1991). *The cultural-historical development of verbal thinking.* Commack, NY: Nova Science Publishers.

Van de Vijver, F. J. R. (1991). *Inductive thinking across cultures: An empirical investigation.* Helmond, the Netherlands: WIBRO.

Van de Vijver, F. J. R. (1993). Factor analysis and intelligence. In M. A. Croon & F. J. R. Van de Vijver (Eds.), *Viability of mathematical models in the social sciences* (pp. 163–183). Lisse, the Netherlands: Swets & Zeitlinger.

Van de Vijver, F. J. R., & Willemsen, M. E. (1993). Abstract thinking. In J. Altarriba (Ed.), *Cognition and culture: A cross-cultural approach to cognitive psychology* (pp. 317–342). Amsterdam: North Holland.

Vernon, P. A. (Ed.). (1987). *Speed of information processing and intelligence.* Norwood, NJ: Ablex.

Vygotsky, L. S. (1978). *Mind in society: The development of higher psychological processes.* Cambridge, MA: Harvard University Press.

Wagner, D. A. (1981). Culture and memory development. In H. C. Triandis & A. Heron (Eds.), *Handbook of cross-cultural psychology* (Vol. 4, pp. 187–232). Boston: Allyn & Bacon.

Weinberg, R. A. (1989). Intelligence and IQ: Landmark issues and great debates. *American Psychologist, 44,* 98–104.

Wright, J., & Cashdan, A. (1991). Training metacognitive skills in backward readers: A pilot study. *Educational Psychology in Practice, 7,* 153–162.

PART 2

Development and Literacy in Cultural Context: Empirical Issues

CHAPTER SEVEN

Facilitating Language Development Promotes Literacy Learning

Catherine E. Snow

The basic premise of this chapter is that literacy development and school success are most effectively promoted during the preschool period by attention to the development of oral language skills. The contrary assumption might seem much more logical—that ultimate success in literacy would be promoted by the early facilitation of skills directly related to the process of decoding. There is much evidence to suggest that children who know the alphabet on arrival in school, or who have some basic phoneme segmentation skills, end up as better readers, so it seems obvious that we should promote letter recognition and phoneme segmentation skills during the preschool years. In contrast, I will argue that premature attention to print skills and to some others typically subsumed under the rubric "reading readiness" or "emergent literacy" can absorb time and attention better spent on the child's access to experiences which help develop much more crucial oral language skills.

The chapter is organized in the following way. First, I will present a model of literacy development, with special attention to the role played by oral language skills in literacy and school achievement. Second, I will outline a model for the emergence of language. I will then summarize evidence from the early stages of a longitudinal study we have carried out about the social-interactive experiences that support optimal oral language development and thus contribute to literacy outcomes. Finally, I will discuss the ways in which the social-interactive environments of preschool children—particularly in group settings—can be designed to optimize those aspects of language development most relevant to later school performance, as well as ways in which parent education or family intervention programs might be designed so as to optimize children's ultimate school achievement.

A MODEL OF READING

The model to be presented presumes the necessity of a componential analysis both of language and of literacy (see Snow, 1991a, 1991b, 1991c, and Snow & Dickinson, 1991, for more extensive presentations of the componential model). Whereas literacy skill is often represented in educational research by a single number—a score on a test, or the grade level at which a child is reading—on the contrary, I argue that reading should be seen as a set of skills, each of which could be assessed independently and all of which may have somewhat different developmental histories.

Skilled reading requires the integration of many individual skills, including at least the following:

- Rapid letter recognition

- Automated word recognition

- Accessing word meaning

- Syntactic processing of sentences

- Processing of discourse markers and cohesive relations among sentences

- Extraction and evaluation of new information

- Integration of new information with previously stored information

- Identification of authorial stance and perspective

- Development of a reaction to the material read

In addition to these reading skills, efficient reading also requires metaliteracy skills—identifying what sort of text one is being exposed to; and deciding whether one wants to study it deeply or scan it, read it for knowledge or entertainment, or take it as literal or as evocative. Furthermore, a central characteristic of good readers is that their skills buffer them against specific deficits of knowledge. Good readers can, for example, acquire new words and figure out their meanings from texts if they understand the context in which the new word is presented. The fact that such a wide array of skills is involved in reading raises the strong possibility that an individual reader might be much better at some aspects of reading than at others; in fact, the clinical literature confirms the existence of children who do quite well at word recognition but have particular difficulty with comprehension (Yuill & Oakhill, 1991).

At the early stages of reading development, many of the skills noted above are unnecessary for adequate performance. A second or third-grade reader is not expected to read words or process information from texts that go beyond what is already under the child's oral control. Beginning reading texts use words that children already know,— whereas older readers often encounter in print words they have never heard and would not use orally. Beginning readers are exposed to simple stories or expositions about familiar topics, not to novel information or new ideas.

Nonetheless, even young readers must integrate an array of skills to be effective users of literacy. These skills can be thought of as falling into three categories.

Print Skills

Print skills are those most closely related to the writing system itself, and reflect a knowledge of the orthographic system used to represent one's language. Good predictors of these print skills for alphabetic languages include the ability to recognize and name letters, being able to write one's own name, recognizing words frequently encountered in the environment (such as Coca-Cola or McDonald's), and sounding out simple words. Young children growing up in highly literate environments practice print skills with alphabet blocks, plastic "refrigerator letters," and while being read to from picture books, particularly alphabet books. Many children, however, only have the opportunity to develop print skills when they are first exposed to formal schooling.

Language Analysis Skills

Units of print, in any kind of writing system, map onto units of language. The most transparent mappings are from logograms to morphemes, as in Chinese. Mappings from spoken syllables to syllabic script units, as in the Japanese syllabaries, are also relatively accessible even to young children, because syllables are psychologically real units of speech production; even 2-year-olds can learn to segment their speech into syllables. The most difficult language analysis task is posed by the need to segment speech into phonemes—most of which are unpronounceable in isolation—for mapping onto letters in an alphabetic system. Some understanding of phoneme segmentation is a prerequisite to understanding the nature of an alphabetic system, and to being able to benefit from instruction using methods like phonics. Phoneme segmentation is typically assessed by asking children to produce rhymes, or to pronounce words without the initial or final sounds (e.g., What's Fred without the "f"? What's bark without the "k"?). In addition to not having mastered phoneme segmentation, though, young children are often baffled by the status of function words, by the meanings of terms like "word," and by aspects of written language that deviate from spoken forms ("want to" instead of "wanna" or "would have" instead of "would of," for example). Segmentation and language analysis skills are developed in the context of talk about language; exposure to rhymes, alliteration, and play with language; and during spontaneous playful writing activities.

Culture of Literacy

In addition to skills with print and skills in analyzing language so as to understand the relation of oral to printed forms, children who are going to be successful in learning to read need to understand what reading is all about. They must understand that reading and writing are communicative activities, and that distanced communication is different in some ways from face-to-face communication. They need to have some sense of the sorts of functions that print serves—for example, that books can amuse and entertain; that reference books are organized differently from books of fiction; that one can seek information or learn new things from books, magazines, and newspapers. Children growing up in literate households have many opportunities to observe how adults use print, but some children arrive at school and are plunged into reading instruction with little understanding of the ways in which knowing how to read will benefit them. Indeed, as Purcell-Gates (1995) has shown, some children even in modern, Western societies come from families which do not share at all in the culture of literacy, for whom the print encountered in signs, in mail, or in notes from school is essentially invisible. Absence of the understanding that literacy is useful, and that school activities are directed toward the development of literacy, becomes a particular problem if early reading instruction is heavily focused on the mechanics of decoding, with little attention to meaning. This is because learning the mechanics of decoding is an unmotivated and puzzling task to children who do not understand what reading is for.

The major argument to be made in this chapter is that these three domains of literacy skills, assuming normal age-appropriate cognitive and linguistic skills, are adequate for initial reading success. However, as children get older and are expected to read ever more challenging material, these skills are not enough. Children need high levels of language skills—in particular, skills with what we call "decontextualized language"—in order to become fully proficient readers and school learners.

Decontextualized language skills are a prerequisite for high levels of literacy because decontextualized oral language tasks conform to the same rules as literate language use. Certain oral language tasks depend heavily on the pragmatic skills of the conversationalist—for example, reacting to the interlocutor; exploiting shared experiences; and utilizing back channels, questions, and comprehension checks (Schley & Snow, 1992). Other oral language tasks require recognizing the reality (or maintaining the fiction) that (1) one's audience is distant, unknown, and nonresponsive; (2) one cannot presume shared background knowledge with the audience; and (3) the goal full comprehension of explicit information by the audience (De Temple, Wu, & Snow, 1991; Snow, 1990). The pragmatic demands of this second set of oral language tasks is much more similar to the demands of literate discourse. There is considerable evidence that children who do well in literacy achievement have higher levels of control over these pragmatic orientations in oral contexts (Snow, 1990; Snow, Cancino, De Temple, & Schley, 1991; Snow, Cancino, González, & Shriberg, 1989).

Vocabulary and world knowledge are also crucial to advanced literacy achievement. In fact, the best single predictor of reading success is vocabulary size (Anderson & Freebody, 1981); however, this relationship probably reflects the role of more than just simple word knowledge. Knowing words is an index for knowing about the world, and wide-ranging world knowledge may be an important route to literacy success. As noted above, early reading texts are largely limited to words present in children's oral vocabularies. More advanced literacy achievement, though, requires understanding relatively rare words and understanding texts about complex matters. Previous oral exposure to these words and to relevant background information greatly increases children's comprehension of these texts. It is possible, of course, to acquire new vocabulary through reading—probably the vast majority of the vocabulary items of literate adults were first learned from text. Such learning, however, also requires an analytic orientation to word meaning and efficient strategies for comprehension from partial information (Snow, Barnes, Chandler, Hemphill, & Goodman, 1991).

THE EMERGENCE OF ORAL LANGUAGE SKILLS

The emergence of oral language abilities occurs simultaneously in several different dimensions—increasing control over adult rules for phonology, morphology, and syntax, for example, as well as expanding knowledge of vocabulary. I argue that one dimension highly relevant to literacy and school success is the pragmatic dimension—increasing control over the appropriate use of language in a variety of situations (Ninio & Snow, 1996; Snow, 1996). Consider the linguistically sophisticated 2-year-old, she can talk comprehensibly about what she is doing, the objects that are present in the room, and events that occur in the present or immediate past. Her talk occurs in the context of conversations with familiar adults—adults who support the child's language performance by asking appropriate questions, filling in missing information, offering interpretations that clarify imprecise utterances, and scaffolding the child's contribution in other ways. The young child's talk is effective because it is contextualized spatially, temporally, and conversationally. Even sophisticated 2-year-olds cannot report about past events in extended discourses without prompts and other kinds of support from an adult, nor explain complex matters, nor even, in most cases, talk comprehensibly to strangers.

As children get older, though, they become capable of appropriate and communicatively effective speech in situations and about topics that are increasingly decontextualized. They can talk about spatially distant objects and places, about abstract entities, and even about the nonreal in ways that clearly mark the difference between reality and fantasy. They can talk about distant past and future, and about both hypothetical and contrary-to-fact conditions. Perhaps most relevant to literacy, they can construct extended discourses autonomously without depending on the collaboration of an adult to help provide global structuring, to ensure completeness of information, or to repair miscommunications.

Certain formal aspects of the language system must develop to support these decontextualized uses of language: past and future tenses, perfect and progressive aspects, and subjunctive mood, for example, are crucial to representing complex temporal and conditional relations; sophisticated vocabulary items must be acquired to support the discussion of abstract topics; and devices for establishing relationships across utterances (e.g., relational terms like "moreover" and "nonetheless" must be acquired to maintain cohesion in extended discourses. An important question to consider is where children learn these more sophisticated aspects of the language system. What sorts of social interactions support these developments?

Linguistic input of a sufficiently clear, rich, and interpretable type is a prerequisite for the development of an adequate phonological and grammatical system, but these two systems also show characteristics suggesting they are relatively buffered against impoverishment of the linguistic input (Snow, 1994). That is to say, while severe disruption of the social environment (e.g., extreme isolation or profound deafness) causes deficits in the acquisition of basic oral vocabulary and grammar, a meager social-linguistic environment can be adequate for supporting basic language development. Lexical and pragmatic development, on the other hand, are massively susceptible to environmental influences (Snow, 1989). These systems show very large social class differences (Dickinson & Snow, 1987). For example, Hart and Risley (1995) found that middle-class children had heard ten times as many words as welfare children by the time they had entered school, and their own vocabularies were comparably greater. Because vocabulary is so dependent on input, it readily shows the consequences of interventions such as attendance at language-enriched preschool classrooms (Cazden, Snow, & Heise-Baigorria, 1990; De Temple & Beals, 1991; Dickinson & Smith, 1991; Dickinson & Tabors, 1991; and Snow, 1991c). Continued acquisition of vocabulary and the acquisition of control over the more sophisticated uses of language in decontextualized situations seem to be quite heavily dependent on children's access to particular social-interactive contexts, such as reading books with adults, participating in one-on-one conversations with adults, and engaging in family talk at the dinner table. Clearly, by identifying these contexts for enriched language use, we can help to ensure their availability to all children through family intervention programs or the design of group care settings.

HOME-SCHOOL STUDY OF LANGUAGE AND LITERACY DEVELOPMENT[1]

Seeking the Sources of Literacy and Language Skills

In order to study the factors affecting the emergence of literacy skills, and in particular, to seek the role of language skills in literacy accomplishments, the Home-School Study of Language and Literacy Development was started in 1986. The study was designed to collect data on three domains: 1) children's interactions at home with their parents, analyzed for support of the development of language and literacy skills; 2) children's opportunities to acquire language and literacy skills at preschool, and literacy skills during the elementary years at school; 3) children's language and literacy skills, assessed yearly starting when the children were five.

Subjects

To collect this information, 84 children from 81 low-income families were visited at home and at (pre)school, starting at age 3. During home visits, interactive language data was collected from mothers and children during structured activities like book-reading, toy play, and elicited reports, and from the families at mealtimes. During school visits, interactive data was collected during free play periods in preschool and kindergarten, and measures were taken of the classroom environment each year. Parents and teachers were also interviewed during each visit. Starting at age 5, the children were been given a battery of language and literacy tests each year.

All families whose children are participants in the Home-School Study were contacted through Head Start or other preschool programs when the children were 3 years old. In order to be eligible for the study, the families needed to identify themselves as speaking English at home and as being eligible for Head Start or subsidized day care. At the first home visit, just under half of the families in the study were on welfare; over a third of the families were single-parent families; and a third of the children were from a racial minority group. Mothers' education was as follows: 28.4 percent had not completed high school, 43.2 percent had graduated from high school, and 28.4 percent had completed some post-graduation education.

Attrition had reduced the size of the sample by about 30 percent by the time the children were in fourth grade, but did not affect its composition of the sample. While home observations are being carried out during alternate years until the children reach seventh grade, and interview data from teachers is also collected on a yearly basis, I will focus here on the results from the preschool and kindergarten period, when the children were 3 through 5 years old. Observational settings change radically as the children get older, after they have learned to read, and as their teachers become decreasingly willing to allow classroom observations. Thus, the types of data available and the procedures for analyzing the data from these children as they got older shifted, leading to a picture that is much too complex if we consider predictors from across the entire age span studied.

Home Observations

Home observations carried out when the children were 3, 4, and 5 involved a series of structured tasks designed to offer the mother the opportunity to demonstrate her interactive style during focused interaction with her child. At each of the home visits, the mother was asked to play with a set of toys with her child and to read a book to her child. At home visits when the child was 3 and 4, the mother was asked to elicit from the child a report of some recent, interesting event. At age 5, the experimenter elicited the personal report by telling a story of a scary event that had supposedly just happened to him and encouraging the child to respond by telling his/her own scary story. At the end of each visit, the observer left a tape recorder with the mother and asked her to tape a dinner table conversation at which the whole family was present. When the children were 5, the visit included two novel settings. The child was asked to "read" the book back to the mother, and mother and child were also asked to play with a set of objects that included a powerful magnet, and smaller metal and nonmetal objects including some small magnets. The magnet session was designed to elicit scientific talk, as a complement to the fantasy or narrative talk that the toy play session tended to generate. While many families taped the mealtime conversations as requested, a relatively high number did not manage to do so in any given year, so there is considerable missing data about mealtimes.

Analyzing the Home Interactions

Methods of coding and analyzing the talk transcribed from the home interactions were designed to reflect both the pragmatic orientations adopted and the availability of vocabulary and world knowledge crucial to literacy. In particular, we coded the interactions for the occurrence of decontextualized talk—talk that involves extended discourse about a single topic, and talk that goes beyond the here-and-now. For book-reading, the type of talk that was hypothesized to be most helpful was "nonimmediate" talk, or talk that went beyond discussions of the pictures and information presented in the book, including discussions of connections to the child's life and experiences, predictions, evaluations, motivations, or causes (De Temple, 1994). For toy play, the occurrence of talk that created a fantasy world, rather than talk that discussed the visible or concrete aspects of the toys, was coded. For the magnet session, talk that dealt with scientific process (questions, hypotheses, categorization) was coded (Snow & Kurland, 1996). From the mealtime transcripts, talk that was narrative or explanatory was coded, since the narrative and explanatory segments constituted the only chunks of extended discourse that occurred at mealtimes (Beals & Snow, 1994). Furthermore, in all these contexts the maternal talk has been analyzed for the occurrence of relatively low-frequency vocabulary items, as one index of the sophistication of the talk occurring in these families (Beals & Tabors, 1993; Weizman, 1995).

Observations at School

Because of the much greater complexity of the multichild classroom environment, data about classroom interactions is derived from both transcripts (e.g., of whole-group book-reading) and from catalogues of how classroom time was spent (e.g., in small group topic-focused talk, in fantasy, and in activities with little language support). In addition, teachers were interviewed about their pedagogical orientations and their curricular foci (Dickinson, Cote & Smith, in press). Talk occurring in classrooms has also been analyzed in ways analogous to those used for the home data for the presence of low-frequency vocabulary items (Smith, 1996).

Language and Literacy Battery

The children's language and literacy skills were assessed using an individually administered battery called the School-Home Early Language and Literacy (SHELL) assessment. While some components of the SHELL have remained the same whenever administered across the years (definitions, picture description, and the Peabody Picture Vocabulary Test (PPVT), other tasks have been modified to reflect newly developing abilities (the narrative task and the literacy assessments). The SHELL was designed in an attempt to include assessments of children's abilities with decontextualized language differentiated by genre (giving definitions, picture descriptions, and narratives), as well as of their skills with emergent and conventional literacy. For literacy assessments we used the Comprehensive Assessment Profile (CAP) at kindergarten, the Gray Oral and Wide Range Achievement Test during the primary years, and some text-interpretation tasks to help see where comprehension was breaking down (Snow, Tabors, Nicholson, & Kurland, 1995).

Findings from the Home-School Study of Language and Literacy Development

Obviously, the Home-School Study has by now generated many and complex findings, so a detailed review of the results would extend beyond the boundaries of a single chapter. Instead, I will focus on just a few issues—namely, the value of preschool experiences with nonimmediate talk, with extended discourse, and with rare vocabulary items, for the later development of both language and literacy skills.

Book-reading as a Predictor

It is widely accepted that book-reading, particularly dialogic book-reading, promotes young children's language and preliteracy development (see Debaryshe, 1993; Bus, van IJzendoorn, & Pellegrini, 1995; Goldfield & Snow, 1984 for reviews; see Scarborough & Dobrich, 1994a, 1994b for a dissenting view). Results from the study suggest that, in particular, engagement during book-reading in talk that goes beyond the immediate demands of the text, to include inference, prediction, and connection to world knowledge, promotes vocabulary acquisition and story comprehension (De Temple, 1994; De Temple & Beals, 1991). An example of the kind of talk De Temple has found relates to child outcomes is cited here (from Snow & Kurland, 1996). Note how George's mother asks George to interpret the events, and uses the book-reading as a context for talking about connections between the book and George's experience of the world:

Example 1. George at 5 years, book-reading.

Mother:	"that night he had a stomachache."
Mother:	he ate all those things.
Child:	wow.
Mother:	"the next day was Sunday again."
Mother:	one week later.
Mother:	"the caterpillar ate through one nice green leaf, and after that he felt much better."
Mother:	why do you think he felt better?
Child:	because he ate all those things.
Mother:	(be)cause that's his real food right?
Mother:	and all this other junk (pause) is for us not for caterpillars right?
Child:	right.

Reasons why these relationships emerge are no doubt complex. It is of course the case that families in which more sophisticated book-reading occurs are those in which more books are present and reading is more frequent as well; the effects of style of book-reading combine with those of exposure to literacy. It is, however, reasonable to think that children whose exposure to books includes modelling of reading as an active process that involves prediction, reflection, and integration of new knowledge with old will end up as better comprehenders in general, and that such children are exposed to new vocabulary in the more engaging conversations that generate learning.

Exposure to Extended Discourse as a Predictor

Participation in family conversations that include many stretches of connected discourse, such as occur during narratives or explanations, helps children acquire the linguistic devices needed to express the pragmatics of distanced communication (Beals, 1991), as revealed in effects two years later on the quality of children's extended discourse in narratives and definitions (De Temple & Beals, 1991). Dinner-table conversations often offer opportunities for talking about events of the day, or discussing why and how things happen, as in the following excerpt from a dinner conversation between George and his mother (from Snow & Kurland, 1996):

Example 2. George at 4 years, mealtime.

Mother:	Okay well we still have to wait.
Child:	Wait for what?
Mother:	Can't go can't go swimmin(g) right after you eat.
Mother:	You have to wait a little while so you won't get cramps.
Child:	Huh?
Mother:	You have to wait a little while so you don't get cramps.
Child:	What's cramps?
Mother:	Cramps are when your stomach feels all tight, and it hurts (be)cause you have food in it.
Mother:	And you're in the water (trailing off) . . .

Maternal use of talk about scientific processes, hypothesis testing, and prediction of likely events during play with a magnet related to children's control over the production of extended discourse as well (Snow & Kurland, 1996). The following example shows Kurt and his mother approaching the magnet play by invoking relevant world knowledge.

Example 3. Kurt at 5 years playing with magnets.

Mother:	Those keep sticking to it huh?
Child:	Mmhm.
Mother:	You know why?
Child:	Why?
Mother:	Think.
Mother:	What do you think is inside that black box?
Child:	Metal?
Mother:	What?
Mother:	We've talked about this before.
Mother:	What's inside?
Mother:	That makes everything stick like that [laughs]?
Mother:	Like on our refrigerator?
Child:	Magnets.
Mother:	Very good.

George and his mother use the magnet play session to test hypotheses and analyze how things work.

Example 4. George at 5 years playing with magnets.

Mother:	How come, how come all the silver colored ones stick but the money doesn't stick? (putting nuts and a nickle on the base)
Mother:	Hmm?
Mother:	You know why?
Child:	I don't know how it does.
Mother:	You think money has, is a magnet?
Child:	No.
Mother:	(Be)cause it's a different metal?
Child:	Yeah.
Mother:	But it's the same color.
Child:	Yeah.

No matter what the specific context, talk that extends a topic beyond a single utterance or turn provides a model for the child of how to organize information in longer stretches. The relevance of experience with such models to performance in sharing-time turns at kindergarten, or to writing stories in first grade, is obvious.

The impact of frequency of exposure to stretches of extended discourse on children's performance suggests that practice with these extended discourse forms is important. In other words, understanding the structural features of extended discourse is not enough; producing extended discourse requires planning and ordering the information to be exchanged, assessment of the state of knowledge of the listener, and adherence to the genre-specific rules of narrative or explanation. Integrating these complex tasks requires previous practice in hearing, participating in, and producing extended discourse forms.

Exposure to Rare Vocabulary Items

The use of rare, sophisticated vocabulary items by family members related to children's scores on the Peabody Picture Vocabulary Test as well as to the sophistication of the definitions they offered two years later (Beals & Tabors, 1993; Weizman, 1995). Furthermore, while density of rare words explained some of the variance in vocabulary outcomes, the occurrence of rare words in informative contexts (i.e., in stretches of talk that gave information about the word meanings) explained even more of the variance in vocabulary (Weizman, 1995). Note how George's mother, in the dinner table conversation cited above, provides rich information about the new vocabulary item "cramps" and uses technical terms like "magnet" and "metal" while playing with magnets. These relationships between aspects of family talk and child vocabulary outcomes become particularly important precisely because vocabulary is so key to children's literacy success during the later grades of elementary school.

IMPLICATIONS

Implications for the Design of Preschool Classrooms

Preschool classrooms or group care settings can provide many of the same language enrichment experiences of the best homes, but many do not. In careful analyses of the preschool experiences of a sample of low-income American children, half of which were attending Head Start (the same children whose home experiences were reported above), Dickinson and his colleagues have found certain settings and certain kinds of talk that promote children's vocabulary and their extended discourse skills. During large group settings, a common preschool activity is reading books with children. As at home, book-reading at preschool promotes language and literacy skills. However, Dickinson and Smith (1994) have found that not all styles of book-reading work equally well. A didactic style, in which teachers regularly probe for children's literal comprehension of the text, is less productive than a performance-oriented style, in which teachers read dramatically with relatively few interruptions, then engage in discussion afterwards (when it does not disrupt the flow of the narrative that is less tied to specific textual details). The strongest single predictor of childrens language outcomes from the book-reading sessions was the percent of "child-involved analytic talk," or teacher talk that went beyond literal comprehension questions to include topics that were nonimmediate and in which children were actively and enthusiastically involved. In the larger group setting of the preschool reading, this type of talk provides the same sort of stimulus to development that De Temple (1994) found for nonimmediate talk in the dyadic setting.

Beyond book-reading, many large- and small-group activities typically are planned for preschool settings. Do some of these settings have more value than others for children's development? Dickinson's findings (Dickinson, 1994; Dickinson & Smith, 1991, 1994; Dickinson, Cote, & Smith, 1993; Smith & Dickinson, 1994; see also Smith, 1996) suggest that small group activities—one teacher working with three to six children—are the most productive in terms of long-term language outcomes. The percent of cognitively challenging talk was also positively related to language outcomes—talk that was coded as cognitively challenging was, of course, likely to occur during small-group activities, and less likely to occur when children were playing without an adult present. Yet, at least, 3-year-olds, seemed to benefit from the opportunity for pretend play; percent of time in pretend play at age 3 related to language and literacy outcomes. This finding might reflect the contribution of child language sophistication—the more sophisticated 3-year-olds were more likely to engage in pretense and more likely to score well two years later. Finally, Dickinson and his colleagues found that the amount of time teachers scheduled for free play was negatively related to long-term outcomes, while the presence of an explained pedagogical focus on language and literacy had a positive effect.

Implications for the Design of Family Intervention Programs

Our focus on ways to provide language-enrichment activities in the context of preschool programs or group care settings reflects the widespread use of such programs to "compensate" for perceived inadequacies in the quality of interaction in the home. In reality, most parents are capable of providing linguistic environments in the home that are enriched enough to support their preschoolers' development of the decontextualized language skills. The failure of impoverished and poorly educated parents to do so may reflect their absorption in the more pressing demands of ensuring basic care to their children, rather than neglect of linguistic and cognitive development. If, however, parents do not understand the importance of extended language interactions with their children, then home-based intervention programs designed to alert parents to the value of such interactions can be helpful. But, like classroom-based interventions such programs may be a waste of time if they focus on "academic skills" (alphabet, counting, colors) rather than on the opportunities for extended discourse provided by storytelling, fantasy play, book-reading, and discussions of ongoing events.

What is the role of parents in supporting their preschoolers' language development if the children will attend school in a language different from that spoken at home? A very large percentage of young children in the world today speak one language at home and another at school; it is perhaps not surprising that many parents attempt to help prepare their children for school by switching to the school language at home. Such a strategy is, however, counterproductive unless the parents speak the school language very well. If they speak the school language poorly, they will be unable to provide the interesting discussions, the elaborated narratives, and the sophisticated vocabulary that children require. Their children will have some familiarity with the basics of the school language, but not with the language skills they most desperately need. If children acquire the pragmatic rules underlying decontextualized language in their first language, they will be able to use those skills in a second language (Cummins, 1981; Lanauze & Snow, 1989).

CONCLUSION

Literacy requires print skills, language analysis skills, cultural understandings, and control over the production and comprehension of extended discourse and complex vocabulary. Successfully literate individuals control the ability to interpret print, an understanding of the language structures that are utilized for literate purposes, and an understanding of the broader cultural purposes and meaning of literacy. Educators, particularly preschool and primary school educators, often either ignore or presuppose linguistic and cultural understandings, and focus instead on teaching print skills. On the contrary for children who have arrived at school with little previous exposure to a wide variety of literacy activities—children who have had little chance to develop the language skills and world knowledge crucial to literate use—these two components of literacy are considerably more challenging and troublesome than is the task of acquiring orthographic and word-reading skills. Paradoxically though, these children often receive very little teaching that is focused on these challenges.

In family intervention and preschool literacy preparation programs, much time and attention are typically focused on print skills, phonics, numbers, and colors. This focus diverts attention from activities that develop competence with complex, connected discourse designed for a distant audience. Compensatory preschool curricula tend to devote a great deal of time to teaching the alphabet, perhaps some letter-sound combinations, and basic vocabulary or concepts that educators assume are important for school. Exposure of preschool children to the language structures necessary for communicating effectively with a distant audience with whom background knowledge is not shared would be much more valuable, as would exposure to rich vocabulary and information structures. Activities that support language and literacy development include, in addition to dialogic book-reading, discussions around science, cooking, or construction projects; development through teacher intervention of naturally occurring sociodramatic play; projects such as making videotapes and writing class letters to send to "distant audiences," and encouraging children to tell, act out, and dictate stories. Teaching the print skills needed for literacy can safely be postponed until all children are 6 or 7; the preschool years should be reserved for language-rich experiences, storytelling, fantasy, and learning about the world.

NOTES

1. The Home-School Study has been directed by David Dickinson, Catherine Snow, and Patton Tabors, and has benefitted from the hard work and intellectual contributions of many students and research assistants, including Diane Beals, Jeanne De Temple, Christine Hérot, Jane Katz, Brenda Kurland, Petra Nicholson, Kevin Roach, Stephanie Ross, Miriam Smith, and Zehava Weizman. Funding for the project at various stages from the Ford Foundation, the Spencer Foundation, and the W.T. Grant Foundation is gratefully acknowledged, as is the collaboration between the families and the many classroom teachers we have interviewed.

REFERENCES

Anderson, R. C., & Freebody, P. (1981). Vocabulary knowledge. In J. T. Guthrie (Ed.), Comprehension and teaching: research reviews. Newark, DE: International Reading Association.

Beals, D. (1991). "I know who makes ice cream": Explanations in mealtime conversations of low-income families of preschoolers. Unpublished doctoral dissertation, Harvard Graduate School of Education.

Beals, D. E., & Snow, C. E. (1994). "Thunder is when the angels are upstairs bowling": Narratives and explanations at the dinner table. *Journal of Narrative and Life History, 4*, 331–352.

Beals, D. E., & Tabors, P. O. (1993). Arboretum, bureaucratic, and carbohydrates: Preschoolers' exposure to rare vocabulary at home. *First Language, 15*, 57–76.

Bus, A., van IJzendoorn, M. H., & Pellegrini, A. D. (1995). Joint book reading makes for success in learning to read: A meta-analysis on the intergenerational transmission of literacy. *Review of Educational Research, 65,* 1–21.

Cazden, C. B., Snow, C. E., & Heise-Baigorria, C. (1990). Language planning in preschool education. Report prepared at request of Consultative Group on Early Childhood Care and Development, UNICEF.

Cummins, J. (1981). The role of primary language development in promoting educational success for language minority students. In a publication of the National Evaluation, Dissemination and Assessment Center. *Schooling and language minority students: A theoretical framework.* Los Angeles: California State University.

Debaryshe, B. D. (1993). Joint picture-book reading correlates of early oral language skill. *Journal of Child Language, 20,* 455–462.

De Temple, J. M. (1994). Book reading interaction among low-income mothers with preschoolers and children—s later literacy skills. Unpublished doctoral dissertation. Harvard Graduate School of Education.

De Temple, J., & Beals, D. E. (1991). Family talk: Sources of support for the development of decontextualized language skills. *Journal of Research in Childhood Education, 6,* 11–19.

De Temple, J., Wu, H. F., & Snow, C. E. (1991). Papa Pig just left for Pigtown: children's oral and written picture descriptions under varying instructions. *Discourse Processes, 14,* 469–495.

Dickinson, D. K. (1994). Features of early childhood classroom environments that support development of language and literacy. In J. Duchan, R. Sonnenmeier, & L. Hewitt (Eds.), *Pragmatics: From theory to practice* (pp. 185–201). Englewood Cliffs, NJ: Prentice Hall.

Dickinson, D. K., Cote, L., & Smith, M. W. (1993). Not by print alone: Oral language supports for early literacy development. In C. Daiute, (Ed.), *The development of literacy through social interaction* (pp. 67–78). San Francisco: Jossey-Bass.

Dickinson, D. K., Cote, L., & Smith, M. W. (in press). Preschool classroom as lexical environments: Long term effects of patterns of vocabulary use on low-income children's language development. *Merrill-Palmer Quarterly.*

Dickinson, D. K., & Smith, M. W. (1991). Preschool talk: Patterns of teacher-child interaction in early childhood classrooms. *Journal of Research in Childhood Education, 6,* 20–29.

Dickinson, D. K., & Smith, M. W. (1994). Long-term effects of preschool teachers' book readings on low-income children's vocabulary and story understanding. *Reading Research Quarterly, 29,* 105–122.

Dickinson, D. K., & Snow, C. E. (1987). Interrelationships among prereading and oral language skills in kindergartners from two social classes. *Research on Childhood Education Quarterly, 2*, 1–25.

Dickinson, D. K., & Tabors, P. O. (1991). Early literacy: Linkages between home, school and literacy achievement at age five. *Journal of Research in Childhood Education, 6*, 30–46.

Goldfield, B. A., & Snow, C. E. (1984). Reading books with children: The mechanics of parental influence on children's reading achievement. In J. Flood (Ed.), *Promoting reading comprehension* (pp. 204–215). Newark, DE: International Reading Association.

Hart, B., & Risley, T. (1995). *Meaningful differences in the everyday experience of young American children*. Baltimore: P. H. Brookes.

Lanauze, M., & Snow, C. E. (1989). The relation between first- and second-language writing skills: Evidence from Puerto Rican elementary school children in bilingual programs. *Linguistics and Education, 1*, 323–340.

Ninio, A., & Snow, C. (1996). *Pragmatic development*. Boulder, CO: Westview Press.

Purcell-Gates, V. (1995). *Other people's words: The cycle of low literacy*. Cambridge, MA: Harvard University Press.

Scarborough, H. S., & Dobrich, W. (1994a). Another look at parent-preschooler bookreading: How naked is the emperor? *Developmental Review, 14*, 340–47.

Scarborough, H. S., & Dobrich, W. (1994b). On the efficacy of reading to preschoolers. *Developmental Review, 14*, 245–302.

Schley, S., & Snow, C. E. (1992). The conversational skills of school-aged children. *Social Development, 1*, 18–35.

Smith, M. W. (1996). *Teacher-child interaction in early childhood education classrooms: Theoretical and practical perspectives*. Unpublished doctoral dissertation, Clark University.

Smith, M. W., & Dickinson, D. K. (1994). Describing oral language opportunities and environments in Head Start and other preschool classrooms. *Early Childhood Research Quarterly, 9* (3 & 4), 345–366.

Snow, C. E. (1989). Understanding social interaction and language acquisition: Sentences are not enough. In M. Bornstein & J. Bruner (Eds.), *Interaction in human development* (pp. 83–103). Hillsdale, NJ: Erlbaum.

Snow, C. E. (1990). The development of definitional skill. *Journal of Child Language, 17*, 697–710.

Snow, C. E. (1991a). Diverse conversational contexts for the acquisition of various language skills. In J. Miller (Ed.), *Research on child language disorders: A decade of progress* (pp. 105–124). Austin, TX: Pro-Ed.

Snow, C. E. (1991b). Language proficiency: towards a definition. In G. Appel & H. Dechert (Eds.), *A case for psycholinguistic cases*. Amsterdam: John Benjamins.

Snow, C. E. (1991c). The theoretical basis for relationships between language and literacy in development. *Journal of Research in Childhood Education*, *6*, 5–10.

Snow, C. E. (1994). What is so hard about learning to read? A pragmatic analysis. In J. Duchan, R. Sonnemeier, & L. Hewitt (Eds.), *Pragmatics: From theory to practice* (pp. 164–184). Englewood, NJ: Prentice Hall.

Snow, C. E. (1996). Change in child language and child linguists. In H. Coleman & L. Cameron (Eds.), *Change and language* (pp. 75–88). Clevedon, UK: British Association of Applied Linguists.

Snow, C. E., Barnes, W. S., Chandler, J., Hemphill, L., & Goodman, I. F. (1991). *Unfulfilled expectations: Home and school influences on literacy*. Cambridge, MA: Harvard University Press.

Snow, C. E., Cancino, H., De Temple, J., & Schley, S. (1991). Giving formal definitions: a linguistic or metalinguistic skill? In E. Bialystok (Ed.), *Language processing and language awareness by bilingual children*. New York: Cambridge University Press.

Snow, C., Cancino, H., Gonzalez, P., & Shriberg, E. (1989). Giving formal definitions: an oral language correlate of school literacy. In D. Bloome (Ed.), *Classrooms and literacy* (pp. 233–249). Norwood, NJ: Ablex.

Snow, C. E., & Dickinson, D. K. (1991). Skills that aren't basic in a new conception of literacy. In A. Purves & T. Jennings (Eds.), *Literate systems and individual lives: perspectives on literacy and schooling*. Albany: SUNY Press.

Snow, C. E., & Kurland, B. (1996). Sticking to the point: Talk about magnets as a preparation for literacy. In D. Hicks (Ed.), *Child discourse and social learning: An interdisciplinary perspective*. New York: Cambridge University Press.

Snow, C. E., Tabors, P. O., Nicholson, P. A., & Kurland, B. F. (1995). SHELL: Oral language and early literacy skills in kindergarten and first-grade children. *Journal of Research in Childhood Education*, *10*, 37–48.

Weizman, Z. (1995). *Sophistication in maternal literacy input at home: Does it affect low-income children's vocbulary, literacy and language success at school?* Unpublished doctoral dissertation. Harvard Graduate School of Education.

Yuill, N., & Oakhill, J. (1991). *Children's problems in reading comprehension: An experimental investigation*. Cambridge: Cambridge University Press.

CHAPTER EIGHT

Home and School Literacy in a Multicultural Society

Paul P. M. Leseman

HOME AND SCHOOL LITERACY

Becoming literate starts long before children enter school. Yet although early introduction to books and early participation in literate or literacy-related interactions in the home environment are seen as most important to prepare young children for literacy instruction at school, the widespread consensus about the importance of home literacy is not supported by the available evidence. This will become clear below, when the validity of these strong claims regarding home literacy is examined in a multicultural context, using families and communities that have traditionally different attitudes toward the "culture of literacy."

Preparing for School Literacy

Many countries face the problem of young children being unequally prepared for school. Socially disadvantaged children and children from ethnic-cultural and language minorities do not have an optimal start in formal education. As their school careers unfold, it becomes increasingly clear that this suboptimal start largely determines school performance many years later. Instead of disappearing under the influence of schooling, early educational lags tend to increase (Stanovich, 1986).

Of the differences in developmental domains, it is early differences in language and preliteracy skills that have attracted much attention; as a result, various programs to promote home literacy in disadvantaged families are now being implemented. These programs differ vastly in their basic intervention strategy, aims, delivery systems, target groups, timing, and intensity. In some, the main objective is to introduce children's books into the home and to make parents aware of the importance of reading to children (e.g., the Dutch Project Boekenpret; see Veen, Overmars, & de Glopper, 1995), whereas others attempt to improve the quality of shared book-reading interactions between parents and children (Arnold & Whitehurst, 1994). However, with a few promising exceptions the results to date have not been very encouraging (cf., Darling & Paull, 1994; for the Netherlands, see de Glopper, 1993, and Veen et al., 1995). This calls for a further analysis of the relationships between home literacy, language development, and literacy achievement at school.

Home literacy programs are administered to target populations that often have very different traditions regarding the use of written language, and whose living and working circumstances are not favorable for home literacy. Even in industrialized countries, which have accessible and extensive compulsory education systems, large sections of the adult population can be considered to be functionally illiterate, both because of their low reading and writing proficiency and the marginal role of literacy in their daily lives. Some of this is attributable to immigration. Many immigrants from countries with low schooling and traditional agricultural economies arrive in the new country without being able to read or write functionally. There are also indigenous populations in the industrialized country that can be characterized as semi-illiterate. Though it is clear from nationwide assessment studies that full illiteracy (inability to read and write simple texts) is incidental among indigenous populations (Doets, 1992; Kirsch & Jungbluth, 1987; Leseman, 1994a; Ortiz, 1989), literacy (i.e., reading books for pleasure or writing as means of communication) may not be at the heart of family life.

The success of early educational interventions to promote literacy preparation at home depends on many factors, but the basic presupposition of this chapter is that sensitivity to the family's culture and the wider social-cultural context is crucial to success. The present chapter is intended to further understanding of theoretical and empirical issues relating to this needed cultural sensitivity.

Issues of Home and School Literacy

In a recent review, Scarborough and Dobrich (1994) concluded that there is a reliable relationship with a median correlation size of .28 between home literacy and several outcome measures, including reading and writing at school. Applying a different approach of statistical meta-analysis, Bus, van IJzendoorn, and Pellegrini (1995) arrived at the same conclusion with a similar estimate of the mean strength of the relationships (.27 to .33). This implies that home literacy matters, but the size of its effects are small.

In the same vein, the disappointing results of home literacy programs (and early educational intervention programs in general) raise the basic question of whether intervention strategies, the focus of the intervention, the delivery system, and other program characteristics are sufficiently well-tailored to the target groups and their sociocultural context. Put differently, early intervention in the domains of literacy, preliteracy, and literacy-related skills to support subsequent schooling needs a stronger theoretical basis. Below, I will address three basic issues that seem to me to need further consideration in order to strengthen the basis of context-sensitive early intervention programs in the realm of home literacy.

The first issue concerns the effective ingredients; that is to say, the possible causal or constructive processes that underlie the relationship between home literacy (and related educational activities), and developmental and educational outcomes. At present, knowledge about what works is limited (Scarborough & Dobrich, 1994). Questions arise as to what effective home literacy essentially is, or what it consists of. Is it mere exposure and modelling of certain behaviors, or co-constructive interaction leading to higher levels of knowledge? Is it primarily instruction of content and skill in the domains of language and literacy, or an emotional-motivational experience presumably also related to motivation vis-à-vis literacy in school?

The second issue is related to the first. It concerns the relation of home literacy in a more narrow sense (e.g., joint storybook-reading) with other everyday situations of informal education, such as conversation, joint play, joint practical problemsolving in household routines, and religious practice. Literacy situations in a narrow sense and the situations intended here probably have much in common, such as the use of language to establish, explain, coordinate, and evaluate complex activities, and the underlying social-emotional bond between parent and child, with similar implications for the development of social-emotional dispositions that may facilitate school learning. Questions arise as to the relative contributions of the different forms of informal education at home in preparing children for formal literacy education at school. How important is home literacy in a narrow sense? Are there perhaps other routes of preparation for literacy acquisition at school? Should we extend our definition of home literacy to include play, ordinary (mealtime) talk, and everyday household problem-solving?

The third issue concerns the contextuality of home literacy and related informal education. The home environment, seen as a social microsystem for young children to acquire all kinds of skills that are relevant for school learning, cannot be separated from the surrounding social and cultural contexts constituted by parents' education, work, social networks, and cultural practices (cf., Bronfenbrenner, 1989). For instance, if parents have low literacy, the opportunities for literacy-related interactions at home are strongly limited. Similarly, economic pressure forces parents to go out to work and reduces the time remaining for informal educational interactions with children. Seen from this angle, changing one or more facets of the home microsystem as part of an early intervention program is doomed to be relatively ineffective unless important context factors support or are made to support the intervention. Questions arise as to the functional and systemic relationships between educational practices at home and the social and cultural context surrounding the family.

To deal with the issues raised here, I will first outline a theoretical view on home literacy in a broad sense, including other educationally relevant activities that also occur in the home. In the next section, I will present research findings supporting the general theoretical view based on a study in a multicultural sample in the Netherlands. In the final section, I will discuss the implications for early intervention programs.

THEORETICAL CONSIDERATIONS

Young children's home environment can be characterized by opportunities to participate in literate or literacy-related practices and by the processes of appropriation of the knowledge, skills, and values involved in these practices through participation, interpersonal instruction, and guidance by more experienced persons such as parents and older siblings (Rogoff, 1990; Rogoff, Mistry, Goncü, & Mosier,

1993). Starting from this social-constructivist point of view, I further assume that there are functional and meaningful relations between the literacy and informal education practices on the microsocial plane, and the practices, processes, and structures on the sociohistorical plane (Rogoff et al., 1993). That is to say, microsocial processes are closely related to the social and cultural context of the family. Finally, I assume that, other things being equal, differences in the opportunities for participation and in the characteristics of the interpersonal instruction and guidance determine differential developmental outcomes.

Home Literacy and Informal Education as Apprenticeships

Social-constructivistic theory views learning and development as consisting of transactional processes of co-construction of knowledge in interaction with the physical, social, and symbolic environment. To a certain extent, young children acquire knowledge and skills spontaneously in constructive interactions with the immediate environment; that is to say, without explicit, intentional social mediation by a parent or teacher. Beyond this, however, the acquisition of knowledge and skills, especially those that are decontextualized and culture-loaded, needs to be mediated in co-constructive social interactions. Co-construction essentially means that before being internalized, the knowledge and skills concerned are created in an interpsychological form shared by the participants, such as in a dialogue or in a coordinated sequence of actions (Wertsch, 1985; Wertsch & Bivens, 1992).

Concerning the question of the effective ingredients of educational, in particular literacy-related, interactions, there are at least three dimensions or facets that should be mentioned here as the key parameters of the informal education system constituted by the family.

Opportunity

In order for (co-)constructive processes to take place, there must be at least some opportunities for interaction with or centered around literacy of whatever kind, in whatever shape. If sufficiently frequent, opportunities to observe parents reading and writing, be it a TV schedule or a shopping list, makes literacy familiar and may foster positive attitudes toward acquiring literacy. In this respect literacy is a broad concept, involving not only co-constructive joint reading of high-quality books but also interaction with all kinds of environmental print and literacy technologies that pervade the home (Anderson & Stokes, 1984; Heath, 1983; Purcell-Gates, 1996). This perspective can easily be extended even further to include opportunities for co-constructive interactions with physical and symbolic materials (as in play), and for joint problem-solving in the contexts of housekeeping and domestic industry.

Instruction Quality

In addition to spontaneously constructing knowledge and skills by observing and participating without guidance, the things that children learn beyond what is within their reach from all potentially educational opportunities at home are dependent upon the guidance they receive from experienced others such as their parents. Co-constructive learning experiences under guidance and instruction by the parents may be manifold, but confined to the perspective of preparation for school learning, they can perhaps be reduced to one or a few basic dimensions.

Following distancing theory developed by Sigel and colleagues, I consider that the basic underlying dimension of joint book-reading and other types of educational interactions is how cognitively demanding these activities are (Leseman & Sijsling, 1996; McGillicuddy-DeLisi & Sigel, 1991; Pelligrini, Galda, Jones, & Perlmutter, 1995; Sigel, 1982). The key concept for evaluating parental strategies in educational interactions with young children is distancing—that is to say, the degree to which parents stimulate thinking and high level communication.

Social-emotional Quality

Co-constructive interactions are collaborative enterprises requiring that the participants are willing to cooperate. In this sense, they are also affective experiences created by the participants. Interactions at home that are less rewarding social-emotionally may lead to a negative attitude toward school literacy and reduce motivation to learn, which in turn affects achievement (de Jong, Leseman, & van der Leij, 1997; cf., Dweck, 1986). Starting from the point of view of attachment theory, Bus and van IJzendoorn (1995) argued that insecurely attached dyads will have less rewarding and satisfying interactions, leading to a lower frequency of such interactions and less optimal learning experiences (see also Denham, Renwick, & Holt, 1991; de Ruiter & van IJzendoorn, 1993; Erickson, Sroufe, & Egeland, 1985).

Contexts of Literacy and Informal Education at Home

The family's informal education system, including home literacy, is embedded in a wider social and cultural context. Besides background factors such as social class, ethnicity, race, religion, etc., which can be considered macrosystems operative at a certain "distance" (cf., Bradley & Caldwell, 1995; Bronfenbrenner, 1989) and only indirectly influencing educational home processes, I assume that the family's immediate sociocultural context essentially consists of three distinct but interrelated components: parents' own literacy practices and the models of literacy use available to them; their more general ideas about appropriate ways to interact with children of young ages; and the constellation of the family in relation to the socioeconomic circumstances, concerning in particular the effects of economic hardship and related risk factors. In multilingual societies a fourth component should be added: the language used at home and in the wider community, which may not be the language of literacy instruction at school.

Parents' Literacy Use and Literacy Models

The opportunities provided for participation in literacy practices in the home environment are closely related to the parents' own literacy use at home and the forms of literacy invading from the wider social environment of the family (Heath, 1983, 1986; Leseman & de Jong, 1998). Heath (1983) depicted the effects of involvement in the social (family) network and its traditions of oral language and literacy use on literacy and language use with children. The way parent-child literacy-related interactions are framed, (i.e., the kinds of apprenticeships that are offered to young children), depends on the models or examples of literacy use and appropriate behavioral roles offered in the diverse contexts of literacy use in which parents are involved. For instance, Heath (1983) described how white lower-class parents' questions and evaluations of children's answers during shared book-reading reflected bible-related interactions in the religious meetings they attended, with a strong emphasis on "true" interpretations and staying close to the literal text.

In similar ways, the contexts of the parents' jobs, the social and cultural practices in the social network and wider community, and intergenerationally transmitted traditions of craft and domestic industry influence parents' perceptions of potentially educational activities such as play and practical problem-solving, and offer behavioral models (and inherent but largely implicit didactical strategies) for interacting with the child regarding these activities (Leseman & Sijsling, 1996; Hoogsteder, Maier, & Elbers, 1996; Wertsch, Minick, & Arns, 1984).

Parents' Child-Rearing Beliefs

Literacy and educational interactions cannot be separated from general features of the parent-child relationship and the predominant child-rearing strategies of the parent. Following work in the area of parental belief systems (e.g., Goodnow, 1990; Harkness & Super, 1992, this volume; Palacios, 1990; Rubin & Mills, 1992), basic ideas of the parents and the wider community on the nature of intellectual and personal development, the role of caregivers in development, beliefs about what is age-appropriate behavior, and acceptable strategies to modify behavior, are at the root of the instruction and affective quality of parent-child interactions. Palacios (1990) found that the modernity of parents' beliefs about development and learning affected their interaction (teaching) styles, especially their age-appropriate use of distancing strategies and allowing the child to take initiatives, following the child's activities and scaffolding high-level involvement in play and book-reading interactions.

Family Constellation Characteristics and Socioeconomic Risks

Family constellation characteristics such as the number of children, single parenthood, constraints concerning time to be shared with children, and socioeconomic factors such as income, employment, and time at work potentially affect all three facets of the home as a system of informal education. Temporary or enduring psychological stress on the family and the parents, in particular stress resulting from socioeconomic hardship and other risk factors (Richter, this volume; Sameroff, Seifer, Baldwin, & Baldwin, 1993), may fundamentally influence the opportunities, time, and patience for instruction, the willingness to cooperate, and the social-emotional bond between parents and children (e.g., Crnic & Greenberg, 1993; Erickson et al., 1985). Single parenthood, a large family, and lack of support in child-rearing may have similar impact on the opportunity and quality facets.

Home Language

Though having a home language different than that of the majority language needs not in itself adversely influence the acquisition of literacy, children who speak a minority language are faced with the dual task of learning the majority language and becoming literate in the majority language. Bilingual children from low-income families are reported to face more difficulties in acquiring literacy in school because the school language is their second language (cf., McLaughlin, 1987; Ortiz, 1989; Verhoeven, this volume).

LITERACY AT HOME AND AT SCHOOL: AN EMPIRICAL DEMONSTRATION

In the next sections I will report and discuss findings from a study conducted in the Netherlands that are pertinent to the three core issues raised here, and which offer support for most theoretical considerations put forward in the preceding sections. In this study, the effects of home literacy and related informal educational practices at home on language development and early school achievement were determined, controlling for alternative explanations. Furthermore, the study related several facets of informal education in the home environment, including literacy, to the family's social and cultural context, and to children's reading and math-learning in school.

Sample, Design, and Measurements[1]

The study involved a cohort of 125 children of 4–7 years of age. The sample was socioeconomically and ethnic-culturally varied, consisting of four subsamples. The first subsample comprised indigenous Dutch middle-class families. The second consisted of Dutch lower-class families, and the other two subsamples were composed of immigrant families from Surinam and Turkey. (For more information on present-day Dutch multicultural society, see Eldering, 1996.)

The children attended 28 inner-city primary schools, and the families were recruited via the schools. In the Netherlands, primary school begins at the age of 4. The first two years encompass kindergarten. Formal instruction in reading, writing, and math does not usually start before the third year, or first grade.

The study was designed as longitudinal research, with three waves of measurements. The first visit to a family was scheduled around the time the child entered primary school, which was usually directly after the fourth birthday. On the first measurement occasion, age of the children was on average 4.3 years. Home visits were repeated twice when the children were about 5 and about 6 years of age. In the second semester of first grade, just under a year after the last home visit, children were tested in reading (word decoding, reading comprehension) and math (knowledge of arithmetical facts).

Each family was visited by a female researcher of the same ethnic origin. At each visit the primary caretaker of the child (in all but two cases the mother) was interviewed about the family's socioeconomic and ethnic background, parents' child-rearing beliefs, family composition, family's cultural features, and the opportunities provided for play and literacy-related interactions. Video recordings were made of a book-reading and joint play interaction (solving a categorization game). Data was collected by means of interview and video observation at home. Tests were administered at school.

Background Characteristics

The sociocultural context characteristics of the families measured in this study were divided into three categories. The first category concerned socioeconomic characteristics; that is to say, characteristics that reflect the family's socioeconomic status (SES) and participation in the economy, and which are indicative of income and prosperity. Variables falling into this category were parents' educational level (combined to an index of SES), the symbolic (e.g., literate, accounting, and computer-related) content of the parents' jobs (in the case of unemployment this concerned the former job), and unemployment of the principal breadwinner. Job content was assessed by a questionnaire determining the everyday literate and symbolic information processing demands of the job (cf., Kohn & Schooler, 1983).

The second category concerned parents' cultural practices relating to literacy, and their pedagogical beliefs. Though related to the family's socioeconomic background, the cultural family characteristics brought to attention here were assumed to reflect more directly dynamic features of everyday family life, including leisure time activities and styles of interaction with the children. Variables included in this category were parents' own literacy activities at home. These were measured using a list of different kinds of literacy use; for instance, asking whether they read books, and newspapers, and asking them to indicate how frequently they were involved in the activity mentioned. Language use at home was considered a cultural characteristic, as well. Parents were asked which language they used in a number of common situations in family life such as mealtime conversations and family visits. Finally, Schaefer and Edgerton's (1985) Parental Modernity Scale was used to assess parents' ideas and opinions on a large number of child-rearing and child development issues concerning appropriate behavior and behavioral dispositions (such as obedience and respect for authority), acceptable disciplining strategies, the role of parents in development, and the preferred division of roles of parents and teachers in educating the child.

The third main category of family background characteristics concerned a mixture of family constellation variables that were assumed to be somehow important for child-rearing and educational processes at home. These included variables indicating whether the family was a single-parent family (in the present study, always mother-headed); the number of children living at home; and a measure of the total amount of time per week that the principal caregiver was working out of home, which presumably would affect time to be shared with the children. Also included were two measures of support received in everyday child-rearing, namely the use of child care (day care, preschool, host parents) and the extent to which principal caregivers were assisted by others (e.g., husband, parents and parents-in-law, friends) in everyday child-rearing.

Literacy and Informal Education at Home

Three basic facets of the proximal processes of the family as a social microsystem in which children construct knowledge and skills and develop affective dispositions were measured with regard to two broad domains of informal learning, namely, literacy and play.

Opportunity

Opportunity for literacy interactions was measured on a scale administered during the interview. Parents were asked to rate the occurrence of a number of literacy-related activities such as reading books or newspapers in the child's vicinity, reading storybooks to the child, reading "environmental print" such as advertising magazines in the child's presence, and acknowledging spontaneous prereading (i.e., "as if" reading) and prewriting by the child.

In the same way, parents were asked to rate the occurrence of play and everyday practical problem-solving activities, such as playing with dolls, toy cars, jigsaw puzzles, and construction materials (wooden blocks, Lego); memory and thinking games; painting and drawing; and situations of child and parent together being involved in practical problem-solving (e.g., sewing, knitting, carpentry, cooking, shopping).

Social-emotional Quality

Socioemotional quality was assessed by observations of parent-child interactions during joint book-reading and solving a categorization task yielding two measures for each task. The rating scales of Erickson et al. (1985) were used to evaluate mother's behavior toward the child in both situations. The scales referred to the degree to which mothers supported an emotionally positive and instructive experience during joint book-reading.

Instruction Quality

A coding scheme based on distancing theory was developed to evaluate instruction level of book-reading. Several types of acts and utterances by the mother were distinguished and pooled into two categories. The first category was denoted as low distancing. The acts and utterances in this category were either unrelated to the narrative or related to the narrative but closely connected to the pictures, such as pointing, "see that?" questions, and labelling, or repeating of the text word for word. The second category reflected high distancing utterances comprising explanatory, evaluative, narrative-extending and topical-extending utterances. Instruction quality was defined as the proportion of higher distancing level utterances out of all coded narrative-related utterances.

A coding scheme that distinguished between task instruction at the start of the session (the mother explaining the purpose, rules, and principles of the task in advance), instructions and strategic suggestions during the game (giving direct instructions, providing cues for search strategies, and giving rationales for certain choices), and extensions (labelling the pictures, providing information on definitional characteristics, giving formal definitions, and extending with general world knowledge) was developed to assess the quality of mother's instruction to the child during the categorization game. Underlying the scheme were notions derived from Markman (1989) on the development of categorization skill, evolving from no categorization, via perception-based syntagmatic, to paradigmatic categorization, that is to say, to the use of semantic-taxonomic categories. The hierarchy implied here was compatible with the distancing dimension. Instruction quality was computed as the sum of the score for the advance task instruction plus the proportion of semantic-taxonomic instruction and higher-level extensions during task completion.

Stability of Home Educational Processes

All facets of the informal home education processes were measured three times. The mean cross-lag correlations obtained for each facet on the three occasions were rather high-ranging, from .46 to .66, indicating a fairly stable home environment across time. Therefore, to reduce the number of variables in subsequent analyses the measures for every facet were combined into single indexes representing the mean of the scores obtained on the three measurement occasions.

School Literacy and Math Achievement

Vocabulary and Nonverbal Intelligence at Age 4

A few months after the children entered school, their receptive vocabulary and nonverbal intelligence was tested. The vocabulary test had the same format as the well-known Peabody Picture Vocabulary Test (PPVT) and consisted of 48 items. A block-design test, which was part of a norm-referenced intelligence test for young children, was used to measure nonverbal spatial intelligence.

School Achievement at Age 7

At the end of first grade, when the children were about 7 years old, norm-referenced tests were administered to assess receptive vocabulary, reading achievement (decoding and reading comprehension), and math achievement. The tests are all widely used in the Netherlands (for more details, see Leseman & de Jong, 1998, and de Jong, 1997). All tests were in Dutch.

RESULTS

Comparing the Four Groups

The family's *socioeconomic status* showed the expected differences between the four groups, amounting to more than one and a half standard deviations between the Dutch middle-class families and the Turkish families. The symbolic job-content measure was related to socioeconomic status. The kinds of jobs held by Dutch middle-class parents outranked the jobs of the other groups in the degree of literate and symbolic information-processing demanded. The jobs of the Turkish parents had the least symbolic content (the mean score is close to the minimum value of the scale). Unemployment rates were highest in the Turkish group, which fit in well with national statistics (see also Eldering & Vedder, this volume). No unemployment was reported in the Dutch middle-class group.

The *cultural characteristics* of the family covered parents' literacy activities at home, home language, and child-rearing beliefs. Literacy use at home for varied purposes (information and education, instrumental use and recreation) differed clearly between the four groups. As was expected, the highest level was found in the Dutch middle-class homes, the lowest level in the Turkish families.

Differences between the groups were especially strong regarding home language and parental beliefs. In these cases, Turkish and Surinamese parents as a group deviated greatly from Dutch parents. With a few exceptions, Turkish was the predominant language for conversation in Turkish homes. In some of the Surinamese homes, Surinamese Creole or Surinamese Hindi were spoken. Finally, the child-rearing beliefs of the Surinamese and Turkish parents, especially of the latter, tended to be more authoritarian than the child-rearing beliefs of the Dutch parents, appreciating more values such as obedience, respect for adults and authorities etc. .

Concerning the *family constellation characteristics,* there were differences between the groups in proportion of single-parent families (relatively high in the Surinamese group) and use of child day care (relatively high in the Dutch middle-class group and in the Surinamese group).

Important differences were also found regarding the home environment as a system of informal learning, indicating that families prepare children differentially for school learning. With respect to opportunity, differences were greatest regarding literacy, but small and insignificant regarding play. Literacy opportunities in Turkish and, to a lesser degree, in Surinamese homes were relatively scarce. The differences between Dutch middle-class families and Dutch working-class families were negligible. Typically, on closer scrutiny, it appeared that of the list of presented literacy events it was those concerned with reading books either alone (with the child present) or to the child, and writing letters or postcards that accounted for the biggest difference between the groups, whereas interaction with environmental print and written language use for instrumental purposes (e.g., writing a shopping list) did not differ significantly between the groups.

Regarding play and practical problem-solving, the most pronounced differences concerned joint play with dolls, toys, and construction materials. According to the reports this play occured least in the Turkish homes and most in the Dutch working-class homes. Overall, the differences were small.

The two measures of instruction quality regarding book-reading and the categorization task, respectively, revealed rather large differences between the groups. In terms of the share of higher-level instruction in joint book-reading and the categorization game, the Turkish mothers came last and the Dutch middle-class mothers first. The most pronounced differences in joint book-reading concerned the comparatively high proportions of procedural negotiation in the Turkish families, of repeating (or having the child repeat) read sentences word by word in both the Turkish and Surinamese families, and of narrative extensions and evaluations in the Dutch middle-class families (for a more extensive discussion, see Leseman & de Jong, 1998). The high proportion of procedural utterances in the Turkish families was indicative of the difficulties the mothers had in dealing with the child's spontaneous reactions to the book-reading event. Turkish children, like Dutch and Surinamese children, wanted to look at the pictures, turn the pages, and take the book, but their mothers apparently quite often regarded this as inappropriate. This sometimes resulted in rather lengthy negotiations, in difficulties in getting started, and a few times in a complete failure of the book-reading event.

The most pronounced difference between the four groups in the categorization game concerned the quality of the advance task instruction, which was highest in Dutch middle-class families and lowest in Turkish families. Furthermore, differences were found, though less pronounced, regarding the use of irrelevant instructions (comparatively high in Turkish and Surinamese families), thematic instructions (high in Dutch lower-class families), semantic-taxonomic directions, and definitory extensions (high in Dutch middle-class families), and labelling of the pictures (high in Turkish families).

Finally, the groups also differed very markedly in the social-emotional quality facet of the book-reading interaction and joint categorization game, with the same pattern of findings: the highest scores were obtained by the Dutch middle-class parents, with Dutch working-class parents about a half standard deviation lower, the Surinamese a further half standard deviation below that, and the Turks a further one standard deviation below that.

Correlational and Structural Analysis

Correlational analysis and structural equations analysis were performed to gain more insight into the relationships between contextual factors and home education processes and in the effects of home education processes on school achievement.

Correlational Analysis

The correlations between background characteristics and home informal education measures and predicted variances per category of background characteristics presented in Table 8-1 show that socioeconomic status, job content, parents' own literacy, home language, and parents' child-rearing beliefs can be seen as explaining most of the differences in the six facets of home education that were assessed. These characteristics correlated strongest with the measure of literacy opportunity. The correlations with the degree of opportunities for play and problem-solving interactions, however, were much smaller (and neither showed strong differences between the four groups). The correlations of socioeconomic status, job content, and cultural family characteristics with the instruction quality and social-emotional quality of book-reading and play were also all rather strong. Correlations of socioeconomic and family constellation risk factors (unemployment, time at work of the principal caregiver, single parenthood, number of children) and protective factors (child-rearing support, use of child center care) with the home informal education facets were rather small overall.

Elsewhere, the same data was analyzed using structural equations technique (Leseman & de Jong, 1998). Support was found for the view that the effects of (static) structural and nonpsychological characteristics such as class or socioeconomic status and minority status are mediated, first, by (dynamic) everyday social and cultural practices within the settings of the job, the social (family) network, religious community, and forms of leisure time spending; second, by the caregiver's psychology (see also Harkness & Super, 1992, this volume), that is to say, the parents' child-rearing beliefs; and, third, by practical constraints and family constellation characteristics (money, time, arrangements for child care, number of children, availability of child-rearing support.

Table 8-2 presents the correlations found between the informal home education facets and the developmental and school achievement measures. In general, correlations were modest, although the combined, multivariate prediction, as represented by the R^2 statistic, is substantial for most outcome measures. The correlations with Dutch vocabulary were the strongest, which may be partly due to confounding with the effects of home language. Regarding reading achievement, both expected and unexpected patterns of associations were found. Opportunity for literacy, the instruction quality of book-reading, and the social-emotional quality of book-reading correlated statistically significantly, though modestly, with technical reading (word decoding), but weakly with reading comprehension and zero with math achievement. In contrast, the instruction quality and social-emotional quality of play (i.e., jointly solving a categorization problem) correlated stronger overall with both language and nonverbal intelligence at age four, and with both reading and math achievement measures taken at age seven.

Structural Analysis

A structural model was analyzed to examine further the multivariate structure of home literacy and home education as related to school achievement. Overall, correlations between these facets and school achievement were moderately strong. However, strictly speaking, this provides no evidence for a causal relationship. For instance, the correlation between facets of informal home education and school achievement may be attributable to genetic factors that covary with home education and school achievement (Scarr, 1992), or else to a nonmeasured home factor. Or the correlation may point to effects of the home environment at earlier stages. To rule out these alternative explanations, vocabulary and nonverbal intelligence at age 4 were taken as developmental precursors of school achievement at age 7. Further, because of the strong intercorrelations, the measures of instruction quality and social-emotional quality were combined, separately for book-reading and play. The measure of opportunity for play was

Table 8-1. Pearson Correlations of Family Background Characteristics, Including Ethnicity, with Facets of Informal Home Education; Also Presented is the Total Amount of Predicted Variance R^2 per Block of Predictor Variables

Predictors	Home Informal Education Facets					
	Oppor-tunity for Literacy	Oppor-tunity for Play	Instruct Quality Reading	Instruct Quality Play	Emotion Quality Reading	Emotion Quality Play
Surinamese	.01	-.12	-.25 **	-.15 *	-.18 *	-.29 **
Turkish	-.45 **	-.16 *	-.37 **	-.39 **	-.44 **	-.34 **
SES	.37 **	.09	.35 **	.46 **	.49 **	.43 **
Symbolic job content	.40 **	.14	.45 **	.46 **	.55 **	.46 **
Unemployment breadwinner	-.29 **	-.06	-.15 *	-.21 **	-.14	-.10
R^2	.27 **	.08 *	.24 **	.28 **	.36 **	.25 **
Informational literacy	.63 **	.28 **	.37 **	.43 **	.37 **	.34 **
Recreational literacy	.55 **	.18 **	.43 **	.36 **	.33 **	.32 **
Home language	.46 **	.20 **	.44 **	.43 **	.53 **	.43 **
Modern child-rearing beliefs	.47 **	.20 **	.43 **	.51 **	.51 **	.50 **
R^2	.47 **	.09 *	.27 **	.31 **	.35 **	.30 **
Single parent family	.06	.05	-.08	-.00	-.09	-.15 *
Number of children	-.08	-.11	-.10	-.06	-.00	.01
Caregivers' work time	-.05	-.13	-.11	.03	-.03	.03
Intensity of child care	.04	-.16 *	.21 **	.27 **	.23 **	.36 **
Child-rearing support	-.00	-.17 *	-.05	-.02	-.03	.06
R^2	.03	.07	.08 *	.07	.07	.15 **

* p < .05; ** p < .01

Table 8-2. Pearson Correlations of the Facets of Informal Home Education With Measures of Development at Age 4 and School Achievement Measures at Age 7.

Predictors	Cognitive-verbal Development and School Achievement					
Informal Home Education Facets	Age 4 Vocabulary	Age 4 Nonvb. Intell.	Age 7 Vocabulary	Age 7 Word Decoding	Age 7 Reading Compreh.	Age 7 Math
Opportunity for literacy	.47 **	.09 *	.30 **	.35 **	.29 **	.06
Opportunity for play	.01	.01	.06	.19 *	.04	-.02
Instruction quality reading	.25 **	.04	.43 **	.24 *	.04	.07
Instruction quality play	.18 *	.19 *	.40 **	.44 **	.24 *	.28 **
Emotional quality reading	.18 *	.09	.47 **	.24 *	.10	.11
Emotional quality play	.15	.16	.39 **	.29 **	.16	.22 *
R^2	.20 **	.06	.33 **	.24 **	.16 *	.12 *

* $p < .05$; ** $p < .01$

excluded from the structural analysis because of low intercorrelations with all other measures. The model was analyzed separately for word decoding, reading comprehension, and math. Finally, as all tests were administered in Dutch, home language was included as a control variable. Figure 8-1 summarizes the results. Presented are the standardized regression-weights (path-coefficients). All models were fitting satisfactorily.

The results of the model analysis confirmed the expectation that home education facets contributed to children's differential development between ages 4 and 7. The sum of the squared regression-coefficients indicates how much additional variance is predicted by the home education facets in the school achievement measures. The amount of explained variance is statistically insignificant in the case of reading comprehension (additional predicted variance is .03) and modest in the two other cases (.10 for math and .13 for word decoding). Home language, opportunity for literacy, and instruction quality of joint book-reading explained part of the variance in reading achievement, but not in math achievement. Instruction quality of play interaction explained part of the variance in both reading and math achievement. It is interesting to note here that the quality of play had a stronger effect on the reading achievement measures than did the quality of book-reading.

Summary of the Results

The results presented above suggest that quality facets, in particular, the instruction quality, of both literacy and more general educational play interactions probably contribute to cognitive-verbal development and can be seen as prepatory for acquiring literacy and math in school. After controlling for previous differences in the verbal and nonverbal developmental domains and for home language, the differential development between first and final measurement occasion was explained to about 3 percent (in the case of reading comprehension) to 13 percent of the variance in total (in the case of word decoding).

Joint book-reading quality was found to be less important for early school achievement (reading and math achievement) than the quality of joint play. A possible explanation is that the potential of joint book-reading as an apprenticeship for general cognitive-verbal development is limited to younger ages.

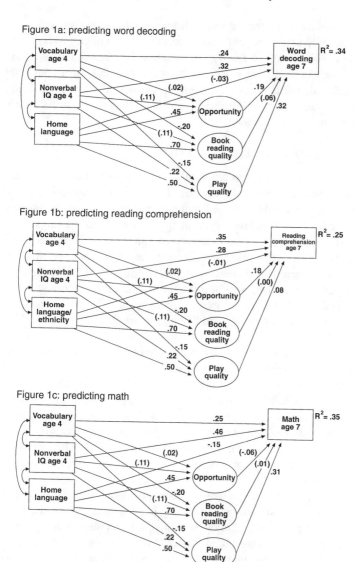

Figure 1a: predicting word decoding

Figure 1b: predicting reading comprehension

Figure 1c: predicting math

Figure 8-1. Results of structural equations analysis of home education (a) predicting word-decoding, (b) reading comprehension, and (c) math skills.

The facets of the family's informal education system were satisfactorily explained by the socioeconomic and cultural background factors. The effects of family constellation and associated risk (and protective) factors were small overall, compared to educational level and cultural characteristics. Note that this result might be specifically related to the Dutch welfare state, which protects most families from extreme poverty and parenting stress.

CONCLUSIONS AND IMPLICATIONS

The research findings reported in this chapter are pertinent to the three issues identified earlier concerning the processes underlying home literacy, the multiple routes of home preparation for school literacy learning, and the contextuality of home literacy. Three findings stand out. The first concerns the multifaceted nature of home literacy and related cognitive apprenticeships. The separate bivariate correlations of the home literacy and education facets with school achievement measures were in the range of .00 to .47. Most of them corresponded reasonably well with the average correlations of .27 to .33 reported in reviews by Bus et al. (1995) and Scarborough and Dobrich (1994). The results of the multiple regression analyses, however, gave an impression of the combined effects of different facets of home literacy. The multiple correlations (computed as the square roots of the R^2's) with age seven outcome measures were overall much stronger, ranging from .35 to .57. With respect to the issue of effective ingredients, therefore, it can be concluded that home literacy and informal education at home in general are multifaceted phenomena involving opportunities, instruction quality, and affective quality. The results fit in well with the social-constructivist theory outlined in the first part of this chapter.

The second finding is that in addition to home literacy, informal learning in other situations concerning play involving both the joint construction and application of problem-solving strategies and general world knowledge contributed equally, if not more, to the child's cognitive-verbal development and school achievement in reading and math. Bearing in mind that the observation procedures and coding schemes used to assess instruction quality and social-emotional quality of book-reading and play interactions were either the same (in the case of social-emotional quality) or developed on the same theoretical basis (in the case of instruction quality), this result suggests that parents scoring low in one situation did not necessarily score low in the other situation.

The third finding concerns the embeddedness of home educational processes in the family's socioeconomic and cultural context. Socioeconomic status, represented by the educational level of both parents and, in particular, the degree of symbolic job content; parents' literacy practices; and parents' child-rearing beliefs appeared to be strong determinants of the various facets of the informal home education system. There was no marked difference between the contextual embeddedness of literacy and play, except for the opportunity for play facet, which was less well-explained, but did not differ very strongly between the families, either. The explanation by "dynamic" socioeconomic (e.g., job content) and cultural context factors was overall stronger than the explanation by class and ethnicity as such.

Home literacy and informal home education in general are multifaceted phenomena, involving opportunities for interaction, instruction, and affective experiences. The core of the informal home education system consists of co-constructive interactions between children and their parents (and by theoretical extension, between children and other adults or older siblings who might be present). In the samples examined, the instruction facet was the most effective ingredient, but other facets, especially opportunity for literacy interactions, improve the statistical prediction of the measures of school achievement significantly. In designing home literacy programs, it is therefore advisable to adopt an approach involving all relevant facets of home literacy.

There are probably more routes of preparation for schooling than home literacy in a narrow sense. A narrow focus on literacy is perhaps not the best strategy to obtain more sizeable effects. Extrapolating from the present findings, it seems likely that enhancing opportunity and quality of play and problem-solving interactions, conversations, oral storytelling, singing nursery rhymes, and so on may contribute to preparing young children for acquiring literacy and learning other school subjects (e.g., math) as well (see also Snow, this volume). It may be recommendable to focus even more on other prepatory routes to school literacy, especially in the case of families and communities with a low literacy level, living in a social-cultural context that is not conducive to literacy.

The strong link between facets of home literacy and home education in general, and the parents' educational history, job content, cultural life styles, and the influence of child-rearing beliefs raises the question of whether a narrow focus on promoting literacy interactions with children is sufficient to bring about lasting effects. Attention should be paid to changing the wider sociocultural context of home literacy interactions as well. For example, combinations with adult literacy programs, adult basic education, child-rearing consultancy, and family support programs may be necessary to obtain long-term effects (Darling & Paull, 1994; Delgado-Gaitan, 1995; Weiss & Kagen, 1989; for a related argument, see Yoshikawa, 1994).

NOTES

1. The study was carried out in collaboration with P. F. de Jong and A. van der Leij of the Free University of Amsterdam, the Netherlands. Other publications on parts of the study are Leseman, 1994b; Leseman & de Jong, 1998; Leseman, Sijsling, Jap-A-Joe, & Şahin, 1995. For full technical reports, see Leseman, 1997, and de Jong, 1997.

REFERENCES

Anderson, A. B., & Stokes, S. J. (1984). Social and institutional influences on the development and practice of literacy. In H. Goelman, A. Oberg, & F. Smith (Eds.), *Awakening to literacy* (pp. 24–37). London: Heinemann.

Arnold, D. S., & Whitehurst, G. J. (1994). Accelerating language development through picture book reading: A summary of dialogic reading and its effects. In D. K. Dickinson (Ed.), *Bridges to literacy: Children, families, and schools* (pp. 103–128). Cambridge, MA: Blackwell.

Bradley, R., & Caldwell, B. (1995). Caregiving and regulation of child growth and development: Describing proximal aspects of caregiving systems. *Developmental Review, 15,* 38–85.

Bronfenbrenner, U. (1989). Ecological systems theory. *Annals of Child Development, 6,* 187–249.

Bus, A. G., & van IJzendoorn, M. H. (1995). Mothers' reading to their 3-year-olds: The role of mother-child attachment security in becoming literate. *Reading Research Quarterly, 30*(4), 998–1015.

Bus, A. G., van IJzendoorn, M. H., & Pellegrini, A. D. (1995). Joint book-reading makes for success in learning to read: A meta-analysis on intergenerational transmission of literacy. *Review of Educational Research, 65,* 1–21.

Crnic, K. A., & Greenberg, M. T. (1993). Minor parenting stresses with young children. *Child Development, 61*, 1628–1637.

Darling, S., & Paull, S. (1994). Implications for family literacy programs. In D. K. Dickinson (Ed.), *Bridges to literacy* (pp. 273–284). Cambridge, MA: Blackwell.

de Glopper, K. (1993). Grenzen aan leesbevordering [The limits of literacy promotion]. In M. Koren (Ed.), *Leesbevordering aan de grens* (pp. 15–28). The Hague, the Netherlands: NBLC.

de Jong, P. F. (1997). *Schoolcareers from 4–7: The relationships between cognitive development and the acquisition of reading and arithmetics.* Amsterdam: Department of Psychology and Pedagogics of the Free University.

de Jong, P. F., Leseman, P. P. M., & van der Leij, A. (1997). Affective quality of mother-child interaction as a predictor of children's school achievement: Evidence for a situation specific relationship. In W. Koops, J. B. Hoeksma, & D. C. van den Boom (Eds.), *Early mother-child interaction and attachment: Traditional and nontraditional approaches* (pp. 313–314). Amsterdam: Elsevier North Holland.

Delgado-Gaitan, C. (1995). *Protean literacy. Extending the discourse on empowerment.* London: The Falmer Press.

de Ruiter, C., & van IJzendoorn, M. H. (1993). Attachment and cognition: A review of literature. *International Journal of Educational Research, 19*, 5–20.

Denham, S. A., Renwick, S. M., & Holt, R. W. (1991). Working and playing together: prediction of preschool social-emotional competence from mother-child interaction. *Child Development, 62*, 242–249.

Doets, C. (1992). Functionele ongeletterdheid onder volwassen Nederlanders [Functional illiteracy among adults in the Netherlands]. *Pedagogische Studiën, 69*(5), 388–399.

Dweck, C. S. (1986). Motivational process affecting learning. *American Psychologist, 41* (10), 1040–1048.

Eldering, L. (1996). Multiculturalism and Multicultural Education in an International Perspective. *Anthropology and Education Quarterly, 27*(3), 315–330.

Erickson, M. F., Sroufe, L. A., & Egeland, B. (1985). The relationship between quality of attachment and behavior problems in preschool in a high-risk sample. In I. Bretherton & E. Waters (Eds.), Growing points of attachment theory and research. *Monographs of the Society for Research in Child Development, 50*.

Goodnow, J.J. (1990). The socialization of cognition. In J. W. Stigler, R.A. Schweder, & G. Herdt (Eds.), *Cultural psychology: Essays on comparative human development* (pp. 259–286). Cambridge: Cambridge University Press.

Harkness, S., & Super C. M. (1992). Parental ethnotheories in action. In I. E. Sigel, A. V. McGillicuddy-DeLisi, & J. J. Goodnow (Eds.), *Parental belief systems: The psychological consequences for children* (2nd ed., pp. 373–391). Hillsdale, NJ: Erlbaum.

Heath, S. B. (1983). *Ways with words*. Cambridge: Cambridge University Press.

Heath, S. B. (1986). Critical factors in literacy development. In S. de Castell, A. Luke, & K. Egan (Eds.), *Literacy, society, and schooling: A reader* (pp. 209–229). Cambridge: Cambridge University Press.

Hoogsteder, M., Maier, R., & Elbers, E. (1996). The architecture of adult-child interaction. Joint problem solving and the structure of cooperation. *Learning and Instruction*, 6(4), 345–358.

Kirsch, I. S., & Jungebluth, A. (1987). *Literacy: Profiles of America's young adults. National assessment of educational progress*. Washington, DC: Educational Testing Service.

Kohn, M. L., & Schooler, C. (1983). *Work and personality: An inquiry into the impact of social stratification*. Norwood, NJ: Ablex.

Leseman, P. (1994a). Socio-cultural determinants of literacy development. In L. Verhoeven (Ed.), *Functional literacy: Theoretical issues and educational implications* (pp. 163–184). Amsterdam: John Benjamins.

Leseman, P. P. M. (1994b). Parent-child interactions as a system of informal education. In F. Laevers (Ed.), *Defining and assesing quality in early childhood education* (pp. 263–277). Leuven, Belgium: Leuven University Press.

Leseman, P. P. M. (1997). *Schoolcareers from 4–7: Informal home education in Dutch, Surinamese, and Turkish families*. Amsterdam: SCO Kohnstamm Institute.

Leseman, P. P. M., Sijsling, F. F., Jap-A-Joe, S. R., & Şahin, S. (1995). Gezinsdeterminanten van de cognitieve ontwikkeling van vierjarige Nederlandse, Surinaamse en Turkse kleuters [Home influences on four year old Dutch, Surinamese-Dutch, and Turkish-Dutch children's cognitive development]. *Pedagogische Studiën*, 72(3), 186–205.

Leseman, P. P. M., & Sijsling, F. F. (1996). Cooperation and instruction in practical problem-solving: Differences in interaction styles of mother-child dyads as related to socio-economic background and cognitive development. *Learning and Instruction*, 6(4), 307–323.

Leseman, P. P. M., & de Jong, P. F. (1998). Home literacy: Opportunity, instruction, cooperation, and social-emotional quality predicting early reading achievement. *Reading Research Quarterly 33* (3), 294–318.

Markman, E. M. (1989). *Categorization and naming in children.* Cambridge, MA: MIT Press.

McGillicuddy-DeLisi, A. V., & Sigel, I. E. (1991). Family environments and children's representational thinking. In S. B. Silvern & B. A. Hutson (Eds.), *Advances in reading/language research* (Vol. 5, pp. 63–90). Greenwich, CT: JAI Press.

McLaughlin, B. (1987). Reading in a second language: Studies with adult and child learners. In S. R. Goldman & H. T. Trueba (Eds.), *Becoming literate in English as a second language* (pp. 57–70). Norwood, NJ: Ablex.

Ortiz, V. (1989). Language background and literacy among hispanic young adults. *Social Problems, 36*(2), 1–20.

Palacios, J. (1990). Parents' ideas about development and education of their children: Answers to some questions. *International Journal of Behavioral Development, 13*, 137–155.

Pellegrini, A. D., Galda, L., Jones, I., & Perlmutter, J. (1995). Joint reading between mothers and their Head Start children: Vocabulary development in two text formats. *Discourse Processes, 19,* 441–463.

Purcell-Gates, V. (1996). Stories, coupons, and the TV guide: Relationships between home literacy experiences and emergent literacy knowledge. *Reading Research Quarterly, 31,* 406–428.

Rogoff, B. (1990). *Apprenticeship in thinking. Cognitive development in social context.* New York: Oxford University Press.

Rogoff, B., Mistry, J., Göncü, A., & Mosier, C. (1993). Guided participation in cultural activity by toddlers and caregivers. *Monographs of the Society for Research in Child Development, 158.*

Rubin, K. H., & Mills, R. S. L. (1992). Parents' thoughts about children's socially adaptive and maladaptive behaviors: Stability, change, and individual differences. In I. E. Sigel, A. V. McGillicuddy-DeLisi, & J. J. Goodnow (Eds.), *Parental belief systems: The psychological consequences for children* (2nd ed., pp. 41–69). Hillsdale, NJ: Erlbaum.

Sameroff, A., Seifer, R., Baldwin, A., & Baldwin, C. (1993). Stability of intelligence from preschool to adolescence: The influence of social and family risk factors. *Child Development, 64,* 80–97.

Scarr, S. (1992). Developmental theories for the 1990s: Development and individual differences. *Child Development, 63,* 1–19.

Scarborough, H. S., & Dobrich, W. (1994). On the efficacy of reading to preschoolers. *Developmental Review, 14,* 245–302.

Schaefer, E. S., & Edgerton, M. (1985). Parent and child correlates of parental modernity. In I. E. Sigel (Ed.), *Parental belief systems: The psychological consequences for children* (pp. 287–318). Hillsdale, NJ: Erlbaum.

Sigel, I. E. (1982). The relationship between parental distancing strategies and the child's cognitive behaviour. In L. M. Laosa & I. E. Sigel (Eds.), *Families as learning environments for children* (pp. 47–86). New York: Plenum Press.

Stanovich, K. E. (1986). Matthew effects in reading: Some consequences of individual differences in the acquisition of literacy. *Reading Research Quarterly, 21*(4), 360–406.

Veen, A., Overmars, A., & de Glopper, K. (1995). *Boekenpret belicht. Onderzoek naar een project leesbevordering voor 0–6-jarigen* [The project "Books are Fun". Evaluation of a literacy promotion project]. Utrecht, the Netherlands: ISOR.

Weiss, B., & Kagen, S. L. (1989). Family support programs: Catalysts for change. *American Journal of Orthopsychiatry, 59*(1), 20–31.

Wertsch, J. V. (1985). *Vygotsky and the social formation of the mind.* Cambridge, MA: Harvard University Press.

Wertsch, J. V., & Bivens, J. A. (1992). The social origins of individual mental functioning: Alternatives and perspectives. *The Quarterly Newsletter of the Laboratory of Comparative Human Cognition, 14*(2), 35–44.

Wertsch, J. V., Minick, N., & Arns, F. J. (1984). The creation of context in joint problem solving. In B. Rogoff & J. Lave (Eds.), *Everyday cognition: Its development in social context.* Cambridge, MA: Harvard University Press.

Yoshikawa, H. (1994). Prevention as cumulative risk protection: Effects of early family support and education on chronic delinquency and its risks. *Psychological Bulletin, 115*(1), 28–54.

Parenting in Poverty: Young Children and Their Families in South Africa

Linda M. Richter

Countless people in developing countries are desperately poor. This means they have little or no access to materials, facilities, and services that they can use to safeguard their social and economic resources, improve their circumstances, or bootstrap their children's chances for a better life. Nonetheless, many people, at least in South Africa, do improve their lives and those of their children. And they did, even during the most stifling years of Grand Apartheid; this is clear from the descriptions given by people like Sindiwe Magona (1990) of the way families, and particularly women, persevere in their efforts to educate and advance themselves and their children. This fact is testimony to the hidden potential of knowledge, skills, and resources in people, families, and communities.

In South Africa this potential has been obscured from us by a number of things. First, we have tended to maintain a conscious blindness to individual differences in people's adaptation to poverty and hardship, for fear that recognition and discussion of them might support the tendency of government to "individualize" social problems and blame those who suffer most for their own situation. Second, both colonialism and apartheid have fostered an unconscious blindness to the psychological substance of poor (and especially, in South Africa, black) people. Instead, we have tended to see people in terms that parody Abraham Maslow's (1970) need hierarchy theory.

We have been inclined to view economically deprived people as entities who operate from a predetermined hierarchy of needs, the activation of each higher level being dependent on the fulfillment of lower level needs. We have tended to presume that belongingness, self-esteem and hope come into play only when hunger, thirst, physical safety, and shelter are assured. By this reasoning, we are led to presume that poor people have a greater need for food, clean water, and shelter, than a need to feel loved by others and respect for themselves. By extension, we also seem to operate on the assumption that there is a hierarchy of psychological functions; that one cannot feel shy, hopeful, or humiliated when one is hungry, thirsty, or cold. An extreme illustration of this point is the long time it has taken for depressive illnesses to be recognized in Africa (Weiss & Kleinman, 1988). In truth, all these needs operate simultaneously in human beings, and life is lived by people who synchronously exercise their psychological, social, and physical capacities. It is our blindness that prevents us from recognizing the psychological life of economically deprived people and, by implication, their psychological resources. However, perhaps it is also more comfortable for us that way. It is less complicated to provide a tap, a meal, or a book than to meet head-on the shame, distress, and helplessness experienced by many poor people.

Another reason why we have tended to overlook the social and psychological essence of poor and oppressed people is because we have subscribed to a kind of cultural anthropology and cross-cultural psychology that amplifies cultural differences and frequently bypasses psychological depth in family relationships and parent-child interaction in non-Western cultures (e.g., LeVine, 1990). Socialization, a process credited with great complexity in our own society, is often taken to be understandable according to only a few principles in other cultures—for example, that African child-rearing can be characterized by the importance of compliance, which is enforced through corporal punishment. In contrast to this view, Welch (1978), for example, has asserted that there is less divergence between the socialization practices of African and non-African societies than is generally believed.

In this chapter, I would like to play down the influence of specific cultural influences and, instead, point out that, first, in South Africa there is a great deal of individual variation in coping with economic hardship, particularly with regard to the provision of nurturing and instructive experiences for young children, and that these differences are attributable to individual and social factors; second, that women, who are responsible for the care and guidance of young children, are increasingly burdened also with sole financial responsibility for children; third, that some women, without sufficient material and social resources, are psychologically overcome by adversity and their demoralization reduces their effectiveness as caregivers; fourth, caregiving dysfunctions place at risk the social and psychological capacities of young children necessary for optimal participation and learning when given educational opportunities; and, finally, apart from providing preschool and educational facilities and compensating for past inequalities, interventions need to be directed at caregivers by strengthening family ties, promoting paternal commitment to children, assisting vulnerable women in ways that increase their confidence and emotional engagement with their children, and increasing women's education and income-earning capacities.

THEORETICAL ORIENTATION

The theoretical background to these ideas originates in the paradigm of social constructivism, according to which one takes children's development to be determined by experiences that are mediated or socially constructed by significant social agents in the environment (Vygotsky, 1978). More specifically, at the level of the child's day-to-day experiences, the approach is based on a conception of caregiving as a regulator of human development (Bradley & Caldwell, 1995). According to the analysis offered by Bradley and Caldwell (1995), caregiving conditions and actions can be classified into five primary caregiving tasks: sustenance, stimulation, support, structure, and surveillance; and the caregiving environment can be viewed as complementary to the human psychobiological system. In this sense, the model developed by Bradley and Caldwell is compatible with the bioecological paradigm proposed by Bronfenbrenner and Ceci (1994). In the latter model, adult-child interactions in caregiving (such as responsiveness to the child's needs and interests) are conceptualized as proximal processes, through which genetic potentials for psychological functions are actualized.

In Bronfenbrenner and Ceci's model, genetic actualization is increased with increases in magnitude of proximal processes, taking into account also the stability of proximal processes, the environmental contexts in which they take place, the characteristics of the persons involved, and the nature of the psychological function being considered. According to this view, adult-child interaction is not merely an environmental influence, but a process occurring within an immediate setting, which itself is situated within a broader sociocultural context. The Bronfenbrenner and Ceci model is significant in that it specifically articulates testable hypotheses regarding the size and degree of impact of interventions in the most disadvantaged environments. In this regard, it draws attention to features of the wider social context infrequently addressed by targeted interventions, including resources and opportunity structures, to which disadvantaged parents need access to expand and secure the proximal processes in which they are engaged with their children. The model emphasizes the environmental stability necessary for proximal processes to operate successfully, and they observe that "it is environmental conditions and events originating outside the family that are likely to be the most powerful and pervasive disrupters of family processes affecting human development throughout the life course" (Bronfenbrenner & Ceci, 1994, p. 576). Stability, in the model, is also important for another principle of the bioecological model, which is that the elements combine in nonadditive synergistic fashion; that is, they have the capacity to generalize across psychological functions. In conclusion, Bronfenbrenner and Ceci express the conviction that the model, if found to be valid, provides a basis for designing more effective strategies to counteract the social changes (including in developing societies) which have undermined conditions necessary for health psychological development, through the provision of environments in which proximal processes can be enhanced (p. 584).

Both the Bronfenbrenner and Ceci (1994) model, and the more specific model of Bradley and Caldwell (1995), address what the latter authors call "near universals"—components of caregiving that apply across most caregiving systems. The bioecological model is an attempt to theorize about the fundamental processes of translation between human genetics and psychological phenotypes; in this sense, its approach is universal. Culture, from the point of view of the model, would constitute one influence among others (including political, economic, and social systems) in determining whether "the environments in which human beings are living allow and instigate the actualization of particular inherited abilities and behavioral dispositions" (p. 583). Similarly, the present chapter is concerned with processes in adult-child interaction that are assumed to be universally involved in the actualization of developmental outcomes. The chapter further outlines the way in which those developmental processes (for example, emotional availability) are undermined, disrupted, and rendered unstable by the environmental context in which they occur.

Little attention is given in the ensuing discussion to the specific influence of culture on what Bronfenbrenner and Ceci would call proximal processes. The chapter by Harkness and Super deals in detail with culturally determined parental belief systems and socialization goals as they contribute to creating a "developmental niche" in which young children acquire culturally specific competencies.

Culture is a highly problematic concept, and definitions of it have variously stressed shared behaviors, competencies, cognitive systems, and meanings or symbolic systems. According to Triandis (1996), culture consists of shared elements "that provide the standards for perceiving, believing, evaluating, communicating, and acting among those who share a language, a historic period, and a geographic location" (p. 408). Triandis concedes that cultures vary in terms of their homogeneity and the strength of norms, and that simple cultures, in contrast to complex cultures, exercise tight constraint over beliefs and behavior. In a country like South Africa, which is undergoing extremely rapid political, economic, and cultural transformations concurrently along a number of dimensions, it is extremely difficult to apply cultural models. First, there is little uniformity in cultural experience: people who speak the same language might live in different locations under different economic conditions. Second, because of the country's history and the ideological commitment by the majority of the population to a united South Africa, there is individual and collective resistance to assigned ethnic or cultural identities.

While interventions, including those to promote literacy, need to be essentially culture-sensitive in their design and application, culture is not as useful a unit of analysis for diagnosing what requires intervention as are, what Poortinga (this volume) calls, "prevailing external conditions." Poortinga concedes that it is axiomatic that cross-cultural differences are manifestations of differences in internalized values, norms, beliefs, or attitudes; but, he argues, "in many instances a more parsimonious explanation is possible by postulating a direct link between the actions of persons and the external circumstances they are living in" (Poortinga, this volume). In addition to assuming that certain features of adult-child interactions are universally necessary for the development of psychological functions, the approach taken in this chapter is that a first analysis of cross-cultural differences should include a recognition of socioeconomic conditions. With respect to the caregiving behaviors of black South African parents, for example, cultural analyses should be contained within investigations of the effects of poverty, discrimination, and marginalization on parental behaviors (Richter, 1996).

Poortinga (this volume) makes a distinction between three paradigmatic perspectives on culture—relativism, absolutism, and moderate universalism. He stresses that these perspectives are complimentary, rather than mutually exclusive. This implies that one orientation, for example, cultural relativism, may provide an appropriate framework for understanding parental belief systems, while another, say absolutism or universalism, may be more suitable as a starting point for comprehending the processes of early language development. In this chapter the orientation adopted is that of moderate universalism, in which it is assumed, for example, that psychological functions such as self-consciousness are dependent upon universal features of early adult-child interaction. In a paper specifically addressing the issue of universality in adult-infant interactions (Richter, 1995), both argument and evidence is adduced to show that very strong similarities exist in the behavioral patterns of very young infants across the world, as well as in the parenting behaviors of older children and adults who care for infants. Poortinga points out that one of the major advantages of adopting a position of moderate universalism is that the extent of cultural variation becomes an empirical issue and not one predetermined by a priori viewpoints.

Leseman (this volume) hypothesizes that differences exist between families from different sociocultural backgrounds in opportunities, instruction quality, and social-emotional quality of potentially stimulating interactions in the home that explain early differences in cognitive and language abilities. In the reasoning developed here, with respect to impoverished South African families, it is argued that stimulation itself is dependent on a more basic parental affective availability, and that adult emotional involvement and responsiveness to young children is highly vulnerable to conditions of poverty and stress.

VARIATIONS IN CHILD-REARING ENVIRONMENTS IN SOUTH AFRICA

There have been very few studies of the home environments of young children in South Africa. Nonetheless, anyone familiar with townships, squatter settlements, and subsistence plots knows that side-by-side one may find stands, houses, and people very different from one another. One dwelling may rest on a barren, dusty stand, its interior dirty and dismal and its occupants inert and demoralized; next door may be a cultivated square on which stands a cardboard and corrugated iron house, its interior clean and cared for, inhabited by poor but spirited people (du Toit, 1993).

Psychologists, however, have been slow to respond to these differences. For example, on the basis of not finding any significant relationships between infant competence and socioeconomic factors in a group of Soweto children, Miller (1976) concluded that poverty precludes variations in lifestyle of much consequence for child development. In contrast, our own study of young children living in black townships indicates substantial effects of home environments on children's developmental levels, which are independent of measures of socioeconomic status.

In a study that examined the interrelationships between parental socioeconomic status, home environment, and infant mental and psychomotor development and growth, 305 African infants aged 2 to 30 months were tested on the Bayley Scales of Infant Development and their mothers interviewed regarding family and home background. Home environment was assessed using the Home Screening Questionnaire (Coons, Frankenburg, Gay, Fandal, Lefly, & Ker, 1982). The sample was drawn from well-baby clinics in the urban black townships surrounding the core industrialization sites in South Africa, including Johannesburg, Pretoria, and Durban-Pietermaritzburg. The Home Screening Questionnaire (HSQ, a proxy measure for Betty Caldwell's HOME Inventory) was translated into Sizulu and Setswana, the major languages used in the areas surveyed, and translated back for checking.

In summary, the analyses of this study (Grieve & Richter, 1990; Richter & Grieve, 1991) suggested three major conclusions. First, the HSQ appears to reflect the same major factors in black South African communities as those identified in the United States. The primary factor evident in home environment scores in South Africa was labelled

Opportunities for Stimulation, and included items that tap caregivers' ability to structure the environment for learning and promote development by becoming involved in children's activities.

Second, there are wide variations in home environments and parental behaviors, both between and within different socioeconomic groups of people living in black township areas. Items tapping, for example, the kinds of playthings provided for a child, frequency of adult play with a child, and the extent of father (or other male) involvement in caregiving (on which there were wide variation between families), were not found to be related to socioeconomic status.

Finally, none of the home environments examined in black townships provided what, by Western middle-class standards, would be called enriched environments. Nonetheless, the differences in home environments and day-to-day experiences of children that were found were shown to be important correlates of children's developmental status. Bayley Scale indices showed significant positive correlations with home environment scores in the first two to three years of life, but were not significantly associated with parental measures of socioeconomic status (occupation, income, and education). These results were taken to support the conclusion drawn by Bradley et al. (1989) that "within a very broad range of environments, differences in the home environment are associated with differences in cognitive development irrespective of average level of environmental quality that is observed in a particular subgroup" (p. 232).

In a separate study of the home environments of malnourished children (Richter, 1992a), the HSQ, together with several other measures, was administered to 135 mothers of infants between 3 and 18 months of age who had been admitted to a short-stay hospital ward with a primary diagnosis of protein-energy malnutrition (PEM). A comparison group of infants resident in the same community outside Pretoria, with no history of hospitalization or PEM, was selected from the sample described above. The home environments of malnourished children could be distinguished, at a high level of accuracy, from the home environments of matched children with normal growth living in the same community, particularly on the primary factor of the HSQ called Opportunities for Stimulation. A model using items comprising this factor provided a significant separation of the malnourished and comparison groups, with an 85 percent level of specificity and sensitivity. That is, although no causal relationship is implied by the findings, features of the home environment of small children were found to be associated with health and developmental risks for young children, at least as expressed in protein-energy malnutrition.

It is clear that "different levels of socioeconomic status offer children experiences which are both different and unequal with respect to the resources and rewards of the society" (Hess, 1970, p. 457). However, without wishing to minimize the influence of harsh physical environments on the psyches of the small children who have to endure them, it is also necessary to assert, as Urie Bronfenbrenner (1979) puts it, "the primacy of the phenomenological over the real environment in steering behavior" (p. 24). For young children, the experienced environment is one that is basically socially constituted. It is constructed from the interactions that children have with other people around them; for very young children, it is largely created by the involvement and responsiveness of their mothers and other primary caregivers. What the findings discussed above show is that, despite material poverty and low levels of education, some South African mothers are highly responsive to the social and cognitive needs of their young children, and provide day-to-day experiences for their children that are known to support and stimulate intellectual development. What is not entirely clear is which social and psychological factors are associated with caregiver differences in sensitivity and responsiveness to the needs of infants and young children.

THE STRESSES AND RESPONSIBILITIES OF WOMEN

The position of women and children in South Africa is made especially vulnerable by the prevailing nature and structure of the black family (Howell, 1992). Only about 58 percent of black women over the age of 18 have ever been married (Central Statistical Services, 1993) and, depending on the area, between 20 percent and 60 percent of black households are single-parent female-headed (Simkins, 1986). Even when men and women are married, housing shortages and migrant labor prevent about a third of them from living together (Simkins, 1986). As a corollary, men and women sometimes live together for varying lengths of time, perhaps having one or more children together, without ever getting married. Whether men and women live together or not, it is not always possible for them to have their children with them, mainly for reasons of lack of accommodation and child care. For example, it has been estimated that nearly 20 percent of children under the age of 15 live apart from their parents (Simkins, 1986; UNICEF, 1993).

While there are social, economic, and historical factors why some black people in South Africa have insecure partnerships, the instability of family life frequently forces women to assume sole responsibility for supporting their children economically. Most black women are restricted in their occupational choices, however, by their low levels of education and because there are not adequate child-care provisions for working women. For example, nearly half of all women in the "homelands" and about 15 percent of women in urban areas are illiterate, and in 1991, only 10 percent of women in South Africa had completed a secondary school education (Central Statistical Services, 1991). With regard to child care, two studies in Soweto (Cock, Emdon, & Klugman, 1986; Richter, 1996) indicate that 20 percent of mothers went back to work when their last child was less than two months old, and more than half when their last child was age 6 months or less. The majority of these women were forced to pay for child-care facilities outside of the family.

In addition to earning a living, urban women have to do their domestic chores and care for their children. The same Sowetan studies found that the majority of working women worked for 16–18 hours a day. In rural areas women are agriculturalists, in addition to which they have to collect water and fuel, do the laundry and cooking, and care for small children as well as the sick and aged. In one area of KwaZulu it was found that women had to walk 8 kilometers to collect one headload of wood, an activity that took more than four and a half hours to complete (Wilson & Ramphele, 1989).

Black South African women are undoubtedly overworked, underpaid, and insufficiently supported, both economically and in their role of caring for and rearing children, by either the men in their lives or by the state. Despite the hardships that single women face, they nonetheless have the advantage of being able to make autonomous decisions about their income and their activities. Some studies indicate that children may be better off in women-headed households. For example, research in Kenya and Malawi (Kennedy & Peters, 1992) has found that some female-headed households with very low incomes have lower levels of preschooler malnutrition than higher-income male-headed households. This is attributed to the fact that women tend to allocate proportionately more of their incomes to food and proportionately more of the available household food to children. In

endemic adversity → parental
economic oppression → distress
political

addition, the nurturing of children may be increased in female-headed households.

VULNERABLE CAREGIVERS—VULNERABLE CHILDREN

Despite the hardship of their lives, most South African women cope with these conditions. They make personal and physical sacrifices to earn a living, they rear their children as devoted mothers, and they maintain their homes conscientiously; many are also committed members of women's groups and church and community groups, which actively serve people in more precarious situations than their own. Nonetheless, hardship takes its toll on many South Africans, including women. A large number of black people interviewed as part of a national study complained of sleep disturbances (>50 percent), depression (31 percent) and tension (26 percent) (Olivier, 1989).

For some women, the load becomes too heavy. Their constant struggle, the scarcity of their social supports, and their lack of prospects makes them demoralized, withdrawn and depressed. It is the resultant diminished psychological capacity of adults for supportive, consistent, and involved parenting that primarily threatens the well-being of small children (McLoyd, 1990). It is proposed here the mediating link between caregiving and child effects is parental psychological distress originating from endemic adversity. Being part of the African culture, being black and politically oppressed, and being poor does not necessarily imply that young children will be deprived of sufficient appropriate experiences to enable them to cope with the demands of formal education. Neither low social class, nor poverty, nor deprivation (vaguely defined) have been shown to have an inevitably negative effect on children's social or cognitive development (Richter, 1993). There has been, very rightly, a great deal of criticism of the assumption that poor people or people from outside of the mainstream cultural group necessarily make poor parents who produce children with social and intellectual deficits (Oyemade, 1985).

It is often assumed that caregiver-child relationships in black cultures are different from those observed in white families and, implicitly, that they are not as good for children, particularly from an educational perspective. For example, Robert LeVine (1990) claims that mother-infant "mock conversation" is a population-specific phenomenon that rarely occurs in non-Western societies. Some other studies of child development and early experience conducted in Africa have suggested that mothers might be unaware of, or unconcerned about, the need to stimulate their young children's development (e.g., Goldberg, 1977). The home environment research conducted in South Africa, referred to earlier, challenges the generality of these impressions.

My own observations of interactions between black mothers and their babies over the length of the first year (Richter, Grieve, & Austin, 1988) and of interactions between mothers and their malnourished and healthy children up to the age of 3 years (Richter, 1992b), have convinced me that mothers who are not psychologically distressed engage in playful conversations with their babies, and demonstrate affection, responsivity, sensitivity, and child-centeredness in their interactions with their young children. In the first study, longitudinal observations were made of 14 mother-infant pairs who were videotaped during face-to-face interaction from 3 weeks to 52 weeks of age. The conditions under which interactions took place replicated those used by Colwyn Trevarthen in Edinburgh (see, e.g., Trevarthen, 1987), and included object play with a ring-stacking toy.

On the basis of microanalyses of two-second intervals of mother-infant interactions between dyads engaged in a teaching task during the second half of the infants' first year of life, we concluded that the structure of the processes involved in shared understanding and cooperation were the same among black South African dyads as were those described in the West (Richter et al., 1988). That is, mothers were sensitively responsive to their children's needs and level of skill, they adjusted their instructions and behavior to their children's increasing competence, and so on. In the second study, 26 malnourished children and matched comparison children from the same community were followed longitudinally from 9 to 30 months of age and assessed, on both occasions, on a wide range of social, intellectual, and emotional measures. Mother-infant interactions, during both structured and unstructured play, were recorded at both time periods and subjected to microanalysis. Interactional measures recorded at 9 months of age predicted outcome measures at 30 months among both malnourished and comparison children. That is, malnourished infants who enjoyed responsive relationships with their mothers were found, at 30 months, to show fewer ill-effects at 30 months than malnourished children who were not exposed to this kind of caregiving. Mother-infant interactions were found, in this study, to be statistically associated with rated poverty levels and maternal social supports (Richter, Bac, & Hay, 1990).

This does not mean that African mothers engage in responsive, sensitive, interactional behaviors with as much self-consciousness as Western mothers might. When I questioned mothers about their behavior, the majority stated that they had not previously been aware of intentionally teaching or interacting with their infants in the ways described. Nonetheless, I have observed the interactions between healthy black mothers and their children to be as vocal, playful, responsive, and indulgent as the interactions between Western mothers and babies videotaped in, for example, Oxford and Edinburgh (Richter, 1995).

There is wide agreement that socioeconomic and other stresses can adversely affect caregiving practices through the struggle, fatigue, and demoralization that poor and disadvantaged women endure (Richter, et al., 1990; Scheper-Hughes, 1985). Emotional withdrawal associated with pervasive low-level depression is one of the most common forms of psychological distress found among economically deprived populations that suffer from chronic stress (Fried, 1982). Polansky, Borgman, and De Saix (1972) have suggested that, when faced with severe economic hardship, caregivers may become emotionally unavailable through defensive interpersonal detachment and immobilization (what they refer to as "massive affect inhibition"). Mothers, overwhelmed by the immediate concerns occasioned by their social and economic circumstances, lack the energy normally available for investment in child care, and become emotionally detached and psychologically inaccessible to their children. They feel helpless and hopeless and lose any sense of confidence that they can do something about their child's health and development. As Fried (1982) describes it, they become resigned to the reduced options available in their lives and paralyzed by their sense of futility about altering their restrictive circumstances.

Parental distress in the form of emotional detachment and depression is capable of affecting children's behavior through a number of routes, including seeing children's behavior in an increasingly negative light (Belle, 1990); being passive and inappropriate in interactions with children; and being punitive, inconsistent, and unresponsive (McLoyd, 1990). Dix (1991) has proposed a model of parenting in which he argues that positive emotional states are vital to effective parenting. In parenting, argues Dix, emotions must be empathic, and organized to a large extent around concerns relevant to children's well-being and developmental outcomes. When invested in the interests of children, emotions organize sensitive, responsive parenting. Such emotional states promote surveillance of the child's needs, as well as the willingness and patience to comfort, encourage, and teach young children. There is some support for these ideas in, for example, Osborn's (1990) contention that the results of the Bristol longitudinal study of disadvantaged children indicate that a critical element in childhood resilience is attributable not to any particular caregiving behaviors, but to the communication of an all-pervading parental attitude of interest in, and devotion to, the child. It may be, however, that such parental attitudes are only expressed when the stresses associated with poverty are mitigated by compensatory positive influences, like inspirational belief systems, good interpersonal relationships, and supportive family and friends.

A considerable number of women, especially those with severe economic pressures, find childrearing to be a draining and disheartening activity. Cleaver and Botha (1989), for example, found that 74 percent of the urban black women they interviewed in South Africa had negative or ambivalent feelings towards their babies. Most of the women found the lack of involvement on the part of the father, both financially and personally, to be the most upsetting part of motherhood. In a study of the effects of intervention among malnourished infants, Richter and Mphelo (1991) found that nearly 70 percent of the women admitted with their malnourished children to a nutrition rehabilitation unit rated themselves as depressed. That is, physical and social conditions typically associated with childhood malnutrition are also associated with negative psychological effects on caregivers, who are most often women.

A consciousness on the part of parents of the importance of their behavior to children's development, as well as a belief in their capacity to fulfill children's physical and emotional needs has been found, in several studies, to be the axis around which optimal child care takes place (Tinsley & Holtgrave, 1989). These parental convictions, which entail a sense of pride in themselves and a belief in the meaning of their lives, are in turn a reflection of the wider social relationships in which caregivers participate.

Of all the negative consequences caused by economic stress, hardship, and dependency, the most pertinent to children is the threat these things pose to adequate family and parental functioning. In this way, poverty, socioeconomic disadvantage, and social deprivation confer a general risk possibility on all children. However, it is likely that selective interpersonal and social experiences determine which children are vulnerable and which children remain resilient in the face of adversity. A caregiver's "emotional availability" (Biringen & Robinson, 1991) to a child may be a critical mediating concept for understanding the effects of poverty and deprivation on young children.

In conclusion, it is possible that studies which suggest that cultural differences in early child care may contribute to later intellectual or educational problems experienced by children from developing countries may actually be documenting negative effects on parenting caused by poverty, stress, and family disintegration. The latter can result in parental emotional disengagement from children. Observations of mother-child interactions in South Africa indicate a great similarity between the behaviors of nonstressed African mothers with their young children, and those behaviors described as typical of middle-class Western mothers. Endemic stress impairs the capacity of parents to get involved with their children in ways that are known to promote intellectual development.

INTERVENTIONS TO ASSIST CAREGIVERS

It should be clear from the preceding discussion that structural interventions at a national level should be directed at correcting inequalities in education and providing preschool and child-care facilities. Every attempt should also be made for supplementary feeding of young children and free health and mental health care for children— both of which were introduced in 1995 as priority policies of the democratically elected Government of National Unity in South Africa. However, parents with few financial resources find it difficult to take advantage of services offered by separate organizations at separate times and in separate places. For this reason, as much intersectoral cooperation as possible should be mustered to provide comprehensive care and intervention for young children and their families. As pediatric primary care settings constitute the *de facto* social and mental health services for poor families, it may be advisable to coordinate interventions in concert with primary health care services.

In addition to the above, we need to assist caregivers by promoting family life, encouraging men to take responsibility for the well-being of their children, and decreasing the social isolation of especially vulnerable women and their children. In particular, women's education deserves urgent attention. Apart from the beneficial effects of women's education on childhood mortality, more educated women feel a greater sense of personal responsibility for their children, are less fatalistic, and are more capable of negotiating within the modern world. It is also possible that the education of women, through increasing their social status, changes the traditional balance of family relationships and moves family values toward greater child-centeredness (Caldwell, 1981). We should be especially wary of interventions that help only children, rather than entire families. Interventions of this kind tend to further undermine the fundamental role that parents and other "natural" caregivers play in their children's development. Despite good intentions to the contrary, many preschool programs in South Africa are directed specifically at children rather than at families, and aim to help children overcome the "deficits" of their backgrounds (Jacobs & Davies, 1991). According to the analysis offered here, the nucleus of interventions should comprise emotional, social, and financial support for women and families so that they will be able to exercise appropriately their emotionally and culturally determined child-care functions.

We should also attend seriously to the warning that much of what is done in current health care and education practice, consciously or unconsciously, ignores caregivers' needs and devalues their accomplishments. As Gerry Salole (1992) puts it, "We have systematically allowed people to feel incompetent and inadequate in raising their own children. We have allowed 'modern' education to be juxtaposed with 'traditional' in such a manner that people are actually ashamed and unsure of their intuitive cultural skills" (p. 7). He maintains that we have overemphasized the distinction between the informal education that takes place during children's socialization and the formal instruction that takes place in a classroom. The way that people socialize their children leads to the development of capacities which are necessary for successful participation in formal education. That is, instead of trying to replace or compensate for what is believed to be inadequate socialization, we should be fostering or strengthening the ability of families and caregivers to provide the forms of socialization that are congruent with schooling. The best way to help children may be to help their natural caregivers and to strengthen the social systems of which they are a part.

In reflecting on the lessons learned in the field toward attainment of the goals of the Jomtien Conference on Education for All, John Bennett (1993) from UNESCO reached similar conclusions to the ones expressed above. He argued that, while early child development interventions frequently take the form of preschool programs and preparation for school, this approach might not be responsive to sociocultural context and might not be appropriate for highly disadvantaged communities. In these circumstances, early childhood formal education makes little sense without a strong care component, Bennett argued, and support and education initiatives for parents may be essential conditions for attaining the key goals of education for all.

REFERENCES

Belle, D. (1990). Poverty and women's mental health. *American Psychologist*, *45*, 385–389.

Bennett, J. (1993). Jomtien revisited: A plea for a differential approach. In L. Eldering & P. Leseman (Eds.), *Early intervention and culture— Preparation for literacy: The interface between theory and practice* (pp. 11–19). Paris: Netherlands National Commission for UNESCO, UNESCO Publishing.

Biringen, Z., & Robinson, J. (1991). Emotional availability in mother-child interactions: A reconceptualisation for research. *American Journal of Orthopsychiatry*, *61*, 258–271.

Bradley, R., & Caldwell, B. (1995). Caregiving and the regulation of child growth and development: Describing proximal aspects of caregiving systems. *Developmental Review*, *15*, 38–85.

Bradley, R., Caldwell, B., Rock, S., Ramey, C., Barnard, K., Gray, C., Hammond, M., Mitchell, S., Gottfried, A., Siegel, L., & Johnson, D. (1989). Home environment and cognitive development in the first 3 years of life: A collaborative study involving six sites and three ethnic groups in North America. *Developmental Psychology*, *25*, 217–235.

Bronfenbrenner, U. (1979). *The ecology of human development: Experiments by nature and design*. Cambridge, MA: Harvard University Press.

Bronfenbrenner, U., & Ceci, S. (1994). Nature-nurture reconceptualized in developmental perspective: A bioecological model. *Psychological Review*, *101*, 568–586.

Caldwell, J. (1981). Maternal education as a factor in child mortality. *World Health Forum*, *2*, 75–78.

Central Statistical Services (1991). *1991 Population Census*. Pretoria: Central Statistical Services.

Central Statistical Services (1993). 1991 Population Census, adjusted for undercount. *SA Barometer, 7*, 42–47.

Cleaver, G., & Botha, A. (1989). *Experiences of motherhood amongst a group of Tswana mothers*. Paper presented at the Seventh National Congress of the Psychological Association of South Africa, Durban, South Africa.

Cock, J., Emdon, E., & Klugman, B. (1986). The care of the apartheid child: an urban African study. In S. Burman & P. Reynolds (Eds.), *Divided society: The contexts of childhood in South Africa* (pp. 66–92). Johannesburg: Ravan Press.

Coons, C., Frankenburg, W., Gay, E., Fandal, A., Lefly, D., & Ker, C. (1982). Preliminary results of a combined developmental/environmental screening project. In N. Anastasiouw, W. Frankenburg, & A. Fandal (Eds.), *Identifying the developmentally delayed child* (pp. 101–110). Baltimore: University Park Press.

Dix, T. (1991). The affective organisation of parenting: Adaptive and maladaptive processes. *Psychological Bulletin, 110*, 3–25.

du Toit, M. (1993). *Huis, Paleis, Pondok . . . Kinders in informele woonomstandighede: 'n veldwerkstudie* [House, castle, cabin. A survey into children's informal housing conditions]. (Internal Report 93–01). Pretoria: University of South Africa, Institute for Behavioural Sciences.

Fried, M. (1982). Endemic stress: The psychology of resignation and the politics of scarcity. *American Journal of Orthopsychiatry, 52*, 4–19.

Goldberg, S. (1977). Infant development and mother-infant interaction in urban Zambia. In P. H. Leiderman, S. R. Tulkin, & A. Rosenfeld (Eds.), *Culture and infancy: Variations in the human experience*, (pp. 211–244). New York: Academic Press.

Grieve, K., & Richter, L. M. (1990). A factor analytic study of the Home Screening Questionnaire for infants. *South African Journal of Psychology, 20*, 277–281.

Hess, R. D. (1970). Social class and ethnic influences upon socialization. In P. H. Mussen (Ed.), *Carmichael's manual of child psychology*, (pp. 457–557). New York: Wiley.

Howell, C. (1992). *Family life and the economic status of women and children in South Africa*. Johannesburg: National Committee for the Rights of Children.

Jacobs, F., & Davies, M. (1991). *Rhetoric or reality? Child and family policy in the United States*. Washington: Society for Research in Child Development (Social Policy Report, V).

Kennedy, E., & Peters, P. (1992). Household food security and child nutrition: The interaction of income and gender of household head. *World Development, 20*, 1077–1085.

LeVine, R. (1990). Enculturation: A biosocial perspective on the development of self. In D. Cicchetti & M. Beeghly (Eds.), *The self in transition: Infancy to childhood* (pp. 99–117). Chicago: University of Chicago Press.

Magona, S. (1990). *To my children's children*. Cape Town: David Philip Africasouth New Writing.

Maslow, A. (1970). *Motivation and personality* (Rev. ed.). New York: Harper & Row.

McLoyd, V. (1990). The impact of economic hardship on black families and children: Psychological distress, parenting and socioemotional development. *Child Development, 61*, 311–346.

Miller, R. (1976). *The development of competence and behaviour in infancy*. Unpublished doctoral dissertation, University of the Witwatersrand, Johannesburg, South Africa.

Olivier, L. (1989). *The physical and psychological problems of the peoples of South Africa*. Pretoria: Human Sciences Research Council.

Osborn, A. (1990). Resilient children: A longitudinal study of high achieving socially disadvantaged children. *Early Child Development and Care, 62*, 23–47.

Oyemade, U (1985). The rationale for Head Start as a vehicle for the upward mobility of minority families: A minority perspective. *American Journal of Orthopsychiatry, 55*, 591–602.

Polansky, N., Borgman, R., & De Saix, C. (1972). *Roots of futility*. San Francisco: Jossey-Bass.

Richter, L. M. (1992a). *Home environments of malnourished and healthy infants*. Paper presented at the Sixth International Conference, "Children at Risk: Assessment, Intervention and Monitoring Outcomes," Santa Fe, NM.

Richter, L. M. (1992b). *Attachment and affect in malnourished infants: An 18-month follow-up*. Paper presented at the Fifth World Congress of Infant Psychiatry and Allied Disciplines, Chicago, IL.

Richter, L. M. (1993). Economic stress and its influence on the family and caretaking patterns. In A. Dawes & D. Donald (Eds.), *Childhood and adversity in South Africa* (pp. 28–50). Cape Town: David Philip.

Richter, L. (1995). Are early adult-infant interactions universal? A South African view. *Southern African Journal of Child and Adolescent Psychiatry, 7*, 2–18.

Richter, L. (1996). *Characteristics of the care of children under four years of age in Soweto-Johannesburg: Final report to the Bernard van Leer Foundation.* Pretoria: Medical Research Council.

Richter, L. M., Bac, M., & Hay, I. (1990). Psychological aspects of the health care of young children. *South African Family Practice, 11*, 490–497.

Richter, L. M., & Grieve, K. (1991). Home environments and cognitive development of black infants in impoverished South African families. *Infant Mental Health Journal, 12*, 88–102.

Richter, L. M., Grieve, K., & Austin, D. (1988). Scaffolding by Bantu mothers during object play with their infants. *Early Child Development and Care, 34*, 63–75.

Richter, L. M., & Mphelo, M. (1991). Enhancing mother-child relationships in undernutrition. *Proceedings of the 7th Health Priorities Conference: Urbanisation and Child Health.* Cape Town, South Africa.

Salole, G. (1992). *Building on people's strengths: The case for contextual child development.* The Hague, the Netherlands: Bernard van Leer Foundation Studies and Evaluation Papers 5.

Scheper-Hughes, N. (1985). Culture, scarcity and maternal thinking: Maternal detachment and infant survival in a Brazilian shantytown. *Ethos, 13*, 291–317.

Simkins, C. (1986). Household composition and structure in South Africa. In S. Burman & P. Reynolds (Eds.), *Growing up in a divided South Africa: The contexts of childhood in South Africa* (pp. 16–42). Johannesburg: Ravan Press.

Tinsley, B., & Holtgrave, D. (1989). Maternal health locus of control beliefs, utilization of childhood preventive health services, and infant health. *Journal of Developmental and Behavioral Pediatrics, 10*, 236–241.

Trevarthen, C. (1987). Universal co-operative motives: How infants begin to know the language and culture of their parents. In G. Jahoda & I. Lewis (Eds.), *Acquiring culture: Cross-cultural studies in child development* (pp. 37–90). London: Croom Helm.

Triandis, H. (1996). The psychological measurement of cultural syndromes. *American Psychologist, 51*, 407–415.

UNICEF (1993). *Children and women in South Africa: A situation analysis.* Johannesburg: UNICEF & the National Children's Rights Committee.

Vygotsky, L. (1978). *Mind in society.* Cambridge, MA: Harvard University Press.

Weiss, M., & Kleinman, A. (1988). Depression in cross-cultural perspective: Developing a culturally informed model. In P. Dasen, J. Berry, & N.

Sartorius (Eds.), *Health and Cross-Cultural Psychology: Toward Applications*. New Delhi: Sage.

Welch, M. (1978). Childhood socialisation differences in African and non-African societies. *Journal of Social Psychology*, *106*, 11–15.

Wilson, F., & Ramphele, M. (1989). *Uprooting poverty: The South African challenge*. Cape Town: David Philip.

CHAPTER TEN

Literacy and Schooling in a Multilingual Society
Ludo Verhoeven

In recent decades, literacy has gradually become a major concern all over the world. A general awareness of the number of illiterates and the consequences of being illiterate for personal life has emerged, although literacy is no longer seen as a universal trait. The distribution and degree of literacy varies greatly across countries, which is why a focus on culturally-sensitive accounts of reading and writing is needed. A multiplicity of literacy practices can be distinguished and related to specific cultural contexts, specific power relations, and specific ideologies. As such, literacy can be seen as a context-bound set of practices that may vary as the individual's needs change over time and place.

The specific sociolinguistic position of minorities must be recognized when modelling literacy (cf., Fishman, 1980; Hornberger, 1989, 1990; Verhoeven, 1987a, 1987b; Verhoeven, 1994a). Minority groups are often confronted with communicating in the dominant language of a majority environment in order to cope with daily life. This language is usually learned as a second language, which is why people from linguistic minorities are often referred to as L2 speakers. However, this conception is problematic for at least two reasons (cf., Extra & Verhoeven, 1993a, 1993b). First, not all of the members of a linguistic minority group acquire the dominant language successfully. In fact, L2 acquisition may come to a halt at a stage that is far removed from near-native competence. Second, the first language is typically taken into account as a potential source of unsuccessful transfer in L2 acquisition, and not as a language in its own right. That is, the languages in the countries of origin are often the primary source of socialization, and thus constitute a vital instrument for intragroup communication. These languages also constitute important symbols of ethnic identity.

In a multilingual society, minority groups may use various written codes for at least partially distinct functions. The written code with the highest status will be used primarily in societal institutions; the written code of the minority language will be used primarily for intragroup communication and the expression of one's ethnicity; and yet another written code may be used for religious identification. Therefore, in order to do justice to the literacy needs of minorities, functional literacy should be defined in terms of the multilingual and multicultural backgrounds of the minorities in question. More concretely, it is important to assess the extent to which people belonging to a minority group are literate in their language, in the language of wider communication, or in another language. In other words, the literacy skills in all these languages must be viewed as relevant human resources.

The migration of people profoundly affects the need for literacy education in the host countries. When a speech community moves to a new environment, the schools in that environment should help the immigrant children acquire literacy. The children can be taught to read and write in their mother tongue and in the language spoken in the new environment. Whether one or more languages are used for instruction and exactly which language and literacy skills are taken as the educational objective for minority children largely depends on the language education policies in the new environment.

The present chapter discusses the appropriateness and effectiveness of literacy programs for minority children, with special reference to the outcomes of ongoing and recently completed studies in the Netherlands. After considering the acquisition of language and literacy in a multilingual context, the role of various cognitive and sociopolitical issues related to bilingualism and schooling will be discussed. In conclusion, arguments for bilingual teaching of reading and writing will be presented in the context of a future perspective on literacy education for minority children.

LANGUAGE ACQUISITION AND LITERACY IN A MULTILINGUAL CONTEXT

Early Language and Acquisition of Literacy

The cultural values and language input in the home environment can be expected to result in significant variation in the first- and second-language acquisition patterns among minority groups. In a recent study (Narain & Verhoeven, 1993; Verhoeven, Extra, Konak, Narain, & Zerrouk, 1993), we examined the patterns of first- and second-language development for 91 Turkish, 111 Moroccan, and 104 Antillean children in the Netherlands. Oral language data was collected at three points in this longitudinal study: at the beginning of kindergarten, and after one and two years of school instruction. The Turkish children were found to be quite dominant in their mother tongue at all three measurement points. The same was true (but to a lesser degree) for the Moroccan children. The language proficiency levels of the Antillean children tended to be more balanced; they were proficient in Dutch as well as in Papiamento. The differences in the first and second language-proficiency levels for the three groups can be explained on the one hand by the language input from the family and the wider community, and on the other hand by the cultural orientations of the children and their parents.

Multicultural studies of early literacy show children to be capable of learning the essentials of literacy at a very early age, in spite of differences in cultural background and language learning. Studies by Hanson (1980), Mino Garces (1981), Kupinsky (1983), and Moore (1990) have shown that bilingual children spontaneously acquire literacy skills imparted by parents or older siblings. There are nevertheless large differences in the knowledge of, and desire for, literacy among minority children entering school. These can be explained by the variability of the literacy support provided in the home environment. Wells (1985) and Snow and Ninio (1986) have shown that success in early literacy acquisition is related both to the value attached to literacy in the home and the steps that parents take to explain the value of such literacy to their children. The role of parents in helping children (re)discover the principles of literacy is crucial.

Literacy Development at Kindergarten

For many minority children, the first language (L1) initially starts in a favorable position. Its development clearly benefits from the rich input provided by the family and the neighborhood. Exposure to L1 may decrease and become unfavorable over time, however. At school, the mother tongue may often be banned, or constitute only a minimal portion of the curriculum. In such cases, there is a mismatch between the linguistic abilities that the minority children bring to the classroom, and the language and literacy curriculum of the school. Minority children who receive early L2 literacy instruction are faced with the complex task of learning the structure and functions of literacy in an unfamiliar language. Downing (1984) has argued that the confusing effects of teaching literacy in a second language will primarily pertain to the children's metalinguistic awareness. Such an ability to reflect on the nature, structure, and functions of language plays an important role in the development of literacy and, according to Downing, children's metalinguistic awareness will develop more readily when instruction is based on familiar exemplars from the mother tongue.

In a recent study (Verhoeven & van Kuijk, 1991), the acquisition of metalinguistic knowledge in Dutch as a first and second language was compared. A battery of metalinguistic tasks measuring literacy concepts, literacy conventions, rhyme, word conservation, sentence segmentation, word segmentation, word blending, and knowledge of graphemes was administered to 298 four-year-old children. The informants were divided into three groups: high socioeconomic status (SES) Dutch children, low SES Dutch children, and minority children. The results showed a small effect of SES and a much larger effect of ethnicity. Factor analyses were then conducted on the test scores for the Dutch children and the minority children separately. For the Dutch children, a single factor was found to underlie the metalinguistic tasks: metalinguistic knowledge. For the minority children, two factors were found: metalinguistic knowledge and word-blending skills. In word blending, children must blend individual speech sounds into words. It is clear that this task is difficult because the target Dutch words are not familiar to the minority children. More generally, it can be concluded that the acquisition of metalinguistic skills proceeds slowly in a second language and that word blending may have to be learned as a separate skill. In other words, minority children receiving language and literacy instruction in kindergarten face the dual task of learning the characteristics of a *written* language and the characteristics of an *unfamiliar* language.

Development of Second-Language Literacy

In most places in the world, minority children are immersed in a second-language literacy curriculum. Does the process of learning to read in a second language differ from the process of learning to read in a first language? Restricted background knowledge, interference from L1, and limited proficiency in L2 may contribute to differences. At the onset of literacy acquisition, however, the influence of restricted background knowledge can be considered weak, because very simple narratives are typically employed when teaching children to read. Two possibilities then remain. The question of interference has traditionally been investigated via contrastive analyses, in which the similarities and differences between two or more languages are used to interpret second-language learning problems. Numerous reviews have nevertheless shown that the problems confronted in L2 reading do not stem from L1 interference alone (Hall & Guthrie, 1982; Harris, 1992; Koda, 1994; Shuy, 1979).

A more promising way of looking at problems of L2 literacy is to examine the similarities and differences in the strategies employed for first-language learning and second-language learning. In a longitudinal study of Turkish children's literacy acquisition of Dutch (their L2) and Dutch children's literacy acquisition during the first two grades of primary school (see Verhoeven, 1987a, 1990a, 1990b), the second-language learners were found to be less efficient in various reading and writing subprocesses than their monolingual peers. Differences in efficiency were found at both the lexical and discourse levels of literacy. That is, second-language learners appear to have problems both with lexical access and the use of reading context. With respect to lexical access, it is interesting to note that the nature of the difficulties shifted with development. Second-language learners initially had problems first with the recoding of graphemic strings, next with the application of orthographic constraints, and finally with direct recognition.

As regards the more general cognitive and social development of minority children, it can be argued that the acquisition of literacy will be facilitated when the instruction links up with the linguistic background of the learner. In another study, Verhoeven (1991a) found that a transitional L1/L2 approach to literacy instruction may have beneficial effects. In two small-scale experiments a strong emphasis on instruction in L1 was found to lead to better literacy results in L1, with no retardation of the literacy results in L2. The L2 literacy results in the transitional classes were also found to be better than the literacy results in the regular immersion classes, and the children in the transitional classes tended to develop a more positive orientation toward literacy in both L1 and L2.

One of the practical implications of this research is that the acquisition of literacy in a second language appears to require a certain level of oral proficiency in that language. Children with limited L2 proficiency should be given the opportunity to build up literacy skills in their mother tongue or strengthen their oral L2 skills, prior to formal L2 literacy instruction.

Attaining Literacy in the Minority Language

The level of literacy children immersed in an L2 environment can attain in their first language is an interesting subject. A stagnation in their L1 development can be expected, due to restricted linguistic exposure in the community and lack of support for the mother tongue in educational institutions. In a recent study, however, we discovered that this need not be the case (Aarts, de Ruiter, & Verhoeven, 1993). In this study, both oral and written language data was collected from Turkish and Moroccan children resident in the Netherlands at the end of their primary schooling. In the Dutch schools the children attended, home language instruction was offered for two to four hours a week as part of the school curriculum. The L1 proficiency of these 263 Turkish and 222 Moroccan children in the Netherlands was then compared to that of a reference group of 276 Turkish and 242 Moroccan children in Turkey and Morocco, respectively. The overall results showed that the Turkish children in the Netherlands attained native-like performance in their mother tongue. A remarkable correspondence between the groups in the Netherlands and Turkey was observed in most of the oral and written tasks. The children in the Netherlands were found to have a high level of proficiency not only in typical school tasks, but also in functional literacy. The Moroccan children in the Netherlands showed greater variation in the language-proficiency tasks than their peers in Morocco. They obtained reasonable scores for the oral-language tasks, but their proficiency in written-language tasks lagged far behind their peers in

Morocco. In this study, home language instruction at school was also found to be positively related to the first language proficiency of the two groups of children.

For the group of Turkish pupils in the Netherlands the limited amount of L1 instruction was even sufficient for them to reach an almost native-like level of literacy. This may be because both Turkish and Dutch use the Latin alphabet, so that literacy skills can be easily transferred from one language to the other. The same amount of L1 instruction did not bring about native-like literacy performance among the Moroccan students. This result reflects the great distance between the orthographic systems of Arabic and Dutch, on the one hand, and the large differences between the Moroccan-Arabic dialect spoken at home, and written standard-Arabic, on the other hand. In the next section we will elaborate on various interdependencies that characterize bilingual development.

THE ROLE OF COGNITIVE FACTORS

Interdependencies in Bilingual Development

The notion of interdependency is quite important for explaining the individual variation in literacy success and literacy motivation in a bilingual context. Cummins (1983) has hypothesized the following interdependency in the acquisition of such cognitive/academic language skills as reading and writing: "To the extent that instruction in a certain language is effective in promoting proficiency in that language, transfer of this proficiency to another language will occur, provided there is adequate exposure to that other language (either in the school or environment) and adequate motivation to learn that language" (p. 29). This hypothesis predicts not only transfer from L1 to L2 but also from L2 to L1 unless the exposure and motivation conditions are negative.

In a bilingual program, the interdependency hypothesis predicts that reading instruction in one language can lead to literacy in that language, but also to a deeper conceptual and linguistic proficiency, which may then strongly relate to literacy and general academic skill in the other language. Whereas the surface aspects of linguistic proficiency (such as orthographic skills and fluency) develop separately, an underlying proficiency that is common across languages also develops. This common underlying proficiency is said to facilitate the transfer of the cognitive/academic skills related to literacy across languages.

Cummins (1984) has attempted to conceptualize language proficiency in order to elucidate the developmental interrelationships between academic achievement and language proficiency in both L1 and L2. His earlier distinction between basic interpersonal and cognitive/academic language skills has been integrated into a new theoretical framework in which language proficiency is conceptualized along two continua. The first continuum relates to the range of contextual support for the expression or receipt of meaning. The extremes on this continuum are "context-embedded" versus "context-reduced." In context-embedded communication, meaning is actively negotiated by the participants through the provision of feedback and the supply of paralinguistic cues when the meaning is not fully understood. In context-reduced communication, the participants are entirely dependent on linguistic cues and must often rely upon their knowledge of the world to interpret the communication and understand its meaning.

The second continuum in the theoretical framework proposed by Cummins relates to the developmental aspects of language proficiency in terms of the degree of active cognitive involvement for appropriate performance of a task. Cognitive involvement is conceptualized in terms of the amount of information that must be processed simultaneously or in rapid succession by the individual. The language processes have become largely automatic at the one end of this continuum, and active cognitive involvement is required at the other end.

According to Cummins (1984), the developmental interrelationships between proficiency in L1 and L2 can be conceptualized within this framework. Such interrelationships are assumed to predominate in the case of academic tasks, which become more academic as the context is reduced and the cognitive demands increase. Therefore, the transferability of many of the proficiencies involved in reading and writing is high, because of the degree of context reduction and high cognitive demand. In a review of studies on bilingual development, Cummins (1989, 1991) does indeed conclude that there is consistent support for the principle of interdependency in a variety of linguistic domains, including literacy.

Further evidence to support interdependency comes from the aforementioned study by Narain and Verhoeven (1993), which explored the role of interdependency in the bilingual development of Turkish, Moroccan, and Antillean children in the Netherlands. In each minority group, a substantial transfer from L1 to L2 was observed at the beginning of kindergarten. In the Antillean children, however, the direction of this transfer tended to be reversed after two years of schooling. That is, the children's language proficiency went from dominance in Papiamento to dominance in Dutch during this period. The latter result can be explained by the assumption that the transfer is usually from the dominant language to the weaker language.

Most empirical research on cross-language transfer in reading has focused on the transfer of background knowledge in older students. In these studies, it has been shown that the background knowledge acquired in L1 can facilitate L2 reading (Weber, 1991). The role of language transfer in the initial stages of reading acquisition has only been examined in a small number of studies. Verhoeven (1991a, 1991b; 1994b) found empirical evidence for cross-language transfer in his study of early biliteracy development in Turkish children in the Netherlands. In particular, the word-decoding skills and reading-comprehension skills developed in one language were found to predict the corresponding skills in the other language acquired later. The interdependency found for word decoding can perhaps be explained by the cognitively demanding nature of the metalinguistic skills involved. The decontextualized nature of handling text seems to be the best explanation for the findings relating to reading comprehension.

Bilingualism and School Success

It is also important to consider the implications of biliteracy education. Several studies of children who learn to read and write in two languages have shown that the children benefit in a number of cognitive domains (for an overview, see Bialystok & Ryan, 1985; Cummins, 1989; Hakuta, 1986). One particular domain is metalinguistic awareness, or the conscious understanding and manipulation of the units of language, which is also crucial for grasping the written code.

In Narain and Verhoeven's study (1993) the effects of bilingual development on Turkish, Moroccan, and Antillean children's metalinguistic awareness were also examined. The children in each minority group were divided into three subgroups according to their L1/L2 proficiency: children with above-average scores in both languages, children with above-average scores in either L1 or L2, and children with below-average scores in both languages. In each minority group, the children with a balanced high level of bilingual proficiency tended to obtain the highest scores on the metalinguistic tasks. Their scores were also significantly higher than those of the children with a high proficiency in L1 or L2 alone, which suggests that a balanced high level of bilingual proficiency enhances children's metalinguistic awareness.

In Aarts, de Ruiter, and Verhoeven's study (1993), the first language proficiency of Turkish and Moroccan children at the end of primary school correlated positively with their academic performance later in secondary school. That is, positive correlations were found between the factor scores for oral and written L1 proficiency and academic achievement after one and two years of secondary school. Moreover, multiple regression analyses showed that L2 proficiency, math proficiency, and written L1 proficiency predicted the secondary school performance of Turkish and Moroccan children.

THE ROLE OF SOCIOCULTURAL FACTORS

Literacy Needs

From a sociocultural point of view, minority group members may feel the need to use two (or more) written codes for complementary purposes. The primary function of the majority language will be for intergroup communication in the society as a whole; the primary functions of the minority language will be for intragroup communication and the expression of one's ethnicity (Fishman, 1980). The motivation to learn seems to increase as societal institutions pay greater attention to the native language and culture of the bilingual child. According to Spolsky (1977), knowing that the language in which they have invested so many years is respected by the school system can clearly enhance pupils' self-respect, and thus constitutes a major argument in favor of bilingual education. A meta-analysis of studies conducted by Willig (1985) has also shown that acceptance of the native language and culture of bilingual children positively influences their self-concept.

In a multilingual society, minority groups may use different written codes for different and at least partially distinct functions. For instance, among Turkish immigrants in western Europe, four written codes may be used. The dominant language (i.e., German, or Dutch) is used for interethnic communication in the society where they have settled. Turkish is used for intragroup communication with people in the immigrant and home country and for the expression of one's ethnicity. Arabic provides for religious identification and enables the reading of such religious texts as the Qur'an. Finally, English constitutes the basis of wider international communication.

The written code with the highest status in a society will be used in such vital domains as education, labor, law, and justice. In a democratic society, this will usually be the majority language because this language possesses the largest communicative potential in geographic and social terms. Interethnic communication by means of written documents proceeds best in that language, and the communicative potential of a minority language is thus usually much smaller.

The extent to which the members of a minority group use their own language for written communication appears to depend on two factors: the written codification of the minority language and the background situation of the minority group. The extent to which the minority language has been codified is very important. Rules for codification (e.g., orthographic rules) provide a firm basis for written language use. To give an example, Berber languages, spoken in Morocco, cannot be used for written communication because no standardized written code is available. If the present Berber revival continues with the same intensity, however, the Berber languages will probably pass from the oral stage to the literary stage (Otten & de Ruiter, 1993) and written use of the language will presumably become more widespread.

Several factors relating to the background situation of the relevant minority groups seem to underlie written use of the native language. Group size is important, as smaller groups are in danger of completely losing their language. The structure of the social groups is also relevant, because written text in the native language may be used in religion, education, and mass media. The written code of the minority language may also be used for dealing with foreign officials (e.g., consulates).

In addition to these sociological factors, the use of the written minority language may be motivated by personal needs. A need to communicate with relatives and other people in the country of origin can certainly exist. A need to learn about one's own ethnicity and/or express oneself in the minority language can also exist. The written language can then be seen as a symbol of ethnic identity. As has been shown by Ferguson (1978), members of a minority group can strengthen their group identification and social integration by means of written communication in the minority language. A high level of literacy in the country of origin will normally preserve a relatively high level of first-language literacy in the immigrant country. In her study of an Amish community in the United States, Fishman (1988) showed that positive learning experiences and positive valuing promoted Amish literacy. In another study among the Navajo Indians in the United States, the transformation of Navajo literacy practices in local school settings was shown to enhance community and cultural identity (McLaughlin, 1989).

If members of a minority group feel the need to become biliterate, the written use of the two languages will usually serve complementary purposes. The primary function of the majority language will be for intergroup interaction, while the most important functions of the minority language will be for intragroup communication and the deepening of one's ethnic roots.

Institutional Support

Institutional support can be seen as an important determinant of L1 language maintenance. In the context of child care, institutional support manifests itself in two domains: family intervention programs and formal education. In Figure 10-1, a theoretical framework for the institutional support of minority children's language and literacy learning is outlined. Family intervention can be seen to influence family variables and in turn, children's learning. At the same time, formal education can directly influence children's learning. Research has demonstrated the critical influence of the home and family on the development of language and literacy among children. Fantini (1985) showed that channels of language input in the home environment, such as communication between and with family members and communication with people outside the family, influenced minority children's language development. Moreover, Tosi (1979, 1984) showed that lack of reinforcement for accepted L1 practices and lack of exposure were responsible for retarding L1 development.

Four home factors have been shown to be crucial for children's early literacy acquisition (Teale, 1980; Sulzby & Teale, 1991): the range of printed materials in the home (i.e., written language input); the accessibility of writing materials; the frequency of shared reading; and the responsiveness of parents. With respect to the latter variable, Wells (1985) has shown the manner and extent to which adults adjust their speech to the immaturity of their interlocutors to influence the ease with which children master the language system(s) concerned.

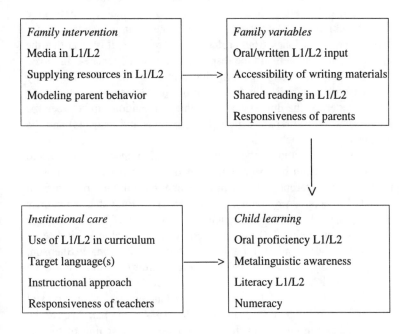

Figure 10-1: The roles of family intervention programs and institutional care in ethnic minority children's language and literacy learning.

The media may also play a significant role in the development of language and literacy. Television programs (e.g., Sesame Street), periodicals, and public libraries can be seen as possible mediators of the oral and written language input in the family. Furthermore, specific programs can be initiated to provide parents with L1/L2 resources (e.g., good quality children's books, tools for drawing and writing), and parental responsiveness can be trained during these programs.

Formal education (day care, kindergarten, and subsequent schooling) appears, to play an important role in children's early language and literacy learning. These institutional contexts give minority children the opportunity to use language in a meaningful way and to receive feedback from professional caretakers. It is clear that the instructional approach and the responsiveness of the teachers involved will play a crucial role. The scaffolding metaphor introduced for family interaction also applies to teacher training. Gaffney and Anderson (1991) underline the importance of an integral relationship between the processes used to prepare experts (both parents and teachers) and the methods used to teach novices.

In evaluation studies, the position of the L2 immersion approach to literacy instruction has been complicated by extremely contradictory results from different settings. In experimental bilingual programs in Canada (immersion programs), children speaking English as a majority language have been found to reach a high level of L2 French literacy skills without their L1 (English) literacy skills lagging behind (e.g., Genesee, 1984; Kendall, Lajeunesse, Chmilar, Shapson, & Shapson, 1987; Lambert & Tucker, 1972). Quite contrary results have been found in studies of direct L2 literacy instruction in the United States and Europe when the L1 was a minority language with low societal prestige. According to Skutnabb-Kangas (1984), this paradox can be solved by assuming that in the latter context the teaching of the L2 proceeds without the support of the L1. Poor results in both languages may also be the consequence of the minority group feeling ambivalent toward the majority group and majority language.

From a sociopolitical point of view, the bilingual education of minority children can be evaluated in terms of socioeconomic and second-language deficits or ethnocultural differences. Policymakers in both North America and Europe tend to view home language instruction as a temporary facility for low SES minority children. The focus has been on bridging the mismatch between language use in the home and the school, while aiming at better results in the majority language. However, home language instruction can also be envisaged in terms of a cultural policy in which minority languages are valued in their own right (cf., Extra & Verhoeven, 1993b). From a cultural perspective, home language instruction can be defined as a facility for children from homes where the language spoken is not the language of society at large; this instruction is independent of socioeconomic background. A contribution to first-language learning can then be defined as an independent goal, and such first-language proficiency can be both seen and evaluated as a legitimate school subject.

A FUTURE PERSPECTIVE ON LITERACY EDUCATION FOR MINORITY CHILDREN

Two worldwide trends can be observed in the use of language and literacy. On the one hand, there are processes of globalization and internationalization via mass media, trade, labor migration, and tourism. On the other hand, there is a growing awareness of significant cultural and linguistic diversity. One of the basic policy questions in the area of institutional support is how the opposing trends of unification and diversification of different communities can be reconciled in multilingual societies. Because language is a prominent feature of both trends and is relatively easy to promote or neglect within the educational context, this question also dominates the language debate.

The debate on bilingual education seems to be about the role of minority languages in an educational language policy aimed at assimilation, and not about the results of empirical research (see Imhoff, 1990; Median & Escamilla, 1992; Padilla et al., 1991). In this light, it is important to realize that minority students have developed attitudes toward their native language/culture and the majority language/culture, and that these attitudes give rise to specific language and literacy needs. A second-language-only approach to literacy intervention programs at home or at school does not seem to fit the linguistic and sociocultural backgrounds of minority children. Given the observation that it is easier for children to build up elementary literacy skills in a language for which they have acquired the basic phonological, lexical, and syntactic skills, it is important to evaluate minority children's oral proficiency in L1 and L2 at the onset of any literacy intervention. The risk of a mismatch between the children's linguistic abilities and the language selected for literacy instruction can then be reduced. Research shows simultaneous and successive literacy interventions in two languages also to be feasible. Such programs improve academic proficiency and do not retard second-language literacy.

Ethnographic studies make clear that literacy in the minority language may help to enhance community and cultural identity. The structure of the social group plays a significant role in this respect. That is, the need for literacy in the mother tongue depends on its use in institutions in the minority community and the need to learn about one's own ethnicity or to express oneself in one's native language. The fulfillment of such needs can prevent a negative self-concept in ethnic communities. In addition to cognitive arguments, thus, anthropological arguments also speak in favor of a biliteracy program for both formal or informal educational settings.

It should nevertheless be acknowledged that language is not the only factor in the intergenerational maintenance of group identity. There are many instances of minority groups with distinct languages, but also many instances of minority groups without distinct languages. Minority languages may naturally shift and even disappear across generations. Boyd (1985, 1993) has identified six major groups of factors determining the rate of shift: historical factors (e.g., the sociolinguistic background of the minority groups in the country of origin, the relationship between the home country and the host country, or the social and linguistic situation of other minority groups that arrived earlier); demographic factors (group size, birth rate, marriage pattern, and length of immigration period); geographic factors (the distance from the country of origin, the concentration of the settlement, and the self-sufficiency of the group); social factors related to the socioeconomic status of the group; institutional factors related to culture, religion, and mass media; and finally, attitudinal factors. It is difficult to determine the relative importance of these factors because they are not mutually exclusive.

Actual educational programs for minority groups are predominantly determined by political factors rather than by linguistic ones. The language policies of local and national authorities determine whether or not minority groups will be in a position to become literate in the majority language and the minority language. Three types of language policy can be distinguished: language segregation, language assimilation, and language maintenance (see Hakuta, 1986; Spolsky, 1977). Language policies in multilingual societies are determined by many factors, including the number and importance of the minority languages in the society, their geographic concentration, the social and religious characteristics of the population, the attitudes of the minority and majority groups, and the availability of teachers and learning materials (Grosjean, 1982). There will be little chance for education in the minority language when policy is strictly directed at assimilation; linguistic diversity in education can only be expected when policy is aimed at the promotion of ethnic identity and language maintenance, and a language maintenance policy will only lead to functional bilingualism and biliteracy if both of the languages find support in the wider community.

REFERENCES

Aarts, R., de Ruiter, J., & Verhoeven, L. (1993). *Tweetaligheid en school succes* [Bilingualism and school success]. Tilburg: Tilburg University Press.

Bialystok, E., & Ryan, E. B. (1985). Metacognitive framework for the development of first and second language skills. In D. L. Forrest-Pressley, G. E. MacKinnon, & T. G. Waller (Eds.), *Metacognition, cognition and human performance*. New York: Academic Press.

Boyd, S. (1985). *Language survival. A study of language contact, language shift and language choice in Sweden*. Unpublished doctoral dissertation. Gothenborg, Sweden: University of Gothenborg.

Boyd, S. (1993). Immigrant minority languages and education in Sweden. In G. Extra & L. Verhoeven (Eds.), *Immigrant languages in Europe*. Clevedon, UK: Multilingual Matters.

Cummins, J. (1983). *Heritage language education: A literature review*. Toronto: Ministry of Education.

Cummins, J. (1984). Wanted: A theoretical framework for relating language proficiency to academic achievement among bilingual students. In C. Rivera (Ed.), *Language Proficiency and Academic Achievement*. Clevedon, UK: Multilingual Matters.

Cummins, J. (1989). Language and literacy acquisition in bilingual contexts. *Journal of Multilingual and Multicultural Development, 10*(1) 17–31.

Cummins, J. (1991). Conversational and academic language proficiency in bilingual contexts. *AILA Review, 8*, 75–89.

Downing, J. (1984). A source of cognitive confusion for beginning readers: Learning in a second language. *Reading Teacher, 37*(4) 366–370.

Extra, G., & Verhoeven, L. (1993a). *Immigrant languages in Europe*. Clevedon, UK: Multilingual Matters.

Extra, G., & Verhoeven, L. (1993b). *Community languages in the Netherlands.* Amsterdam: Swets & Zeitlinger.

Fantini, A. E. (1985). *Language acquisition of a bilingual child.* Clevedon, UK: Multilingual Matters.

Ferguson, C. A. (1978). Patterns of literacy in multilingual situations. In J. Alatis (Ed.), *International dimensions of bilingual education.* Washington, DC: Georgetown University Press.

Fishman, A. R. (1988). *Amish literacy: What and how it means.* Portsmouth, NH: Heinemann.

Fishman, J. (1980). Ethnocultural dimensions in the acquisition and retention of biliteracy. *Journal of Basic Writing, 3,* 48–61.

Gaffney, J. S., & Anderson, R. C. (1991). Two-tiered scaffolding: congruent processes of teaching and learning. In E. H. Hiebert (Ed.), *Literacy for a diverse society.* New York: Teachers College Press.

Genesee, E. (1984). French immersion programs: A Canadian innovation to bilingual education. In S. Shapson & V. D'Oyley (Eds.), *Bilingual and multicultural education: Canadian perspectives.* Clevedon, UK: Multilingual Matters.

Grosjean, F. (1982). *Life with two languages: An introduction to bilingualism.* Cambridge, MA: Harvard University Press.

Hakuta, K. (1986). *Mirror of language: The debate on bilingualism.* New York: Basic Books.

Hall, W. S., & Guthrie, L. F. (1982). On the dialect question and reading. In R. J. Spiro, B. C. Bruce, & W. F. Brewer (Eds.), *Theoretical Issues in Reading Comprehension.* Hillsdale, NJ: LEA.

Hanson, I. A. (1980). *An inquiry how three preschool children acquired literacy in two languages: English and Spanish.* Unpublished doctoral dissertation. Washington, DC: Georgetown University.

Harris, R. J. (1992). *Cognitive processing in bilinguals.* Amsterdam: Elsevier.

Hornberger, N. H. (1989). Continua of biliteracy. *Review of Educational Research, 59*(3) 271–296.

Hornberger, N. H. (1990). Creating successful learning contexts for bilingual literacy. *Teacher College Record, 92,* 1–36.

Imhoff, G. (1990). *Learning in two languages: From conflict to consensus in the organization of schools.* New Brunswick, NJ: Transaction Publishers.

Kendall, J. R., Lajeunesse, G., Chmilar, P., Shapson, L. R., & Shapson, S. M. (1987). English reading skills of French immersion students in kindergarten and grades 1 and 2. *Reading Research Quarterly, 22,* 135–159.

Koda, K. (1994). Second language reading research: Problems and possibilities. *Applied Psycholinguistics, 15,* 1–28.

Kupinsky, B. (1983). Bilingual reading instruction in kindergarten. *Reading Teacher, 37,* 132–137.

Lambert, W. & Tucker, G. (1972). *Bilingual education of children: The St. Lambert Project.* Rowley, MA: Newbury House.

McLaughlin, D. (1989). The sociolinguistics of Navajo literacy. *Anthropology and Education Quarterly, 20*(4) 275–290.

Median, M. J., & Escamilla, K. (1992). Evaluation of transitional and maintenance bilingual programs. *Urban Education, 27,* 263–290.

Mino Garces, F. (1981). *A psycholinguistic analysis of early reading acquisition: six case studies.* Washington, DC: Georgetown University Press.

Moore, A. (1990). *A whole language approach to the teaching of bilingual learners.* Illinois: Center for the Study of Reading.

Narain, G., & Verhoeven, L. (1993). *Ontwikkeling van vroege tweetaligheid* [Development of early bilingualism]. Tilburg: Tilburg University Press.

Otten, R., & de Ruiter, J. (1993). Moroccan Arabic and Berber. In G. Extra & L. Verhoeven (Eds.), *Community languages in the Netherlands.* Amsterdam: Swets & Zeitlinger.

Padilla, A. M., Lindholm, K. J., Chen, A., Duran, R., Hakuta, K., Lambert, W., & Tucker, G. R. (1991). The English-only movement: Myths, reality and implications for psychology. *American Psychologist, 46,* 120–130.

Shuy, R. W. (1979). The mismatch of child language and school language: Implications of beginning reading instruction. In L. Resnick & P. Weaver (Eds.), *Theory and Practice of Early Reading* (Vol 1). Hillsdale, NJ: LEA.

Skutnabb-Kangas, T. (1984). *Bilingualism or not: The education of minorities.* Clevedon, UK: Multilingual Matters.

Snow, C. E., & Ninio, A. (1986). The contracts of literacy: What children learn from learning to read books. In W. Teale & E. Sulzby (Eds.), *Emergent literacy: Writing and reading.* Norwood, NJ: Ablex.

Spolsky, B. (1977). The establishment of language education policy in multilingual societies. In B. Spolsky & R. L. Cooper (Eds.), *Frontiers of bilingual education.* Rowley: Newbury House.

Sulzby, E., & Teale, W. (1991). Emergent literacy. In R. Barr & D. Pearson (Eds.), *Handbook of Reading Research* (Vol. 2). New York: Longman.

Teale, W. (1980). *Early reading: An annotated bibliography.* Newark, DE: International Reading Association.

Tosi, A. (1979). Mother tongue teaching for the children of immigrants. *Language Teaching and Linguistics: Abstracts, 12,* 213–231.

Tosi, A. (1984). *Immigration and bilingual education.* Oxford: Pergamon Press.

Verhoeven, L. (1987a). *Ethnic minority children acquiring literacy.* Berlin: Mouton/De Gruyter.

Verhoeven, L. (1987b). Literacy in a second language context: Teaching immigrant children to read. *Educational Review, 39,* 245–261.

Verhoeven, L. (1990a). Acquisition of reading in a second language. *Reading Research Quarterly, 25*(2) 90–114.

Verhoeven, L. (1990b). Language variation and learning to read. In P. Reitsma & L. Verhoeven (Eds.), *Acquisition of reading in Dutch.* Berlin: De Gruyter.

Verhoeven, L. (1991a). Acquisition of biliteracy. *AILA Review, 8,* 61–74.

Verhoeven, L. (1991b). Predicting minority children's bilingual proficiency: Child, family and institutional factors. *Language Learning, 41*(2) 205–233.

Verhoeven, L. (1994a). Linguistic diversity and literacy development. In L. Verhoeven (Ed.), *Functional literacy: Theoretical issues and educational implications.* Amsterdam/Philadelphia: Benjamins.

Verhoeven, L. (1994b). Transfer in bilingual development. *Language Learning, 44*(3) 381–415.

Verhoeven, L., Extra, G., Konak, O., Narain, G., & Zerrouk, R. (1993). *Peiling van vroege tweetaligheid* [Assessment of early bilingualism proficiency]. Tilburg: Tilburg University Press.

Verhoeven, L., & van Kuijk, J. (1991). Peiling van conceptuele en metalinguïstische kennis bij de aanvang van het basisonderwijs [Assessment of conceptual and metalinguistic awareness at the onset of kindergarten]. *Pedagogische Studiën, 68* (9) 415–425.

Weber, R. (1991). Linguistic diversity and reading in American society. In R. Barr & D. Pearson (Eds.), *Handbook of Reading Research.* New York: Longman.

Wells, G. (1985). *Language development in the preschool years.* Cambridge: Cambridge University Press.

Willig, A. (1985). A meta-analysis of selected studies on the effectiveness of bilingual education. *Review of Educational Research, 55,* 269–317.

PART 3

Strategies of Early Educational Intervention: Cross-Cultural Perspectives

Empowering Parents and Children: The Case of the Turkish Early Enrichment Project

Çiğdem Kağıtçıbaşı

The central theme running through this volume is the enhancement of children's opportunities worldwide through early educational programs. Though this may appear to the uninitiated as a straightforward and uncontroversial issue, it is actually a topic of much debate. Various arenas of contention have emerged from the theory and research of recent decades, one of them being the complex question of whether and how early childhood enrichment works. The issues underlying this are the nature-nurture controversy (Bronfenbrenner & Ceci, 1993; Horowitz, 1993; Wachs, 1993) and the type of intervention, such as center-based vs. home-based; child-focused vs. parent-family focused, etc. (Seitz, 1990; Seitz & Provence, 1990; Yoshikawa, 1994; Zigler, Taussig, & Black, 1992).

Although the question of *whether* early educational intervention works is still being debated, I will not discuss it here in any detail, as elsewhere I have presented ample evidence that it indeed does (Kağıtçıbaşı, 1996, 1997). The fact is that many children grow up in circumstances that do not adequately promote their overall development, which is why environmental intervention is needed. As Bronfenbrenner and Ceci (1993) have eloquently expressed, "Humans have genetic potentials . . . that are appreciably greater than those that are presently realized, and . . . progress toward such realization can be achieved through the provision of environments in which proximal processes can be enhanced, but which are always within the limits of human genetic potential" (p. 315).

On the assumption that early educational intervention works, this chapter will deal with the issue of *how* it works by examining the essential ingredients of an effective program. The main question is whether it is more effective to focus on the child or on the child's environment. Much debate centers on this issue of child-centered vs. parent-family-centered intervention; a related issue is center-based vs. home-based intervention (see Kağıtçıbaşı, 1997 for a review). These debates overlap to a large extent, since most child-centered intervention is also center-based, and most parent-family-focused intervention is home-based, although some parent-family education is carried out not in the home but in community centers or through the media.

The target for the intervention—child or parent—is thus more important than where the intervention takes place. Recent research has shown, however, that it is too simplistic to focus on *either* the child *or* the parent, and that focusing on both as interacting with each other gives the best results (e.g., Kağıtçıbaşı, 1997; Yoshikawa, 1994; Zigler et al., 1992). Interventions with multiple targets and a wider scope do indeed promise to have greater impact. These are some of the essential ingredients of effective programs that are designed to empower parents and to promote the overall development of children.

ESSENTIAL INGREDIENTS OF EFFECTIVE EARLY ENRICHMENT

Based on a review of recent research and evaluations, I recently delineated a number of attributes as "essential ingredients of early enrichment programs" in terms of leading to sustained gains and enhanced opportunities for children (Kağıtçıbaşı, 1997). These attributes are the contextual approach, the whole child approach, multiple targets/goals, empowerment, shared goals, optimal timing, and cost-effectiveness. Of these, the contextual approach will be discussed later at some length, but first the others will be defined briefly.

Whole Child Approach. An effective approach to early education has to assume a whole child approach and must target the child's overall development (social, personal, and emotional), not merely its cognitive development. The reason for this is that if the child's intellectual development is not supplemented by its socioemotional development, the results may be less than optimal. For example, school failure may have as much to do with lack of motivation or poor self-esteem as with cognitive capacity. Thus, the aim must be optimal overall development, in order to increase children's opportunities.

Multiple Goals. A program with multiple goals is bound to be more effective. For example, aiming to enhance the child's abilities, support parents, and improve the family interaction process through working with the child, the parent, and the family is likely to have more of a lasting impact than doing any one of these alone (Seitz, 1990; Yoshikawa, 1994). Such multipurpose approaches are also more cost-effective, as more is achieved with the same investment.

Empowerment. The goal of intervention should be empowerment, not compensation for deficiency. Yet refusing to subscribe to a "deficiency" model does not imply that the existing conditions are adequate; if they were, there would be no need for intervention. Instead, it means that the intervention builds on the existing strengths in changing the conditions to promote optimal development. Empowerment means strengthening what is adaptive in order to change what is maladaptive.

Shared Goals. In order to be effective, the goals of an intervention program must be shared by the people involved. In the case of early enrichment programs, this means parents. When goals are shared, it is easier to work in partnership with parents rather than casting them in a passive recipient role. Schorr (1991) notes, for example, that successful programs emphasize the importance of relationships with the recipients in a flexible structure with a coherent, integrated broad spectrum of services adapted to their needs.

Optimal timing. Timing can be important for the success of programs. When to start an educational intervention is a matter of debate. It is generally assumed that the earlier the intervention, the better it is. However, this depends on the type of intervention (health, nutrition, school preparation, life skills, etc.). Also, some have argued that later preschool intervention that covers the primary school years as well may be more effective (Farran, 1990; Slavin & Madden, this volume), or that later rather than early (infant) intervention produces better results (Yoshikawa, 1994). An important factor is the receptiveness of the parent. For example, Brazelton (1982) talked about "touch points" when parents are most receptive to new information, such as during pregnancy. The period just before school entry may be a touch point for educational interventions.

Cost-Effectiveness. Finally, if they are to reach large numbers of children, educational interventions have to be cost-effective. This concept is relative, not absolute. An inexpensive program, in absolute terms, is costly if it is not effective; a more expensive program with long-range benefits is more cost-effective. In general, group approaches are less costly than individual approaches, and nonformal home-community-based programs, employing paraprofessionals (as well as volunteers, parents, etc.) tend to cost less than formal, center-based preschool programs employing professionals. As Myers (1992) notes, "parent education for early childhood development is the most feasible low-cost approach to programming on a large scale." (p. 121)

These essential ingredients of effective early enrichment need to be taken into consideration when examining programs and approaches used to enhance children's opportunities. They are relevant to the case study of the Turkish Early Enrichment Project described later in this chapter. Of these essential ingredients, a contextual approach is the key to achieving culture-sensitive strategies in intervention.

A CONTEXTUAL APPROACH

Children growing up in poverty are often hampered in their physical and intellectual development. Given the importance of the family context, any intervention to support the child's development has to deal with the child's environment as well. Targeting the child's environment necessitates an interactional-contextual approach. This approach can be used in early childhood care and education programs, whether home- or community-based, and it is quite different from the individualistic approach that abstracts the child from its environment.

Why a contextual-interactional rather than an individualistic model? First of all, providing enrichment to individual children in organized preschool settings is an expensive model of early education. Preschools and kindergartens will probably have low priority for some time to come in the educational policies of many developing countries that have not yet achieved universal primary schooling. Secondly, if the child is provided with intellectual enrichment only in the preschool, but the home environment remains the same, the gains obtained from the preschool may disappear after the completion of the program. This is because the child is left to fall back on its own limited resources, without environmental support. In contrast, if the child's home environment and *significant others* are changed through intervention, they will continue to support the child's development, and thus the cognitive gains will be sustained after the program's completion. Finally, intervention attempts in developing countries need to be especially sensitive to the interdependent human relationships—"the culture of relatedness" (Kağıtçıbaşı, 1990, 1996) prevalent in these societies. In sociocultural contexts where close-knit family, kinship, and community ties exist, it is important to build on these as support mechanisms. Thus, both an empowerment approach and a culture-sensitive approach would implicate contextualism.

Indeed, as already mentioned, research on early enrichment supports the contextual model (Bronfenbrenner, 1979; Kağıtçıbaşı, 1996, 1997; Lombard, 1981, 1994; Myers, 1992; Smilansky, 1979; Yoshikawa, 1994; Zigler et al., 1992). A holistic contextual approach targeting the child in *interaction* with its environment promises to go far because it can promote synergistic dynamics that mutually reinforce developments in both the child and its environment (especially its parents). And because it deals with the child's environment, a contextual approach can also be more sensitive to the cultural characteristics of the family and community than is the case in an individualistic approach.

THE TURKISH EARLY ENRICHMENT PROJECT[1]

The Turkish Early Enrichment Project serves as a case study of how culture-sensitive early education can empower parents and children; it also contains the ingredients essential for effective early enrichment. I and my colleagues Sevda Bekman and Diane Sunar have been involved in this ten-year longitudinal study of early enrichment and its follow-up into adolescence. We began with a four-year (1982–1986) longitudinal study of early childhood enrichment and mother-training in the low-income areas of Istanbul; six years later, we conducted a follow-up study. Only some aspects of this extensive study are dealt with here. For more detailed accounts, see Kağıtçıbaşı, Sunar, and Bekman (1988) and Kağıtçıbaşı (1989, 1991, 1996); and also Bekman (1990, 1993).

We based our purposive sampling on the child day care centers which, under Turkish law, workplaces employing 300 or more women workers are required to run. We selected 3 and 5 year-olds from six such centers in low-income areas of Istanbul. Another group of children not attending day care centers was selected from the neighborhoods in which the day care children lived. All the children were matched for age and their families' socioeconomic status. The mothers of the children selected for the study constituted the mothers' sample. They were mostly of rural origin as were their spouses. Two-thirds of the final mothers' sample were working women (semiskilled or unskilled factory workers), and the remainder were housewives.

The sample was originally drawn to include 280 mother-child pairs, but during the first year this declined to 255, largely by inability (e.g., because of illiteracy, ill health, etc.) or unwillingness (e.g., due to husband's or mother-in-law's objections) to participate in the project.

In the first year the children's level of overall development (cognitive, social-emotional) was assessed by directly testing and observing their behavior, and interviewing their mothers. The mother's child-rearing orientations, lifestyles, worldviews and self-concepts, and the home environment, were assessed through observations and interviews. Baselines were thus established. In the second and third years of the project, home-based intervention (mother-training) was carried out on a *randomly* selected sample of the mothers. The experimental (trained) group consisted of 100 mothers at the beginning of the second year. This number dropped to 90 by the end of the intervention (the attrition rate was low: 10 percent). There were 155 mothers in the control (untrained) group.

In the fourth year, reassessments were carried out to establish the pre and post differences between groups, and also the differences between the control (untrained) and experimental groups. To do this, almost all the assessments used in the first year were repeated, supplemented by extensive school-related assessment (such as school achievement and attitudes toward school).

The intervention program comprised mother-training and had two components: "cognitive training" and "mother enrichment." The cognitive training was the Home Instruction Program for Preschool Youngsters (HIPPY), developed by Lombard (1981) in Israel (see Eldering & Vedder, this volume, for a description of HIPPY). A network of paraprofessional field workers administered the cognitive materials to the mothers at home or in group settings, in alternate weeks, who then administered them to their own children. In this way the mothers assumed the trainer role with their children.

The Mother Enrichment Program was conducted in group discussions. The following topics were covered in the first year—the importance of early years and the role of the mother, child development, social development, toilet training and sex education, children's questions, nutrition, health and child care, importance of children's games, and creative play activities. In the second year, the topics were mother-child interaction, types of negative discipline, types of positive discipline, modifying negative behaviors, accepting the child's behavior, listening to the child, the mother expressing herself (I-messages), generalization (transfer) of learned principles to other interpersonal relations, study habits, and women's needs.

The intervention lasted 60 weeks (30 weeks each year). At the biweekly group discussions, one hour was usually spent on HIPPY, and one to one and a half hours on the Mother Enrichment Program. All the mothers were expected to attend all the group meetings; absenteeism was quite low. If a mother failed to attend a meeting, an aide visited her at home and gave her the cognitive materials.

THE FOURTH YEAR RESULTS

The fourth year results on the project intervention, that is, the mother-training, were remarkable in that they showed very positive effects on children's overall development and school achievement. Children of trained mothers surpassed the control group in most of the measures used (Kağıtçıbaşı, 1991; Kağıtçıbaşı, Sunar, & Bekman 1988). This shows that working only with the mothers, who then work with their children, contributes greatly to children's development. Specifically, significant differences were obtained as predicted, between the trained and control groups of children in cognitive tasks, as measured by the Stanford-Binet IQ scores ($F = 18.36$, $df = 1, 244$, $p = .0001$), as well as in terms of performance on the Analytical Triad ($F = 7.81$, $df= 1, 245$, $p = .006$) and Block Design ($F=16.68$, $df = 1, 246$, $p = .0001$) of WIPPSY. Piaget tests, achievement tests, and school records also showed the trained-mother group scoring better than the control group. The experimental groups outperformed the control group in Piaget classification tasks ($\chi^2 = 7.54$, $df = 1$, $p = .02$). In the Mathematics Achievement Test, there was a near-significant difference between the two groups in the expected direction. This difference was significant for the younger cohort (age 3 at the start of the experiment): $F = 10.59$, $df = 1, 91$, $p = .002$). A General Abilities Test also revealed that the total trained-mother group performed better than the control group ($F = 3.8$, $df = 1, 212$, $p = .05$).

A comparison of school records revealed significant differences within the older cohort (age 5 at the start of the experiment), whose records extended over three years. No significant intergroup differences were found for the younger cohort, who had spent only one year in school. Among the older children, the differences between the experimental and control groups increased with time. Though the trend was in the expected direction in the first grade (after one year of mother-training), the difference was not significant. In the second grade it reached significance in Turkish ($F = 11.19$, $df = 1, 80$, $p = .001$) and near significance in social studies ($F = 3.29$, $df = 1, 79$, $p = .07$), and in the expected direction in mathematics and academic average. In the third grade (a year after the end of mother-training) the significant difference was sustained in Turkish, and the differences in mathematics ($F = 4.28$, $df = 1, 80$, $p = .04$), academic average ($F = 4.50$, $df = 1, 80$, $p = .037$) and deportment grades ($F = 4.22$, $df = 1,79$, $p = .04$) became significant.

Thus, by the fourth year, the children of trained mothers were performing measurably better than the control group in all aspects studied. Furthermore, their school achievement appeared to continue to improve even after the intervention ended, thus resulting in more notable gains for the older cohort for whom school achievement records for three consecutive years were available. During mother-training, this older cohort were 5 and 6 years old. The second year of intervention occurred while they were in the first grade.

If, as Slavin and Madden (this volume) contend, intervention after grade one is less effective, then apparently we just made the "deadline." However, it is important to note the distinctive nature of our intervention: it had a home component. The fact that children's school performance was still improving as much as a year after intervention stopped is evidence of the continuing facilitating role of the changed home environment, especially change in the mother.

As regards socioemotional development, children with trained mothers demonstrated less aggressive ($t = 2.59$, $p = .01$) and somewhat more autonomous behavior ($t = 1.75$, $p = .08$), as well as better self-concept ($F = 3.19$, $df = 1, 191$, $p = .076$) and adjustment to school ($F = 3.06$, $p = .087$) (Kağıtçıbaşı, Sunar, & Bekman, 1988; Kağıtçıbaşı, 1991). Thus, the mother-training had also a positive influence on the children's socio-emotional development, though less so than on cognitive development.

In terms of mothers' interactive styles with their children, we found that trained mothers were more satisfied with their children ($t = 2.16$, $p = .03$), and verbalized and supportively interacted with them more. The latter orientations were apparent in the more positive discipline techniques (reasoning, induction, etc.) and less physical punishment and scolding used by the trained mothers. Trained mothers also had higher educational aspirations ($t = 2.03$, $p = .04$) and expectations ($t = 2.11$, $p = .04$) for their children, as well as better acceptance of their children's autonomy ($\chi^2 = 7.58$, $df = 1$, $p = .006$) These orientations were assessed through questionnaire interviews with mothers, and through observations of mother-child interactions on the Hess and Shipman task (Shipman, Barone, Beaton, Emmerich, & Ward, 1977). For example, responsiveness was measured by recording the frequency of such acts while the mother was teaching a new task to the child, as well as in interviews, using hypothetical situations (more detailed results are provided in Kağıtçıbaşı, Sunar, & Bekman, 1988 and Kağıtçıbaşı, 1991).

Finally, apart from effects on mothers' interactions with their children, there were also direct effects on the trained mothers themselves. Specifically, their intrafamily status vis à vis their husbands became higher than that of the control group, as assessed in terms of joint decision-making, role sharing, and communication with the spouse. They also manifested a more positive outlook on life.

Comparing these results with the results of the application of HIPPY in the Netherlands, evaluated after two years by Vedder and Eldering (1992), HIPPY shows greater gains in Turkey. This is probably because of some significant differences in program implementation in the two countries. The most obvious and important difference is that HIPPY was used only by itself in the Netherlands, but in conjunction with the Mother Enrichment Program in Turkey. The latter program, utilizing participatory learning techniques with the help of "group dynamics," was found to be very effective in changing the mothers and the children's environment. Thus, it had direct positive effects on children. Indeed, almost all the findings referring to children's social development, and to the improvement of women's intrafamily status and their parenting styles and family relations, both in the fourth year posttest and in the follow-up study (see below), provide evidence for the particularly strong impact of the Mother Enrichment Program. The group discussion settings also proved to be a satisfying social experience that helped increase mothers' motivation to continue in the program, which is why the dropout rate was negligible (it was much higher in the Netherlands).

Even though there were group meetings in the Dutch program, too, they were mainly held to explain the application of HIPPY. The other group activities were not well-structured over the two years; often they did not include group discussion or group dynamics techniques, and both the language barriers between the group leaders and the mothers and the "games" played may not have had the intended impact, because of cultural differences.[2] Furthermore, in Turkey, the mothers' progress was monitored more closely. Group leaders made occasional home visits in addition to the regular home visits of the aides. In the Netherlands, the mothers' intensity of participation varied greatly. The evaluation study (Eldering & Vedder, this volume; Vedder & Eldering, 1992) included mothers whose participation was quite low. In the Turkish application, however, intensity of participation was high throughout the program. This important difference probably also accounts for the different outcomes.

DISCUSSION OF THE FOURTH YEAR RESULTS

The Mother Enrichment Program was an empowerment program, which enabled mothers to be more skillful in communicating with their children and with other people (especially their husbands), in expressing their feelings better and in understanding their children. The aim was to empower the mothers to cope with problems and to attend to their children's needs as well as their own needs. Indeed, the "mother enrichment" component best reflects the basic contextual-interactional orientation of the project.

A special effort was made to render the program culturally sensitive. For example, the close-knit family ties and the relatedness values were reinforced, but a new element, "autonomy," was also introduced in child rearing. The fact that the Mother Enrichment Program was "homegrown," not an import, was an asset in rendering it culturally sensitive. Conducting parent education in groups rather than in individual home visits was another culture-sensitive aspect of the program. This is because the groups worked as support mechanisms for the mothers, similar to the familiar community-based women's groups (Aswad, 1974; Kiray, 1981; Olson, 1982). This is not unique to Turkey; for example, Slaughter (1983) has shown that group discussion is a more culturally consonant intervention approach than individual home visits for low-income black mothers in the United States. She notes the importance of women's (family) networks, especially for single black mothers and their female-headed families. Thus, as discussed before, where "natural" groups exist or have the potential to develop, it is sensible to utilize them as facilitators and supporters of change.

The finding about autonomy is important because the first year (pretest) results had shown that autonomy was not valued by the mothers. The trained mothers came to appreciate their children's autonomy while remaining as close to them as the control group of mothers—possibly reflecting an environment promoting something of a synthesis between the "relational self" and the "individuated self." This is in line with a model of family change that I have developed, and I believe it reflects the typical patterns of family change in developing countries (Kağıtçıbaşı, 1990, 1996).

These findings clearly show the empowering effects of the Mother Enrichment Program. It appears that this intervention focusing on the mothers contributed to the well-being of the children by promoting the well-being of the mothers and meeting the intersecting needs of mothers and children.

THE FOLLOW-UP STUDY

Impressive as these findings are, the real test of the impact of intervention lies in long-term evaluation, which is possible only by means of follow-up studies. This is because the immediate gains from an enrichment program may dissipate over time, as has been found in some cases (e.g., Smilansky, 1979). As I indicated before, the subsequent leveling of early gains from intervention programs appear to be due at least partially to two common characteristics of these programs: (1) focusing on cognitive skills exclusively, and (2) focusing on the individual child, abstracting it from its environment. Since our project did not share these characteristics but rather used a contextual approach to the "whole child," we expected that its impact would be sustained. Nevertheless, only empirical follow-up research could confirm this.

Long-term longitudinal study of early childhood programs is rare in developed countries and nonexistent in developing countries, because by definition such research is difficult and time-consuming. A rare example is the Perry Preschool Project, conducted in the United States by the High/Scope Educational Foundation in Ypsilanti, Michigan (Berrueta-Clement, Schweinhart, Barnett, Epstein, & Weikart 1984; Schweinhart & Weikart, 1980), where children who participated in a preschool program were followed through childhood, adolescence, and young adulthood. One of the most remarkable findings of that series of studies is the positive impact of early enrichment on motivational factors (such as commitment to school and valuing education) and on social adjustment to institutions (school, family, the law), rather than on cognitive capacity (IQ). Commitment to schooling, and school achievement mediated between early enrichment and later well-being during adolescence. This is an important finding which points to a chain of interrelated effects deriving from early enrichment and developing into an upward curve.

The fourth year assessments (posttesting) of the Turkish Early Enrichment Project already indicated that such an upward curve began after the children started primary school, as mentioned earlier. The evidence for this was the better adjustment to school and higher school achievement of children with trained mothers, and the trained mothers' expression of greater satisfaction with their children, their higher expectations of school success, and their higher aspirations and expectations of more years of schooling for their children. In addition to the above school-related behaviors and orientations, the trained mothers' interaction styles with and general orientation to their children were also conducive to the children's overall success and well-being.

To test the long-term effects of the project intervention and to determine if the initial gains found a year after the intervention were sustained, we did a follow-up study ten years after the start of the original study (and seven years after the end of the intervention). Our aim was to assess the overall condition of the original children, now adolescents, and of their mothers, and to relate this to the original intervention using a causal model.

A major task of the follow-up study was tracing the original families, which is difficult after so many years, especially for low-income groups that move frequently because people change jobs or become unemployed. Nevertheless, we were able to contact 225 of the original 255 families (a remarkably low attrition rate of only 10 percent). In-depth interviews were conducted individually with the adolescents (then age 13–15), mothers and fathers. They provided a wealth of information about the adolescents, mothers, and family relations. Additionally, extensive school records were obtained for the adolescents. They were also given the vocabulary subtest of the Turkish standardization of the revised Wechsler Intelligense Scale for Children (WISC-R). I will summarize only the main findings here.[3]

THE FOLLOW-UP RESULTS

In a social context where compulsory schooling is only five years (as was the case at the time of this study), the most important indicator of a positive orientation to education in low-income areas is probably just being in school. This is because economic pressure encourages children—especially those who are not performing well or are not highly motivated—to leave school at about the age of 11, after completing compulsory primary education. For this crucial indicator of educational attainment, we found a significant difference between the children whose mothers had been trained in the original study and those whose mothers had not been trained (either in HIPPY or by being "empowered") with 86 percent of the former but only 67 percent of the latter being still in school ($p = .002$) (Table 11-1). This finding alone as an objective measure of outcome demonstrates the policy implications of our contextual model of early enrichment.

Primary school academic performance was the second objective academic indicator on which significant differences were obtained between the experimental (trained mothers) and control groups. Report card grades over five years of primary school revealed that the children with trained mothers surpassed the control group in Turkish, mathematics, and overall academic average (Table 11-1). This finding also provides clear evidence for the value of the intervention model utilized. It shows that the gains obtained from the intervention were not short-lived. Five years of better school performance must have contributed to the experimental group's higher level of school attainment. This implies that better results in school from the outset pave the way for higher educational achievement and more years of schooling.

The difference between the academic performances of the two groups is not significant after primary school. This is largely due to the self-selection factor in the control group, where the less successful students drop out after primary school, whereas the better ones stay on.

Finally, the standardized WISC-R vocabulary scores, as an indicator of cognitive performance, showed a significant difference between the two groups, with the group with trained mothers outperforming the control group (Table 11-1).[4] This is another important finding, especially in view of previous research (Kağıtçıbaşı & Savasir, 1988; Bernstein, 1975) indicating that children from lower

Table 11-1. Adolescents' Academic Performance

	With Trained Mothers $N = 83$		With Untrained Mothers			
*Primary School GPA's**	Mean	SD	Mean	SD	t	p
Turkish	8.85	1.36	8.18	1.41	3.08	.001
Mathematics	8.15	1.75	7.32	1.75	3.01	.001
Overall Academic Performance	8.56	1.45	7.89	1.53	2.82	.002
Cognitive Performance						
WISC-R Vocabulary Score (max. 68)	45.62	10.23	41.92	13.39	F:2.1	.032
Schooling	%	f	%	f	χ^2	p
Is adolescent still in school?						
Yes	86	73	67	88	9.57	.002
No	13	11	32	43		

* Grade Point Average (min. 1, max. 10)

socioeconomic levels have a smaller vocabulary than middle-class children. These results imply that early enrichment, if successful, can have long-term effects. These sustained gains show that the adverse effects of low SES living conditions have been counteracted for the experimental group, whose immediate environment was changed through the project intervention.

The effects of intervention are also visible in adolescents' academic self-esteem and academic orientation (Table 11-2). Thus, the adolescents with trained mothers were more pleased with their school success compared with the control group, and thought that their teachers were pleased with them, too. They also felt that they could be the best in class if they studied hard. Negative or external pressure reasons for going to school (such as having nothing better to do, or parents' wishes) were endorsed more by the control group. Thus, positive orientation to education and self-esteem are concomitant with good academic performance.

The experimental group felt that they were prepared when they started school (97 percent, compared with 22 percent of the control group; $\chi^2 = 150$, df, $p = .000$). They also felt that this preparation helped over a longer period, compared with the control group (Table 11-2). Thus, in retrospect, the intervention was perceived as helpful by the adolescents who were not its direct targets, but who were indirect beneficiaries through mother-training.

As for socioemotional development, the experimental group surpassed the control group in autonomy, as reflected in making their own decisions; and better social integration, in terms of their ideas being accepted by friends and in terms of their mothers' approval of their friends (Table 11-3). Trouble with the law is rare among these adolescents, most of whom have intact families. Nevertheless, the few (6 percent) who had had such a problem were all from the control group (Table 11-3).

Finally, the adolescents' retrospective perception of their mothers gives clear evidence of what our Mother Enrichment Program accomplished (Table 11-4). The adolescents whose mothers had been trained perceived their mothers to be more nurturing and more responsive than the control group. Specifically, the former group retrospectively perceived their mothers as talking to them, consoling

Table 11-2. Adolescents' Academic Orientation

Adolescent's Variables	With Trained Mothers N = 83		With Untrained Mothers N = 134			
	Mean*	SD	Mean*	SD	t	p
Could be best in class if studied hard	4.58	.64	4.38	.81	1.98	.025
Having nothing better to do as a reason for going to school	1.63	1.01	1.99	1.22	-2.22	.015
Parents' wishes as a reason for going to school	2.39	1.31	2.87	1.46	-2.45	.01
How pleased adolescent is with his/her school success	3.64	.86	3.41	.92	1.83	.035
How pleased teachers are with his/her school success	3.63	.74	3.44	.86	1.79	.04
How much preschool preparation helped	4.41	.68	4.15	.95	2.07	.02
How long preschool preparation helped	5.23	1.90	4.31	2.12	3.01	.001

* Scores range 1-5, except for the last one (duration) 1-7.

Source: Adapted from Çiğdem Kağitçibaşi(1996), *Family and human development across cultures: A view from the other side.* Mahwah, NJ: Erlbaum. By permission of the publisher.

Table 11-3. Adolescents' Social Integration and Autonomy

Adolescent Variables	With Trained Mothers N = 83		With Untrained Mothers N = 134			
	Mean*	SD	Mean*	SD	t	p
Are adolescent's ideas accepted by friends?	3.74	.64	3.54	.71	2.06	.02
Adolescent makes decisions on his or her own	3.54	.83	3.32	.96	1.73	.045
Mother Variables	%	f	%	f	χ^2	p
Has child ever been in trouble with the police?						
Yes	0	0	6	8	3.69	.05
No	100	83	94	126		
What mother thinks of adolescent's friends						
Approve highly	56	46	38	51	9.02	.03
Approve somewhat	31	26	33	45		
Not sure	8	7	21	28		
Does not approve	5	4	7	10		

* Scores range 1-5.

Source: Adapted from Çiğdem Kağıtçıbaşı (1996), Family and human development across cultures: A view from the other side. Mahwah, NJ: Erlbaum. By permission of the publisher.

Table 11-4. Adolescents' Perception of Mother

Variables	Trained N = 83 Mean*	SD	Not-Trained N = 134 Mean*	SD	t	p
Mother liked to talk with him/her when little	3.89	.96	3.61	1.06	1.99	.025
Mother used to spank him/her when little	2.00	.96	2.32	1.07	-2.25	.015
Mother used to console him/her when little	4.26	.82	3.93	1.00	2.52	.005
Mother used to appraciate him/her when little	3.94	.84	3.69	.89	1.99	.025
Mother was interested in what he/she did	4.22	.87	4.00	.90	1.75	.040
Mother used to help him/her when little	4.20	.79	4.00	.91	1.69	.045

* Scores range 1-5.

Source: Adapted from Çiğdem Kağıtçıbaşı (1996), *Family and human development across cultures: A view from the other side.* Mahwah, NJ: Erlbaum. By permission of the publisher.

them, appreciating them, and being interested in them more, and as spanking them less than the latter (Table 11-4). Obviously, the trained mothers manifested a different style of parenting. This was probably the key difference between the human environments of the two groups of children.

Much evidence obtained from the mother and father interviews further substantiates the findings from the adolescents. This evidence strongly implies that the changes in the mothers meant changes in the family's emotional atmosphere and family relations, with corresponding changes in children, which I have already described. Significant differences between the two groups emerged in many basic family variables, and in parent-child interaction and parents' perception of their children. Thus, in the experimental group better parent-child communication, better adjustment of the child in the family, less physical punishment, and in general closer and better family relations were reported by both mothers and fathers. Furthermore, trained mothers still enjoyed higher status (vis à vis their husbands) in the family.

The parents in the experimental group also manifested higher educational expectations for their children, were more interested in what was going on in school, and provided the child more help with homework and better environmental stimulation in general. All of these findings, which are statistically significant, attest to the existence of a more supportive and more stimulating home environment—a different family culture in the families with the trained mothers. From this it is clear that such programs, which have a holistic-contextual approach to early childhood development and education, are a viable alternative to formal preschool education in developing countries that targets only the individual child. Their strengths lie in being community-based, parent-family-oriented interactive learning experiences that promote the child's overall optimal development in context. Being cost-effective, they have the potential for wide-scale application, and being community-based, they have the inherent flexibility to benefit from the indigenous culture and to become culturally relevant.

CONCLUSION

This longitudinal study is an example of theoretically informed applied research with important policy implications. These implications have, in fact, been given concrete form as a public service. The mother-training program is now being implemented in many low-income districts of Istanbul and other metropolitan centers, as well as in many smaller cities and towns throughout Turkey, through the adult education centers of the Ministry of Education. The program has been condensed to one year (from two years), because our new Cognitive Training Program is being used instead of HIPPY. This new program is administered in the year just prior to school entry (to 5 year-old children). The program applications have been supported by UNICEF and the World Bank through a private foundation called the Mother-Child Education Foundation, established in 1993 to apply the program. The "mother enrichment" component has been adapted to television. The applications are expanding; over 10,000 mother-child pairs participated in the program in 1995–1996 and this number is expected to double in 1996–1997 (see Kağıtçıbaşı, Bekman, & Göksel, 1995).

Evaluative research is being conducted on the one-year program. Two recent evaluation studies, one on mothers and one on children (Ayçiçeği, 1993; Ercan, 1993, respectively) found evidence of significant benefits from the program, similar to the original project findings discussed above. Another study (Aksu-Koç & Kuşçul, 1994), looking into the specific effects on children's preliteracy skills, found that children who had gone through the program performed better in word recognition tasks than a control group. These evaluation studies, all utilizing quasi-experimental designs, provide evidence for the effectiveness of the current (revised and condensed) program. At the time of writing, a full scale evaluation study was being carried out by Bekman in four different towns; again the initial findings are most encouraging.

On the basis of the research and conceptualizations examined in this chapter, a number of conclusions can be drawn. First, the main question is no longer *whether* early educational programs are effective in enhancing opportunities for children, but rather *which* types of programs are more effective, *why* they are effective, and *how* such programs can be improved to make a greater impact. This allows some essential ingredients of programs that work and the optimal conditions for interventions to be established. The Turkish Early Enrichment Project serves as a case study in which these ingredients and conditions of intervention can be seen. The expanding applications deriving from this project and their initial evaluations provide evidence for the validity of its basic approaches.

Much work is needed to enhance children's opportunities all over the world. A first step toward this goal is scientifically sound research that examines issues in depth and breadth. Such research promises to highlight the main problems and their solutions, and should help to achieve public recognition of the issue. Such recognition will allow headway to be made toward policies designed to ameliorate the problem.

NOTES

1. The original project was funded by the International Development Research Centre of Canada; the follow-up study was funded by the MEAwards Program of the Population Council. Apart from the intervention introduced by the project, that is, mother-training, the effects of children's pre-school environments (home, educational preschool, or custodial preschool) were also studied. However, only the results pertaining to the project intervention are reported here.

2. There is some evidence that the traditional Turkish women do not take "games" seriously, and for this reason do not benefit from them.

3. All the findings presented are statistically significant; the statistics and their significance levels are indicated in the tables.

4. A vocabulary measure was used, because research in this part of the world (reviewed by Kağıtçıbaşı & Savasir, 1988) has pointed to the greater disadvantage of lower SES subjects on performance tests in general and the higher variance explained by the verbal factor of the WISC-R, as evidenced by research from Greece, Israel, and Turkey. The Turkish standardization of the WISC-R had been done with urban low SES norms, appropriate to our sample.

REFERENCES

Aksu-Koç & Kuşçul, H. Ö. (1994, April). *Turkish middle and working-class homes as preliteracy environments and the effects of home enrichment on literacy skills.* Paper presented at the annual meeting of the American Educational Research Association, New Orleans, LA.

Aswad, B. (1974). Visiting patterns among women of the elite in a small Turkish city. *Anthropological Quarterly, 47*, 9–27.

Ayçiçeği, A. (1993). *The effects of the mother training program.* Unpublished master's thesis, Boğaziçi University, Istanbul, Turkey.

Bekman, S. (1990). Alternative to the available: Home-based vs. center-based programs. *Early Childhood Development and Care, 58*, 109–119.

Bekman, S. (1993). The preschool education system in Turkey revisited. *International Journal of Early Childhood OMEP, 25,* 13–19.

Bernstein, B. (1975). *Class, codes and control* (Vol. 3). London: Routledge & Kegan Paul.

Berrueta-Clement, J. R., Schweinhart, L., Barnett, W., Epstein, A., & Weikart, D. (1984). *Changed lives: The effects of the Perry preschool program on youths though age 19.* Ypsilanti, MI: The High/Scope Press.

Brazelton, T. B. (1982). *Early intervention: What does it mean? Theory and research in behavioural pediatrics.* New York: Plenum.

Bronfenbrenner, U. (1979). *The ecology of human development: Experiments by nature and design.* Cambridge, MA: Harvard University Press.

Bronfenbrenner, U., & Ceci, S. J. (1993). Heredity, evironment, and the question of "how?"—A first approximation. In R. Plomin & G. E. McClearn (Eds.), *Nature-nurture* (pp. 313–324). Washington, DC: American Psychological Association.

Ercan, S. (1993). *The short-term effects of the Home Intervention Program on the cognitive development of children.* Unpublished Master's Thesis. Boğaziçi University Istanbul, Turkey.

Farran, D. C. (1990). Effects of intervention with disadvantaged and disabled children: A decade review. In S. J. Meisels & J. P. Shonkoff (Eds.), *Handbook of early childhood intervention* (pp. 501–540). Cambridge: Cambridge University Press.

Horowitz, F. D. (1993). The need for a comprehensive new environmentalism. In R. Plomin & G. E. C. McClearn (Eds.), *Nature-nurture* (pp. 341- 354). Washington, DC: American Psychological Association.

Kağıtçıbaşı, Ç. (1989). Child rearing in Turkey: Implications for immigration and intervention. In L. Eldering & F. Kloprogge (Eds.), *Different cultures same school* (pp. 137–152). Lisse, the Netherlands: Swets and Zeitlinger.

Kağıtçıbaşı, Ç. (1990). Family and socialization in cross-cultural perspective: A model of change. In J. J. Berman (Ed.), *Cross-cultural perspectives: Nebraska symposium on motivation 1989* (pp. 135–200). Lincoln: University of Nebraska Press.

Kağıtçıbaşı, Ç. (1991). The Early Enrichment Project in Turkey. Paris: UNESCO-UNICEF-WFP Notes, Comments . . . No. 193. Reprinted in S. Bekman (Ed.), *Different models in early childhood education.* Ankara, Turkey: UNICEF.

Kağıtçıbaşı, Ç. (1996). *Family and human development across cultures: A view from the other side.* Mahwah, NJ: Erlbaum.

Kağıtçıbaşı, Ç. (1997). Parent education and child development. In M. E. Young (Ed.), *Early child development investing in our children's lecture:*

Proceedings of a World Bank Conference on early child development: Investing in the future. Amsterdam: Elsevier.

Kağıtçıbaşı, Ç., Bekman, S., & Göksel, A. (1995). A multipurpose model of nonformal education: The mother-child education programme. *Coordinators' Notebook: An International Resource for Early Childhood Development, 17,* 25–32.

Kağıtçıbaşı, Ç., & Savasir, I. (1988). Human abilities in the Eastern Mediterranean. In S. H. Irvine & J. W. Berry (Eds.), *Human abilities in cultural context* (pp. 232–262). Cambridge: Cambridge University Press.

Kağıtçıbaşı, Ç., Sunar D. G., & Bekman, S. (1988). *Comprehensive preschool education project: Final report.* Ottawa: International Development Research Centre (Manuscript Report 209e).

Kiray, M. B. (1981). The women of small town. In N. Abadan-Unat (Ed.), *Women in Turkish society* (pp. 259–274) Leiden, the Netherlands: Brill.

Lombard, A. D. (1981). *Success begins at home. Educational foundations of preschoolers.* Massachusetts, Toronto: Lexington Books.

Lombard, A. D. (1994). *Success begins at home: The past, present and future of the Home Instruction Program for Preschool Youngsters.* Guilford, CT: The Dushkin Publishing Group.

Myers, R. (1992). *The twelve who survive: Strengthening programs of early childhood development in the third world.* London: Routledge.

Olson, E. (1982). Duofocal family structure and an alternative model of husband-wife relationship. In Ç. Kağıtçıbaşı (Ed.), *Sex roles, family and community in Turkey* (pp. 33–72). Bloomington, IN: Indiana University Press.

Schorr, L. B. (1991). Effective programs for children growing up in concentrated poverty. In A. C. Huston (Ed.), *Children in poverty: Child development and public policy* (pp. 260–281). Cambridge: Cambridge University Press.

Schweinhart, L. J., & Weikart, D. P. (1980). *Young children grow up: The effects of the Perry Preschool Program an youths through age 15.* Ypsilanti, MI: The High/Scope Press.

Seitz, V. (1990). Intervention programs for impoverished children: A comparison of educational and family support models. *Annals of Child Development, 7,* 73–103.

Seitz, V., & Provence, S. (1990). Caregiver-focused models of early intervention. In S. J. Meisels & J. P. Shonkoff (Eds.), *Handbook of Early Childhood Intervention* (pp. 400–427). Cambridge: Cambridge University Press.

Shipman, V. C., Barone, J., Beaton, A., Emmerich, W., & Ward, W. (1977). *Disadvantaged children and their first school experiences: Structure and development of cognitive competencies and styles prior to school entry. (Head Start Longitudinal Study PR–71–19)*. Princeton, NJ: Educational Testing Service.

Slaughter, D. (1983). Early intervention and its effects on maternal and child development. *Monographs of the Society for Research in Child Development, 48.*

Smilansky, M. (1979). *Priorities in preschool education l, evidence and conclusions.* Washington, DC: World Bank Staff Working Paper No. 323.

Vedder, P. & Eldering, L. (1992, July). *The effects of OPSTAP, a home intervention programme preparing children for school.* Paper presented at the Eleventh International Conference of Cross-Cultural Psychology, Liège, Belgium.

Wachs, T. D. (1993). Determinants of intellectual development: Single determinant research in a multideterminant universe. *Intelligence, 17,* 1–10.

Yoshikawa, H. (1994). Prevention as cumulative protection: Effects of early family support and education on chronic delinquency and its risks. *Psychological Bulletin, 115,* 28–54.

Zigler, E., Taussig, C., & Black, K. (1992). Early childhood intervention: A promising preventative for juvenile delinquency. *American Psychologist, 47*(8), 997–1006.

CHAPTER TWELVE

The Dutch Experience with the Home Intervention Program for Preschool Youngsters (HIPPY)

Lotty Eldering and *Paul Vedder*

There is a great discrepancy between what schools expect of children and what the children of underprivileged parents, especially of ethnic minority parents, can achieve, given what their parents offer them. As a result of their underprivileged background, such children often start their school career with educational arrears. Intervention programs for use in schools or the home have been developed to prevent or rectify such arrears. This chapter focuses on one such program, the Home Intervention Program for Preschool Youngsters (HIPPY). Developed in Israel, HIPPY is currently being implemented in several countries around the world (Lombard, 1994), including the Netherlands, where it has been implemented among ethnic minority groups (Eldering & Vedder, 1992).

Before transferring an intervention program to another country, the societal context of the new country has to be explored in order to ascertain the program's transferability and to identify the most relevant groups to be targeted for intervention. Three clusters of contextual factors influenced the decision to introduce HIPPY in the Netherlands: the low social position of certain immigrant groups and the poor prospects for their children, Dutch government policy on minorities, and the cultural and pedagogical climate in ethnic minority families.

In the first part of this chapter, we sketch the demographic and policy context and describe the groups targeted for intervention in the Netherlands. The second part deals with the Dutch HIPPY experiment from 1987 to 1992 in Amsterdam.[1] We describe how HIPPY was adapted for implementation in ethnic minority groups in the Netherlands, how it was implemented, and its effects on mothers and children both directly after the program and five years later.

DUTCH POLICY CONTEXT AND GROUPS TARGETED FOR INTERVENTION

Immigration and Minorities Policy

Unlike traditional immigration countries, such as the United States, Canada, or Australia, the Netherlands has experienced large-scale immigration only since World War II. Three broad categories of immigrants can be distinguished:

- Immigrants from former colonies, the Dutch East Indies (including the Moluccan Islands), Surinam, and the Netherlands Antilles

- Foreign workers and their families from Mediterranean countries (predominantly Morocco and Turkey)

- Refugees and asylum-seekers from countries with political unrest (predominantly former Yugoslavia, Somalia, Iraq, and Iran)

At present, Surinamese, Antillians, Moluccans, Turks, and Moroccans are the most numerous groups, numbering about 780,000 (5 per cent of the total population of 15.4 million) (CBS, 1995).

In 1983, the Dutch government officially acknowledged that the Netherlands had become a multicultural society and that the *migrants* from former colonies and Mediterranean countries had in fact become *immigrants*. The policy discourse on immigrants centered around two fundamental principles of Dutch society: equality of opportunity and equivalence of cultures. A two-track policy was proposed, aiming at improving the social position of immigrants as well as giving them the opportunity to preserve their cultural identity. Immigrants from Surinam, the Netherlands Antilles, the Moluccan Islands, Mediterranean countries, and refugees and asylum-seekers were designated as the target groups of the minorities policy.

In 1985 the Educational Priority Policy came into effect, aiming at equal opportunities for all students from underprivileged groups. Under this policy, districts and schools with a high percentage of underprivileged students receive extra funds (Eldering, 1989). In addition, a cultural policy, consisting of education in the language and culture of the parents' country of origin is being pursued for students of Mediterranean origin for two and a half hours a week during school hours (monocultural courses) and intercultural education for all students (multicultural courses) (see Eldering, 1996, for an extensive description of Dutch educational policy on minorities).

Low Social Position of First- and Second-Generation Immigrants

The groups targeted by the Dutch minorities policy have, on average, a lower social position than the indigenous Dutch population. There are, however, remarkable differences between the various ethnic minority groups, with the Moroccans and Turks having the lowest position and the Surinamese and Antillians closer to that of the Dutch (Eldering, 1997).

The ethnic minorities tend to concentrate in urban areas. Over half of them live in cities of more than 100,000 inhabitants, compared with only 22 percent of the total Dutch population. Although their housing conditions have improved over the past 10 years, many Moroccans and Turks still live in overcrowded apartments. Only 4 percent of the Moroccans and 7 percent of the Turks are homeowners, compared with 48 percent of the Dutch. The labor market participation of ethnic minorities between 16 and 65 years old is much lower than that of the corresponding Dutch population. The unemployment rates are the highest for the Moroccans and Turks, whereas the Surinamese occupy an intermediate position (CBS, 1995). The educational level shows a similar rank order. More than 60 percent of the Moroccans and Turks have had no education beyond primary education, compared with only 27 percent for the Surinamese and 14 percent for the indigenous Dutch. Many Moroccan women are illiterate.

More than half of the ethnic minority students, particularly those of Moroccan and Turkish origin, perform poorly to very poorly in secondary school, and over half leave school without a diploma (CBS, 1995). A longitudinal evaluation of Dutch Educational Priority Policy showed that over 80 percent of the educational arrears in secondary education originates in primary education and in the preschool period (Kloprogge & Walraven, 1994; Meijnen & Riemersma, 1992). Intervention programs for young children, therefore, have great potential to redress the imbalance. In 1987, the Ministry of Welfare, Public Health, and Culture (WVC) decided to experiment with HIPPY.

Child Rearing in Ethnic Minority Families

With the exception of the Moluccans, the ethnic minority families in the Netherlands consist primarily of immigrant parents, who immigrated voluntarily to the Netherlands, and their children. Most of these immigrants maintain strong relationships with the family they left behind, visit their home country every few years, and invest in land and houses there (although only a minority actually plan to return to their home country). Many Moroccans and Turks want to preserve their cultural and religious traditions and transmit them to their children; many also have an ambivalent attitude toward Dutch society and culture (Eldering, 1997, 1998; Lindo, 1996; Rişvanoğlu, Bilgin, Brouwer, & Priester, 1986; Tesser, 1993).

Below, we give some general information about child rearing in ethnic minority families. We focus on the cultural-ecological aspects relevant for the implementation of HIPPY in the Netherlands (Eldering, 1995; Harkness & Super, 1993).

Household Composition and Size

Surinamese families differ greatly in composition and household size compared with Moroccan and Turkish families. Over a third of the Surinamese families in the Netherlands are female-headed single-parent families, but most Moroccan and Turkish families are headed by two parents (CBS, 1985, 1986; Eldering & Borm, 1996a). The percentages of divorced women in the latter groups, however, are increasing (Eldering & Borm, 1996b). Another striking difference concerns the number of children in the family, with Moroccan and Turkish families having the largest, and the Surinamese the smallest. This factor appears to have great impact on the implementation of HIPPY in Moroccan families, as we will discuss later.

Moroccan and Turkish families generally have a more traditional gender role pattern, with men as the main providers and women as housewives. Women and girls in these families are subordinate to their husbands and fathers, and children are subordinate to their parents (van den Berg-Eldering, 1981; Kağıtçıbaşı, 1996; Pels, 1991). A home intervention program, therefore, can only be implemented in these families after the father has given his consent.

Parental Theories on Education and Children's Development

Immigrant parents initially have high aspirations for their children's education. From experience in their country of origin, they know that education is an effective vehicle for upward mobility, and they hope that their children will achieve a better position in the Netherlands than they have. However, they generally view formal education as the responsibility of the school and the teachers, and are not aware of their own key role in preparing their children for school (Eldering, 1997). Moroccan and Turkish parents see their primary responsibility in their child's moral development and in shaping its social and religious personality (Pels, 1991; de Vries, 1987). Many Moroccan mothers, moreover, never attended school in Morocco.

Ethnic minority families emphasize that their children should be obedient and respectful rather than independent and autonomous (Eldering & Vedder, 1992; Kağıtçıbaşı, 1989, 1996; Mungra, 1990; Pels, 1991). Kağıtçıbaşı (1989; this volume), argues that intervention programs exclusively aimed at children will have no lasting effects, because these programs do not change their parents' (particularly the mothers') attitudes toward children.

Home Language and Preparation for Schooling

Children of immigrant Moroccan and Turkish parents grow up in a non-Dutch-speaking environment and learn either a Moroccan dialect or Turkish as their first language. When speaking with their siblings, however, they tend to switch to Dutch (de Ruiter, 1991; Extra, 1996). Although Dutch was the official language in colonial Surinam, not all Surinamese parents, particularly the Hindustani ones, are fluent in Dutch (CBS, 1986). Nevertheless, most Surinamese children speak Dutch with their mother at home (Extra, 1996). A study on Dutch language proficiency showed that upon entering primary school at age 4, Surinamese and Antillian children were less proficient in Dutch than indigenous Dutch children. Moroccan children scored lower, and Turkish children scored the worst (Boogaard, Damhuis, De Glopper, & Van den Bergh, 1990). Home intervention programs have to take the language situation in the family into account. The way in which this was done in the HIPPY experiment will be discussed later in this chapter.

Many ethnic minority families originate from poor and underdeveloped countries. Parents in these countries are not as focused on preparing their children for school as Western parents are. They buy fewer books and toys for their children, and the verbal interaction in these families is mainly aimed at social and moral modeling rather than at academic learning (Eldering & Vedder, 1992; Pels, 1991). There are, however, some indications of differences between the ethnic minority groups in the "culture of literacy." Surinamese and Moroccans appear to be more oriented to the Dutch media (library membership, reading Dutch journals—especially the Surinamese—and watching Dutch television programs), whereas Turks remain more oriented to Turkish media (reading Turkish newspapers, watching Turkish television programs) (CBS, 1985; van der Wal, 1995).

HIPPY

HIPPY is a two-year program for mothers in underprivileged families and their children aged 4 to 6. It was developed in Israel by Professor Avima Lombard of Hebrew University of Jerusalem for the benefit of immigrant families of oriental origin in Israel (Lombard, 1981; 1994).

The underlying principle of HIPPY is to help the mother educate her preschool child at home. Both mother and child are expected to benefit from the program. The mother will learn new attitudes and skills congruent with the demands of modern schooling and will gain confidence in her ability to help her child learn, and the child will be better prepared for learning in school (Green & Cohen, 1979).

Intervention programs vary in their setting (home-based vs. center-based), structure (structured vs. nonstructured curriculum), scope of activities (limited to language and cognitive development, or focused on the child's total development) and subjects targeted for change (individuals, or families and communities). This variety stems not so much from the ultimate goal that nearly all programs share—that is, improving the chances of underprivileged children at school and in society - as from the diverging views and theories on the appropriate strategies for achieving this goal (Eldering, 1990/1991).

HIPPY uses various strategies to involve the mothers of the target groups. First, HIPPY is carried out in the home. Research on the implementation of center-based community programs has shown that women's attendance rates were poor and irregular (Lombard, 1981). In home programs the pace of learning can be adjusted to the mother's ability, specific problems can be identified and dealt with, and mothers can be supported and encouraged to continue participating in the program.

Second, HIPPY uses a structured curriculum: the program is split into 60 weeks, with a clear assignment for each week, involving five daily activities. When developing HIPPY, the underlying principle was to build up the mothers' confidence as teachers. If they can carry out the activities successfully, they will be satisfied and be motivated to become more involved in the child's education and learning. Furthermore, programmed instruction is considered to be a suitable approach for mothers who have little experience with educational activities at home. Detailed, written instructions are provided for each activity; the mothers merely have to carry them out in the prescribed order.

The third way of involving the mothers of the target groups is to use paraprofessionals as home visitors. These paraprofessionals familiarize the mothers with the weekly materials and activities. They visit the mothers at home to discuss the activities of the previous week and to explain to them how to work with the materials for the next week. The paraprofessionals monitor the progress of mothers and children through the program by making weekly reports. Paraprofessionals are mothers selected from the target group, preferably ones who have a child the same age as the program children. There are two main reasons for using mothers from the target groups as home visitors: they have better access to the families because of their cultural affinity, and they make a program less expensive. Since the HIPPY materials and tasks are prescribed and almost self-explanatory, it is assumed that the program does not need professionals to deliver and explain them.

The curriculum focuses on three major areas of intellectual functioning: language, sensory discrimination, and problem-solving. Language instruction centers around simple story books (18 books in a two-year period). About one-third of the HIPPY materials provide activities in the field of perceptual and sensory discrimination skills (visual, auditory, and tactile skills, in that order). One of the main problem-solving activities in HIPPY involves the extensive use of a series of matrices. The focus during the first year is on books and on the development of discrimination skills, and by the second year the emphasis shifts to problem-solving (Lombard, 1981; 1994).

In the original pilot project in Israel, no group meetings were planned. A comparison between mothers who had participated in

HIPPY with mothers who were not enrolled in the program showed no evidence of any change in the HIPPY mothers' views of themselves as educators (Davis & Kugelmass, 1974), and therefore group meetings were subsequently incorporated in HIPPY in order to enable mothers to share experiences about the program, learn from the experience of others, and internalize some of the program's objectives through active discussions.

From 1969 to 1972, HIPPY was tested on 161 mother-child pairs in several neighborhoods in Tel Aviv. The children were monitored during their primary and secondary school years. The outcomes of this longitudinal evaluation showed that the home-instructed children did significantly better than the control children (Lombard, 1981, 1994). The evaluation of this pilot project in Tel Aviv reflects the way many compensatory and intervention programs were evaluated in the 1960s and 1970s—by means of a pretest-posttest design with experimental and control children, with the emphasis on quantitative effects of the program on the intellectual development of children and their school performance, and with no attention paid to how the program was implemented (Eldering, 1990/1991).

Since 1975, HIPPY has been implemented throughout Israel as part of the Ministry of Education's Welfare Program. Today there are over 75 HIPPY programs involving about 5,500 families, including new immigrants from Ethiopia and the former USSR as well as established Israelis in Arab and Jewish communities (HIPPY International Newsletter, 1997). HIPPY has been exported to other countries since 1982.

THE HIPPY EXPERIMENT IN THE NETHERLANDS

The Dutch HIPPY began in 1987 as an experiment involving Dutch, Surinamese, Turkish, and Moroccan mothers with a 4-year-old child, who were living in ethnically mixed neighborhoods in Amsterdam. The experiment had two main goals: to see whether the HIPPY program could be transferred to ethnic minority groups in the Netherlands, and to study the program's effects on children and mothers. Below we present and discuss the cultural adaptation of HIPPY to the Dutch context, the program's implementation, and its effects on mothers and children.

Cultural Adaptations of HIPPY

Despite similarities in the Israeli and Dutch contexts, cultural differences between the target groups in both countries made a few modifications inevitable. These modifications concerned the languages in which HIPPY was offered to the families, and the decision to use ethnically homogeneous groups and paraprofessionals from the same ethnic backgrounds as the families (Eldering, 1992).

Home Language Approach

In Israel, HIPPY is offered to the Jewish mothers solely in Hebrew. This choice is in line with the official Israeli policy of absorption by providing intensive Hebrew language courses for new immigrants. In the Netherlands, HIPPY is offered to the ethnic minority families in their home language: Dutch for the Dutch and Surinamese families, Turkish for the Turkish families, and Arabic for the Moroccan families. Since it was assumed, and this proved to be the case in the experiment, that most Moroccan and Turkish mothers had little command of the Dutch language and that the children were socialized at home in their parents' first language, the decision to use the home language seemed to be the most practical solution. Another argument in favor of the use of the home language is that Dutch policy on minorities advocates a bilingual approach to young non-Dutch-speaking children. The Turkish groups were able to use the HIPPY books and materials translated into Turkish by Kağıtçıbaşı's project team at Boğaziçi University in Istanbul (see Kağıtçıbaşı, this volume). In the Netherlands, the HIPPY materials were translated into Dutch and into Arabic.

The language chosen for the program proved to be particularly complicated for the Moroccan groups, however, since their mother tongues—Moroccan Arabic and Tarifit Berber—have no standardized written versions. Standard Arabic, the language children learn at school in Arab countries, differs greatly from the national dialect, Moroccan Arabic. A second problem was the high illiteracy rate among Moroccan mothers. For practical reasons, it was decided to offer illiterate and semi-literate mothers the books and materials in Dutch. It was hoped that older siblings of the HIPPY child attending a Dutch school would help the mother with the program.

Ethnicity-Based Program

Offering HIPPY to the immigrant families in the Netherlands in their home language means that it has to operate as an ethnicity-based program as long as the target groups in the Netherlands mainly consist of immigrants lacking proficiency in Dutch. The ethnically homogeneous groups were guided by paraprofessionals from the same ethnic and linguistic background. Ideally, each paraprofessional is responsible for a group of about 15 mothers. However, the decision to operate HIPPY as an ethnicity-based program meant that this ideal was achieved in less than half of the groups in the experiment. In Israel, HIPPY operates as a community-based program, allowing for ethnically mixed groups.

Design and Methods of the Evaluation

In the HIPPY experiment, we studied the implementation and effects of the program on mothers and children. One of the formal eligibility criteria for participation in HIPPY was that the mothers should have received no more than 10 years of schooling. The children had to be no younger than 3 years and 9 months and no older than 4 years and 6 months. This age range was chosen so that children would finish HIPPY just before being transferred to grade three in Dutch primary school, the grade in which formal reading instruction starts.

Baby clinics and kindergartens supplied us with the addresses of about 500 mother-child pairs that satisfied these criteria. About 350 of these 500 families were invited to participate, and of these, 141 mother-child pairs agreed to do so. A nonresponse study established that the participating families did not differ from nonparticipating families in demographic characteristics such as education, rate of unemployment, and number of children. The experiment started with two Dutch groups in 1987 to gain experience with HIPPY. Turkish and Surinamese mothers were involved from 1988, and Moroccan mothers and two new Dutch groups followed in 1989. The Dutch mothers who enrolled in 1987 were not included in the summative evaluation. A comparison of data from several national surveys on demographic characteristics and social position of minority groups in the Netherlands confirmed that the families participating in HIPPY were representative of the entire population of ethnic minorities in the Netherlands (Eldering & Vedder, 1992).

An pretest-posttest control group design was used for the summative evaluation. Control children were selected from the same neighborhoods about eight months after the experimental children had started with HIPPY. The same criteria for age, ethnicity, and mothers' educational level were used as for the experimental children. Budgetary constraints precluded us from having a Dutch control group, but a total of 117 Surinamese, Turkish, and Moroccan control children participated in the study. We used a quasi-experimental design for the Surinamese, Turkish, and Moroccan groups, and a correlational design exploring the correlation between the intensity of participation and effects.

To check the comparability of the experimental and control children, we measured their level of cognitive functioning (K-SON) (Snijders & Snijders-Oomen, 1975) before the start of the program and found no statistically significant differences. A nonverbal test for cognitive functioning (SON-R) (Snijders, Tellegen & Laros, 1988) was also used as a post-test, as well as a Dutch-language test (TAK) (Verhoeven & Vermeer, 1986) and a rating scale for classroom behavior (Schobl-R) (Resing & Bleichrodt, 1991). Effects were analyzed by comparing the experimental and control groups.

Apart from this, we interviewed the mothers at the beginning of the program about their ideas and practices of child rearing, and at the end of the program asked them whether their children and they themselves had learned anything from participating in the program. We administered the HOME (Home Observation for Measurement of the Environment) inventory (Caldwell & Bradley, 1984) in the experimental families at the beginning and at the end of the program to assess the quality of the educational support at home and changes to this after the program ended.

Implementation

The HIPPY experiment in the Netherlands studied the implementation of the program as well as its effects on children and mothers. In this section we report on the dropouts, the intensity of participation by mothers and children, and the involvement of other family members.

Just over 40 percent of the mothers dropped out of the program. The highest dropout rate was in the Dutch group (54 percent) and the lowest in the Moroccan (22 percent). The dropout rates in the Surinamese and Turkish groups were 34 and 39 percent, respectively.

About 80 percent of the dropout occurred in the first year of the program, mostly in the first four months. We used two sources to analyze the dropout: reasons given by the mothers themselves, and a comparison of characteristics between dropout families and families who stayed in the program.

Reasons for Dropping Out

The mothers gave a variety of reasons for dropping out of the program, which broadly fell in two categories: family circumstances (62 percent), and program-related reasons (38 percent). Family circumstances included health problems of the mother (often related to pregnancy) or other problems in the family (marital conflicts, financial or other health problems in the family), and nonproblem-related circumstances (the mothers were too busy with their large households or work, or were themselves attending educational courses). The program-related reasons mostly concerned dissatisfaction with the program or difficulty of the tasks. A few mothers stopped because of problems with the paraprofessional. There were many changes in paraprofessionals during the experiment. Only 5 of the 12 groups had the same paraprofessional throughout the program.

Dropout Families Compared to Nondropout Families

Problematic family circumstances were thus the reasons most frequently given for dropping out of HIPPY. To get a clearer picture of the dropout, we compared dropout families with families who completed the program, using ethnicity, family type, mother's educational level and length of stay in the Netherlands, father's unemployment, quality of educational support at home, birth order, sex, age, and intelligence of the HIPPY child. Dropout appeared not to be correlated with the child's sex, age, or intelligence, nor with the mother's illiteracy and length of stay in the Netherlands, father's unemployment, quality of educational support at home, or family type (two-parent vs. single-parent families).

The child's birth order and mothers' educational level, in contrast, appeared to correlate with dropout. Firstborn children dropped out more often than subsequent children. This is probably due to the greater probability of the mother becoming pregnant again during the program. (We have already mentioned that pregnancy was a reason for dropping out.) Better-educated mothers were more likely to drop out than less well-educated mothers. There was a correlation between education and ethnicity, however. The Dutch mothers in the Dutch HIPPY experiment were both better educated and more likely to drop out of the program.

As a complement to exploring why families dropped out, we also investigated why families completed the program. The main reason given by Turkish, Moroccan, and Surinamese families for continuing the program was that they liked it. They liked receiving the materials and the books and doing the activities. In addition, their children liked the program. Although the reason policymakers decided to introduce the program was to support the children's development and education, only the Turkish mothers frequently mentioned this as a reason. In the other families it hardly played a role in the decision to remain in the program. This suggests that the program failed to make parents fully aware of the program's function for the children's development and school achievement.

Intensity of Participation

Mothers were expected to invest a fair amount of time in carrying out the program: two activities each day for five days a week during 60 weeks over a two-year period. We found that on average, the Dutch, Surinamese, and Turkish mothers worked with over 70 percent of all the week tasks (this is not to say that they did all the activities of each week task). The Moroccan mothers, however, did only just over half of their week tasks. As mentioned earlier, over half of the Moroccan mothers were illiterate. The intensity of participation correlated with the educational level of the mother (better-educated mothers did more week tasks with their children), unemployment of the father (children whose father was unemployed participated less intensively), and the HOME subscale 1 (families with more play and other cognitive stimulating materials at home did more week tasks with their children). In conjunction with the data on dropout, we concluded that although better educated mothers dropped out of the program more often, they worked more intensively with the week tasks if they did stay on. The second conclusion was that unemployment of the father did not seem to have an impact on the dropout, but it could be considered a risk factor in the implementation of the program.

The HIPPY implementation plan prescribed weekly contact between the mother and the paraprofessional, either during a home visit or a group meeting. The functions of the weekly contacts included evaluating the activities of the previous week, explaining the work sheets for the coming week, and instructing the mothers on how to work with the new sheets. With the exception of the Surinamese groups, most groups had a high quotient of contacts with the paraprofessionals (>.86). In the Surinamese group, however, less than half of the planned contacts took place, and many week tasks were not supported by instruction from the paraprofessional. Discrepancy between the number of contacts and the number of week tasks means that the evaluations cannot have taken place every time mothers had finished a week task. And worse, instructions for a new week's task must have sometimes been omitted.

The only ethnic group for which group meetings were not organized was the Moroccan group. Early in the study, these women had indicated that they would probably not attend groups meetings because of their large households and the reluctance of their husbands. The other groups had an average of 8 meetings in the first year, attended by 45 percent of the mothers, and 7 meetings in the second year, with a 55 percent attendance rate. The impact of group meetings on mothers will be discussed in the concluding section.

Involvement of Other Family Members

In over 75 percent of the Dutch, Surinamese, and Turkish families, only mother and child were involved in the program. Sometimes the HIPPY child's father or older sister read the books or did the activities with the child. The situation in the Moroccan families was completely different. In over half of these families an older child, mostly a daughter, helped the mother with the implementation by reading the Dutch books to the HIPPY child and giving her mother instructions about the other activities. One of the Moroccan coordinators even indicated that HIPPY was particularly suitable for Moroccan mothers and children in large families.

Almost 60 percent of all mothers completed the program. This is a major achievement, since the families eligible for participation in HIPPY are generally difficult to reach and to retain in an intervention program (Kloprogge, 1993; Smith & Wells, 1990). The dropout rate in our experiment was comparable to that in the pilot project in Tel Aviv (Lombard, 1981), but high compared with the Turkish program (see Kağıtçıbaşı, this volume). One reason for this difference might be the situation of the mothers. Two-thirds of the mothers in the Turkish project were factory workers who were allowed to attend the group meetings during working hours, whereas about 80 percent of the mothers in the Dutch project were housewives.

Effects on Children and Mothers

To measure the efficacy of the program, we used tests and asked the mothers for their opinion on HIPPY (self-reports).

Mothers

The families who completed the program were generally enthusiastic about HIPPY. Over 90 percent of the mothers were convinced that their children had learned quite a lot from working with HIPPY, and 60 percent reported that they themselves had also profited from the program. Their answers on this last point showed remarkable differences. The Dutch, Surinamese, and Turkish mothers particularly mentioned acquiring pedagogical skills: how to play and be active with children; and how to give them more attention and to find out more about how they feel, think and do things. They also mentioned an increase in their didactic skills, including more patience, new ways of explaining something, reading picture books, and being more responsive to children. Nearly all the Moroccan mothers who answered this question said that they had acquired more school knowledge: Dutch numbers, concepts, and words, and how to read and write. Half of the Turkish mothers and a quarter of the Dutch mothers, however, explicitly stated that they had learned nothing—a remarkable outcome given that the program is supposed to affect parents' pedagogical skills and attitudes. The scores on the HOME, which measures the quality of the educational support at home had not changed during the program.

Children

The test results showed no evidence of HIPPY enhancing the overall cognitive development of children, but we found some minor effects. The Moroccan, Turkish, and Surinamese experimental children showed improved eye-hand coordination. Although most measures of competence in the Dutch language showed no improvement, the Moroccan experimental children did statistically significantly better on a Dutch vocabulary test than the Moroccan control children. Furthermore, after controlling for pretest intelligence scores, we found significant positive correlations between the intensity of participation (number of week tasks mother and children worked with) and the children's cognitive development (SON-R) and classroom behavior (diligence). The intensity of participation, however, did not correlate with the quality of educational support as measured by the HOME at the beginning of the program.

The overall effects of HIPPY were small and only revealed at subgroup or subtest level. The improved eye-hand coordination was attributable to the large number of tasks in the program intended to enhance this skill. The vocabulary effect in the Moroccan group, probably due to the use of Dutch materials in this group, was more encouraging. As pointed out earlier, the Dutch, Surinamese, and Moroccan families received a Dutch version of HIPPY, whereas the Turks used the Turkish version of the program.

Recommendations for Implementation

Since the Dutch Ministry of Welfare, Public Health, and Culture (WVC) decided to implement HIPPY on a national scale long before the report of the HIPPY experiment was published, we recommended improving the program's implementation by:

- Averting and reducing the dropout

- Intensifying the implementation (doing more week tasks, more groups meetings, and more home visits)

- Using Dutch materials in non-Dutch-speaking groups

On the basis of our evaluation, we hypothesized that these aspects would enhance the beneficial impact on children.

School Achievements After Five Years

In 1995 we started a follow-up study involving both the experimental children and the control children. Through the schools, we traced 66 of the 85 minority children who participated in HIPPY (78 percent) and 85 of the 117 control children (73 percent). Thirteen of the 66 HIPPY children had dropped out in either the first or second year of the HIPPY program. We collected data on each child's school career and grade in September 1995. Table 12-1 gives a comparison of short-term effects and the findings in 1995. We ran all analyses for the long-term effects twice: first on the 66 HIPPY children (including the dropouts), and then on the 53 children who had completed the program. In order to control for relevant initial differences between the experimental and control groups we conducted covariance analyses using the children's scores on tests for cognitive functioning assessed when they were about 6 years old as a covariate. Whereas we had found some minor positive effects in the experimental HIPPY children after they had completed the program, we now found no difference, either in type of school (special education or regular education) or in grade (whether or not they had had to repeat a year). The effects on Dutch vocabulary of the Moroccan experimental children were, thus, not converted into an advantage in their school career five years later. We also checked whether there was a correlation between intensity of participation in HIPPY and school career. Again we found no significant correlations.

Factors that appeared to have a correlation (although moderate) with the children's grade were the children's level of cognitive functioning at age 6 (.39, p <.001), teacher's evaluation of children's attitude toward learning in school at age 6 (.45, p <.001), and the quality of educational support at home (HOME scores) when children were 4 (.23-.35, depending on whether total score or subscale scores are used).

These findings suggest that the children's development and education in the kindergarten period correlated with their school career, but that HIPPY had no impact on this relationship. We have to conclude that the overall effects of the Dutch HIPPY experiment in the Netherlands were small in the short term, and that the small effects at the end of the program faded out in five years. The pilot experiment in

Table 12-1. A Comparison of the Short and Long-term Effects of HIPPY

After the Program	Five Years Later
Gains in eye-hand coordination	No conversion into better grades
Positive correlation between intensity of participation and intelligence	No significant correlation between intensity of participation and grades
Positive correlation between intensity of participation and diligence	No significant correlation between intensity of participation and grades
Moroccan experimental children:	
Gains in Dutch vocabulary	No conversion into better grades

Tel Aviv and the Turkish Early Enrichment Project, which included HIPPY, both yielded significant short-term effects on children at the end of the program, and in the Turkish project on mothers as well (Kağıtçıbaşı, this volume; Kağıtçıbaşı, Sunar, & Bekman, 1988; Lombard, 1981, 1994). Here we have a case of a replication of evaluations with different outcomes.

Scaling-up HIPPY

In 1990 the Dutch Ministry of WVC decided to implement HIPPY on a national scale. Since then the number of families participating in HIPPY has increased, from 500 in 1991–1992 to more than 4,000 in 1994 (Averroèsstichting, 1995). The program is being implemented in many cities throughout the Netherlands. A Management Information System (MIS) has been set up to monitor the participating families and their progress through the program. The information system reveals that the program is currently administered primarily to Turkish families and that the percentage of participating Moroccan families is quite low. The percentages of Moroccan and Turkish families involved in HIPPY have declined, but those of Dutch and of other ethnic minority families have been increasing. These changes in ethnic groups are associated with differences in educational level.

The percentage of mothers with 4 or fewer years of schooling has fallen from 23 percent to 16 percent. Concomitantly, the percentage of mothers having more than 10 years of schooling has risen from 14 to 23. This is clearly a shift away from the original target group. One of the formal eligibility criteria for HIPPY is that the mother should have received no more than 10 years of schooling. Thus, although in our evaluation we concluded that HIPPY is a suitable program for poorly educated and even illiterate mothers, these mothers currently tend to participate in HIPPY relatively less often.

In 1996 HIPPY was replaced by a new home intervention program developed in the Netherlands using a similar approach (paraprofessionals, home visits, group meetings, etc.). The effects of this program on children and mothers are not yet known. Given the increased complexity of the materials and tasks of the new program, poorly educated mothers will probably be further excluded from participation.

HIPPY ACROSS COUNTRIES

In 1982, the Hebrew University of Jerusalem decided to implement the two-year HIPPY program outside Israel. The first country to use HIPPY was Turkey in 1983, followed by the United States in 1984. Thus far, the two-year HIPPY model has been implemented in Chile, Mexico, the Netherlands, New Zealand, South Africa, Turkey, and the United States, involving more than 25,000 educationally disadvantaged families. Below, we briefly describe HIPPY's implementation in Turkey and the United States.

HIPPY in Turkey was part of the Comprehensive Early Enrichment Project implemented and evaluated by the Boğaziçi University (Kağıtçıbaşı, this volume; Kağıtçıbaşı, Sunar, & Bekman, 1988; Lombard, 1994). The study was conducted in low-income areas of Istanbul. Two-thirds of the mothers in the sample consisted of semiskilled or unskilled factory workers; one-third were housewives. Most mothers were of rural origin and had a low educational level. Child-care centers, run by the factories, were the starting point for selecting 3 and 5-year-old children and their mothers for the program. The original sample consisted of 280 mother-child pairs. This number had fallen to 225 after two years due to attrition. Most attrition occurred in the first year, mainly for reasons of illiteracy and ill health, or because the husband or mother-in-law objected to participation in the program (Kağıtçıbaşı, 1993). The Turkish project appeared to have had significant short- and long-term effects on children and mothers (see Kağıtçıbaşı, this volume; Lombard, 1994).

Although HIPPY programs were first introduced in the United States in 1984 in Tulsa, Oklahoma, and Richmond, Virginia, it was Arkansas that established the first state-wide program. Initiated by Hillary Rodham Clinton, the wife of the Arkansas governor at that time, the Arkansas governor's office coordinated the expansion of HIPPY from 1986 to 1990. Thousands of children were involved in the program and the demand for the program grew nationwide. By 1992, with over 10,000 families in 17 states participating in the program, HIPPY had become an independent nonprofit organization based in New York. Today, approximately 15,000 educationally disadvantaged families participate in HIPPY programs in rural and urban communities in 28 states. HIPPY runs in English, Spanish, Haitian, and Cambodian (HIPPY International Newsletter, 1997). In the early years of its implementation in the United States, there were a few attempts to evaluate the impact of the program on participating children as part of ongoing evaluations. In 1990, a Research Consortium was established at the NCJW Center for the Child in New York to identify relevant research questions relating to the implementation of HIPPY in the United States and to propose an appropriate program for such research. So far, only a small-scale study in Arkansas and New York has reported on the effects of HIPPY on children's classroom adaptation at school as perceived by their first-grade teachers (Baker & Piotrkowski, 1993).

CONCLUSIONS

In this chapter we have reported how HIPPY, a home intervention program for underprivileged mothers and children developed in Israel, has been implemented in the Netherlands, first experimentally in Amsterdam and a few years later on a national scale. The aim of the experiment involving Dutch mothers and Surinamese, Turkish, and Moroccan mothers from first-generation immigrant families with 4-year-old children was to ascertain whether HIPPY could be transferred to underprivileged families in the Netherlands, and to study the program's effects on children and mothers. We summarize the main conclusions of our evaluation regarding HIPPY's adaptation, implementation, and effects on children and mothers.

HIPPY is operated as a multilingual program in the Netherlands, with paraprofessionals from the same ethnic and linguistic background as the participants. We have pointed out why HIPPY is offered to the immigrant families in their home language (Dutch, Turkish, and Arabic). The home language approach functioned quite well in the Turkish families, but not in the Moroccan groups. So the Moroccan groups mostly used the Dutch HIPPY materials. Another adaptation concerned the decision to implement HIPPY in ethnically homogeneous groups. Since most inner-city neighborhoods in the Netherlands have ethnically mixed populations, it proved to be difficult to find enough mothers in one neighborhood to form an ethnically homogeneous group.

A second issue concerned the target groups for HIPPY, particularly the question of whether or not poorly educated and even illiterate mothers could be involved in the program. The evaluation showed that although they are sometimes hard to reach, poorly educated and illiterate mothers stayed on in the program, whereas better-educated Dutch mothers were more often likely to drop out. Our data did not justify excluding families from participation in the program because of individual risk factors such as mother's illiteracy, father's unemployment, or the absence of a father. Mothers with a firstborn child dropped out of the program more often because of pregnancy than mothers participating with a later-born child. Most mothers dropped out for family reasons (pregnancy, marital conflicts, financial problems, household duties, etc.), and only a minority for program-related reasons. Illiteracy of mothers and unemployment of fathers, however, had a negative impact on progress through the program. Most illiterate mothers relied on an older child to read the books to the HIPPY child.

We conclude that HIPPY can be used by poorly educated and even illiterate mothers, provided that they receive extra help from paraprofessionals and other family members. Furthermore, the paraprofessionals need to have a keen eye for risk factors in the family that may lead to dropout.

In contrast to experiences with HIPPY in Israel and in Turkey, the Dutch HIPPY experiment had no overall effects on children and mothers. The small effects we found directly after the program on Moroccan children and children who worked with more week tasks were not transformed into a better school career five years later. The Dutch HIPPY experiment presents a case of a replication study with different outcomes. Reasons for the disparity between the results of the studies of the Hebrew University, Boğaziçi University, and Leiden University could be the differences in methodology, target groups, language policy, and project organization. Of the three HIPPY applications, HIPPY operated as a monolingual program in Israel and Turkey, but as a multilingual program in the Netherlands. Two-thirds of the mothers participating in the Turkish project were factory workers, whereas about 80 percent of the mothers participating in the Netherlands were housewives. Kağıtçıbaşı (this volume) ascribes the differences in outcomes between the Turkish and the Dutch project to the low attendance rates of the mothers in group meetings in the Netherlands. The Turkish factory workers were allowed to attend group meetings during working hours and they consequently had much higher attendance rates than the immigrant families in the Netherlands. Even if this explains the differences between the Turkish and Dutch project in effects on mothers, the problem remains of accounting for the effects seen on children in the Tel Aviv pilot project, in which no group meetings were held. Finally, differences in the quality of the preschool education in Israel, Turkey, and the Netherlands may have had an impact on the differences in effect on children.

HIPPY is currently being implemented in countries around the world, involving more than 25,000 families from a variety of ethnic and cultural backgrounds. The program is being administered in Hebrew, English, Turkish, Arabic, Dutch, Spanish, Cambodian and Haitian. In spite of its large-scale implementation, HIPPY has not been researched extensively. It is remarkable that HIPPY US, which has involved so many families in the program, has not set up a research program. The main reason for the lack of evaluation studies on HIPPY may be that many projects are struggling to find funds to run the program. Under such conditions, evaluation is a low priority. The Hebrew University in Jerusalem organized an International Research Workshop in 1995, at which researchers from several HIPPY countries discussed ways of improving the comparability of collecting data about HIPPY across countries (Research Institute for Innovation in Education, 1996). Remarkably, no attempt was made to reach agreement on this point, probably because the participants were well aware that HIPPY programs generally experience a shortage of funds. When research has to compete for funding with program implementation, program implementation is likely to win. A home intervention program implemented on such a large scale, however, certainly merits further cross-cultural and cross-national attention from researchers, and research funds.

NOTES

1. The project was developed and implemented by the Averroès Agency in Amsterdam and evaluated by the Center for Intercultural Pedagogics at Leiden University. Both were funded by the Dutch Ministry of Welfare, Public Health, and Culture (WVC) for a five-year period. Although HIPPY is run in the Netherlands under the name OPSTAP, we prefer to use its international name, HIPPY.

REFERENCES

Averroèsstichting (1995). *OPSTAP op weg 3: Monitoring en evaluatie van het OPSTAP-programma in het seizoen 1994–1995* [The project Opstap on the way (3): Implementation-monitoring and evaluation of Opstap (Dutch-HIPPY) in the season 1994–1995]. Amsterdam: Averroèsstichting; Afdeling Evaluatie, Monitoring en Onderzoek.

Baker, A. J. L., & Piotrkowski, C. S. (1993). *The effects of participation in HIPPY on children's classroom adaptation: Teacher ratings* [Initial report]. New York: NCJW Center for the Child.

Boogaard, M., Damhuis, R., De Glopper, K., & Van den Bergh, G. H. (1990). De mondelinge taalvaardigheid van allochtone en Nederlandse kleuters. [Oral language skills of young indigeneous and non-indigeneous Dutch children. In M. du Bois-Reymond & L. Eldering (Eds.), *Nieuwe oriëntaties op school en beroep* (pp. 117–125). Amsterdam: Swets & Zeitlinger.

Caldwell, B. M., & Bradley, R. H. (1984). *Administration manual, revised edition. HOME Observation for Measurement of the Environment.* Little Rock: University of Arkansas.

CBS (1985). *De leefsituatie van Turken en Marokkanen in Nederland, 1984. Deel 1. Eerste uitkomsten* [Conditions of living of Turkish and Moroccan families in the Netherlands, 1984. Part 1. First results]. Den Haag, the Netherlands: Staatsuitgeverij/CBS-publicaties.

CBS (1986). *De leefsituatie van Surinamers en Antillianen in Nederland, 1985. Deel 1. Eerste uitkomsten* [Conditions of living of Surinamese and Antillian families in the Netherlands, 1985. Part 1. First results]. Den Haag, the Netherlands: Staatsuitgeverij/CBS-publicaties.

CBS (1987). *De leefsituatie van Turken en Marokkanen in Nederland, 1984. Deel 3. Huishoudens en migratie* [Conditions of living of Turkish and Moroccan families in the Netherlands, 1984. Part 3. Households and migration]. Den Haag, the Netherlands: Staatsuitgeverij/CBS-publicaties.

CBS (1995). *Allochtonen in Nederland 1995* [Immigrants in the Netherlands 1995]. Voorburg/Heerlen, the Netherlands: Centraal Bureau voor de Statistiek.

Davis, D., & Kugelmass, J. (1974). *Home environment: The impact of the Home Instruction Program for Preschool Youngsters (HIPPY) on the mother's role as an educator.* Jerusalem: Hebrew University.

de Ruiter, J. J. (Ed.). (1991). *Talen in Nederland: Een beschrijving van de taalsituatie van negen etnische groepen* [Languages in the Netherlands: A description of the language situation of nine ethnic groups]. Groningen, the Netherlands: Wolters-Noordhoff.

de Vries, M. (1987). *Ogen in je rug. Turkse meisjes en jonge vrouwen in Nederland* [A stare at your back. Turkish girls and young women in the Netherlands]. Alphen aan den Rijn, the Netherlands: Samsom.

Eldering, L. (1989). Ethnic minority children in Dutch schools. In L. Eldering & J. Kloprogge (Eds.), *Different cultures same school: Ethnic minority children in Europe* (pp. 107–136). Amsterdam/Lisse: Swets & Zeitlinger. Berwyn, PA: Swets North America, Inc.

Eldering, L. (1990/1991). Intervention programmes for preschoolers from immigrant families: The Dutch case. In N. Bleichrodt & P. J. D. Drenth (Eds.), *Contemporary issues in cross-cultural psychology* (pp. 50–63). Amsterdam: Swets & Zeitlinger.

Eldering, L. (1992). Home intervention in ethnic minority families in the Netherlands. In H. de Frankrijker & F. Kieviet (Eds.), *Education in a multicultural society* (pp. 97–118). De Lier, The Netherlands: Academic Book Center.

Eldering, L. (1995). Child rearing in bicultural settings: A culture-ecological approach. *Psychology and Developing Societies: A Journal, 7*(2), 133–153.

Eldering, L. (1996). Multiculturalism and multicultural education in an international perspective. *Anthropology and Education Quarterly, 27*(3), 315–330.

Eldering, L. (1997). Ethnic minority students in the Netherlands from a cultural-ecological perspective. *Anthropology and Education Quarterly, 28*, 330–350.

Eldering, L. (1998). Mixed messages: Moroccan children in the Netherlands living in two worlds. In Henry T. Trueba & Yali Zou (Eds.), *Ethnic identity and power: Cultural contexts of political action in school and society*, pp. 259–282. New York: SUNY.

Eldering, L., & Borm, J. A. (1996a). *Alleenstaande Hindostaanse moeders* [Single Surinamese-Hindustan mothers in the Netherlands]. Utrecht, the Netherlands: Jan van Arkel.

Eldering, L., & Borm, J. A. (1996b). *Alleenstaande Marokkaanse moeders.* [Single Moroccan mothers in the Netherlands]. Utrecht, the Netherlands: Jan van Arkel.

Eldering, L., & Vedder, P. (1992). *OPSTAP, een opstap naar meer schoolsucces voor allochtone kinderen?* [Opstap (Dutch HIPPY), a step up to more success in school?]. Amsterdam: Swets & Zeitlinger.

Extra, G. (1996). *De multiculturele samenleving in ontwikkeling: Feiten, beeldvorming en beleid* [The changing multicultural society: Facts, myths, and policy]. Tilburg, the Netherlands: Tilburg University Press.

Green, H. A., & Cohen, J. (1979). HIPPY: Home instruction program for pre-school youngsters. In H. A. Green & J. Cohen (Eds.), *Research in action* (pp. 17–36). Jerusalem: Hebrew University, School of Education.

Harkness, S., & Super, C. (1993). The developmental niche: Implications for children's literacy development. In L. Eldering & P. Leseman (Eds.),

Early intervention and culture. Preparation for literacy: The interface between theory and practice. (pp. 115–131). Paris: UNESCO.

HIPPY International Newsletter, 1997. Jerusalem: Hebrew University, School of Education, The NCJW Research Institute for Innovation in Education.

Kağıtçıbaşı, Ç. (1989). Child rearing in Turkey: Implications for immigration and intervention. In L. Eldering & J. Kloprogge (Eds.), *Different cultures same school: Ethnic minority children in Europe* (pp. 137–152). Amsterdam: Swets & Zeitlinger.

Kağıtçıbaşı, Ç. (1993). A model of multipurpose non-formal education: The case of the Turkish Early Enrichment Porject. In L. Eldering & P. Leseman (Eds.), *Early intervention and culture. Preparation for literacy: The interface between theory and practice.* (pp. 253–268). Paris: UNESCO.

Kağıtçıbaşı, Ç. (1996). *Family and human development across cultures.* Mahwah, NJ: Erlbaum.

Kağıtçıbaşı, Ç., Sunar D., & Bekman, S. (1988). *Comprehensive preschool education project: Final report.* Ottawa, Canada: International Development Research Centre.

Kloprogge, J. L. (1993). Uit OPSTAP stappen [Dropping out of Dutch HIPPY]. In P. Vedder & B. Bekkers (Eds.), *OPSTAP: Onderzoek en praktijk.* Amsterdam: Averroèsstichting.

Kloprogge, J., & Walraven, G. (1994). *Vernieuwde kaders, veranderende structuren: Notitie over het Onderwijsvoorrangsbeleid 1993* [New frameworks, changing structures: A note on the Educational Priority Policy]. Den Haag, the Netherlands: SVO.

Lindo, F. (1996). *Maakt cultuur verschil? De invloed van groepsspecifieke gedragspatronen op de onderwijsloopbaan van Turkse en Iberische migrantenjongeren* [Does culture make a difference? The effects of group-specific behavioral patterns on immigrant Turkish, Spanish, and Portugese adolescents' school careers]. Amsterdam: Het Spinhuis.

Lombard, A. D. (1981). *Success begins at home: Educational foundations of preschoolers.* Massachusetts Toronto: Lexington Books.

Lombard, A. D. (1994). *Success begins at home: The past, present and future of the Home Instruction Program for Preschool Youngsters.* Guilford, CT: The Dushkin Publishing Group.

Meijnen, G. W., & Riemersma, F. S. J. (1992). *Schoolcarrières: Een klassekwestie? Een literatuurstudie* [Schoolcareers: A matter of class? A review of literature]. Amsterdam/Lisse: Swets & Zeitlinger.

Mungra, G. (1990). *Hindoestaanse gezinnen in Nederland* [Surinamese-Hindustan families in the Netherlands]. Leiden, the Netherlands:

Rijksuniversiteit Leiden, Centrum voor Onderzoek van Maatschappelijke Tegenstellingen.

Pels, T. V. M. (1991). *Marokkaanse kleuters en hun culturele kapitaal: Opvoeden en leren in het gezin en op school* [Moroccan-Dutch children and their cultural capital: Childrearing and education at home and at school]. Amsterdam: Swets & Zeitlinger.

Research Institute for Innovation in Education (1996). *Proceedings of the Second HIPPY International Research Seminar, May 29–31, 1995.* Jerusalem: Hebrew University, School of Education.

Resing, W., & Bleichrodt, N. (1991). Development of a school behaviour judgement list (Schobl-R): A comparison among different ethnic groups. In N. Bleichrodt & P. J. D. Drenth (Eds.), *Contemporary issues in cross-cultural psychology* (pp. 400–411). Amsterdam: Swets & Zeitlinger.

Rişvanoğlu-Bilgin, S., Brouwer, L., & Priester, M. (1986). *Verschillend als de vingers van een hand. Een onderzoek naar het integratieproces van Turkse gezinnen in Nederland* [Different like the fingers of one hand. An inquiry into the social integration of Turkish families in the Netherlands]. Leiden, the Netherlands: Rijksuniversiteit Leiden, Centrum voor Onderzoek van Maatschappelijke Tegenstellingen.

Smith, L. M., & Wells, W. M. (1990). *Difficult to reach, maintain and help urban families in PAT: Issues, dilemmas, strategies and resolutions in parent education.* St. Louis: Washington University Press.

Snijders, J. Th., & Snijders-Oomen, N. (1975). *Snijders-Oomen niet-verbale intelligentieschaal S.O.N. 2–7* [The Snijders-Oomen non-verbal intelligence test S.O.N. age 2–7]. Groningen, the Netherlands: Wolters-Noordhoff.

Snijders, J. Th., Tellegen, P. J., & Laros, J. A. (1988). *Snijders-Oomen niet verbale intelligentie test S.O.N.-R. 5–7: Verantwoording & handleiding* [The Snijders-Oomen non-verbal intelligence test S.O.N. age 5–7. Manual]. Groningen, the Netherlands: Wolters-Noordhoff.

Tesser, P. T. M. (1993). *Rapportage minderheden 1993* [Minorities social-cultural report 1993]. Rijswijk, the Netherlands: Sociaal en Cultureel Planbureau.

van den Berg-Eldering, L. (1981). *Marokkaanse gezinnen in Nederland* [Moroccan families in the Netherlands]. Alphen aan den Rijn, the Netherlands: Samsom Uitgeverij.

van der Wal, G. (1995). *Gemengde berichten. De dilemma's van de omroep in een plurale samenleving* [Miscellaneous news. The national broadcasting company's dilemmas in a multicultural society]. Hilversum, the Netherlands: Nederlandse Programma Stichting.

Verhoeven, L., & Vermeer, A. (1986). *Taaltoets allochtone kinderen, Een diagnostische toets voor de mondelinge taalvaardigheid Nederlands bij allochtone kinderen van 5–9 jaar* [Language test for immigrant children. A diagnostic tool to assess oral Dutch language skills in non-indigeneous children]. Tilburg, the Netherlands: Zwijsen.

CHAPTER THIRTEEN

Integrated Early Childhood Development: The Indian Experience

Rajalakshmi Muralidharan and *Venita Kaul*

EVOLUTION OF CHILD-CARE SERVICES IN INDIA

India is a vast multilingual, multicultural, and multireligious country with a population of about 935.7 million people. Its under-five population is probably the largest in the whole world: approximately 117.4 million. The overall literacy rate as of 1995 averaged 52 percent. The female literacy rate is 38 percent, as against a male literacy rate of 64 percent. Economically, India is a poor country, with about 29 percent in urban and 33 percent in rural situations living below the poverty line (UNICEF, 1997). However, culturally, it is a rich country with its own literature, art forms, festivals, toys, and games.

The responsibility for child-care in India had always rested with the family, but with the changes in the social system such as the breakup of the joint family system, migration from rural to urban areas, and mothers' efforts to take up employment to supplement the family income, more and more families have found themselves unable to look after their young ones and have needed help from outside.

Initially, it was voluntary organizations that pioneered the setting-up of child-care services. After independence, the government of India assumed greater responsibility, establishing the Central Social Welfare Board (CSWB) in 1953 to assist voluntary organizations and mobilize their support and cooperation in the development of services for women and children. In its attempts to reach out to rural women and children, the CSWB set up Welfare Extension Projects that offered services such as maternity and child-care, first aid and primary medical aid, crèches and preschools, supplementary nutrition for children, and craft training and social education for women. The project was evaluated in 1964 and, based on the evaluation, it was decided to develop a countrywide program of integrated welfare services for children, with particular focus on the preschool child. In 1967, the Family and Child Welfare Scheme was launched, with the objectives of providing basic services to children and offering basic training to women in home craft, health, nutrition, child-care, and income-generating activities, as well as extending essential health and maternity services to these population groups. Side by side with these projects, other nutrition projects were also launched to provide supplementary nutrition to preschool children and pregnant and nursing mothers. By 1980, the nutrition projects covered about 8.2 million children and mothers (National Institute of Public Cooperation and Child Development [NIPCCD] 1984).

In 1972 the Planning Commission commissioned eight interministerial teams to review programs for young children and mothers. The report was critical, revealing that the child-care programs were characterized by inadequate coverage, resource constraints, and a basically fragmented approach to the needs of children, and were not having much impact. It became increasingly clear that the probable answer was to organize comprehensive and integrated early childhood services (Sadka, 1984). Taking previous experiences into account, the policy planners and professionals came to the following conclusions: (1) the target group should be children in the 0 to 6 age group, as they are most vulnerable; (2) preschool centers should be the focal point of delivery of services; (3) there should be an integrated package of services for the development of the preschool child whereby all services should converge on the same group of children; and (4) the coverage should be extended to the entire project rather than to only 5 to 10 centers for a population of 100,000 as in the earlier schemes (NIPCCD, 1984).

The mid 1970s also witnessed other important events, such as the declaration of the National Policy for Children, the constitution of the National Children's Board and the setting up of the National Children's Fund. The National Policy for Children recognized children as "the nation's supremely important asset" and declared the nation's responsibility for their "nurture and solicitude." The National Children's Board was set up to focus attention on the welfare and development of children and to ensure continuous planning, review, and coordination of all essential services for children (NIPCCD, 1984).

INTEGRATED CHILD DEVELOPMENT SERVICES (ICDS): AIMS AND OBJECTIVES

In pursuance of the National Policy for Children with its emphasis on the integrated delivery of early childhood services and services for expectant and nursing mothers, the Integrated Child Development Services (ICDS) scheme evolved to make a coordinated effort to deliver a package of services, aiming at the total development of the young children (NIPCCD, 1984). It was launched on an experimental basis in 1975 by setting up 33 projects. Its objectives were:

1. to improve the nutritional and health status of children in the age group 0–6 years;

2. to lay the foundation for the proper psychological, physical, and social development of the child;

3. to reduce the incidence of mortality, morbidity, malnutrition, and school dropout;

4. to achieve effective coordination of policy and implementation among various government departments;

5. to promote child development;

6. to enhance the capability of the mother to look after the normal health and nutritional needs of the child, through proper health and nutrition.

The concept of ICDS is based on the belief that the early years of childhood are crucial for the child because development in early childhood is rapid and cumulative, and any deficits resulting from a deprived and less stimulating environment in these years are likely to affect adversely the child's subsequent development. Any subsequent interventions are thus not likely to yield the desired results unless the early years are adequately attended to.

ICDS caters primarily to the poorest groups, which have the greatest need for this kind of an intervention. It is planned and implemented as an intersectoral program, which is expected to deliver a package of services in an integrated manner. The convergence of services at the same time on the same groups of children is thus likely to yield much higher dividends in terms of their development. ICDS takes a holistic view of the child, and the mother and recognizes the importance of material well-being for the healthy development of the child. It therefore offers a package of services for the children as well as for the mothers and mothers-to-be (Table 13-1). ICDS has now been universalized in the country in all 5,219 community development blocks and 310 major urban slums, thus taking the total number of centers to about 290,700. When selecting the location for a project, preference is given to those areas predominantly inhabited by vulnerable and weaker sections of society, that is, scheduled castes, scheduled tribes, and families in absolute poverty. Such target groups are likely to be found in economically backward areas, drought-prone areas, and areas in which nutritional deficiencies are rampant and social services are poorly developed.

While this applies in general to rural, tribal, and urban situations, there are differences in the sociocultural characteristics of these three target groups. Although 48 percent of the rural households covered under the project are marginal and landless farmers, this figure rises to 69 percent in the tribal areas. The urban projects are located in urban slums that are predominantly inhabited by scheduled castes. The occupational profile is entirely different here, with most falling into the categories of unskilled or semiskilled workers, shopkeepers, or unemployed. Interestingly, the rural projects cater to a higher percentage of social groups other than the scheduled castes and tribes. In terms of educational level, approximately 45 percent of the target group across the three target groups are illiterate, while 49 percent have had some schooling. The national evaluation of ICDS confirms that this program reaches out to the lowest income group, with 77 percent in the rural group, 82.8 percent in the tribal group, and 69.7 percent in the urban group reporting a monthly income of less than Rs. 1,000 per month.

Each ICDS project aims at a total coverage of a compact area, preferably a whole block in rural and tribal areas or a group of slums or wards. The population of such an area is about 100,000 in urban and rural areas and 35,000 in tribal areas. A rural or urban project consists of about 100 centers called Anganwadis (AWs), literally meaning "courtyard centers," while a tribal project consists of about 50 centers. Each center has a staff of one worker and one helper. These tend to be local women who are first sponsored by the community and then

Table 13-1. Services Offered by ICDS

Beneficiary	Services
Children under 3 years of age	Supplementary nutrition
	Immunization
	Health checks
	Referral services
Children 3–6 years of age	All four services
	plus nonformal preschool education
Expectant and nursing mothers	Health checks
	Immunization of expectant mothers against tetanus
	Supplementary nutrition
	Nutrition and health education
Other women 15–45 years	Nutrition and health education

trained for a duration of three months. Each project has about four to five supervisors and one Child Development Project Officer (CDPO) who is in charge of the overall project.

Projects are sanctioned annually by the Department of Women and Child Development of the Ministry of Human Resource Development, Government of India, after discussion with the Planning Commission and state governments. Projects are allocated on the basis of need, demonstrated capability to implement, and commitment to the program. States with greater resources initiate additional projects supported entirely with their own funds. There is normally a time lag of about 12 to 18 months between the sanctioning of a project and the beginning of the delivery of services, which is the time required to identify project sites and establish the Anganwadis (Department of Women and Child Development, 1991).

PRESCHOOL EDUCATION COMPONENT IN ICDS

The Early Childhood Education (ECE) component of the ICDS, known as its "nonformal preschool education component," may well be considered the very backbone of the program, since all six of its services tend to converge on the Anganwadi or its preschool education center. It is this center that provides access to young children and their mothers, thus serving as an entry point for various interventions. The

ECE component is conceived of as a preparation for primary education, and is aimed at reducing school dropout rate and improving retention in grades one and two of the primary schools. With an approximate 48 percent of children on average dropping out between grades one and five, this dropout phenomenon has become a major national concern. One of the reasons for this large-scale exodus from schools in the early grades is the lack of cognitive, linguistic, socioemotional, and psychomotor readiness in children to meet the demands of primary schooling. Preschool education is envisaged as a program for helping children develop this preparedness, and is therefore considered a significant input for the universalization of elementary education in the country. It is also expected to facilitate extension of elementary education to girls by providing substitute care to the younger sibling, thus leaving older girls free to attend school. To ensure this facility, it is essential to have the Anganwadi schedule coincide with the primary school schedule. To this end, the curriculum for the preschool education component is advocated to be development-oriented, focusing on the promotion of the social, emotional, cognitive, physical, and aesthetic development of the children. The curriculum rests on a theoretical framework that is now termed "progressive" and is a blend of various approaches. Initially, it was influenced largely by the Froebellian and Montessori methods, with an emphasis on learning and development through a balance of free and structured play directed toward the developmental objectives. The stress tended to be more on psychosocial development through opportunities for peer interaction. But over the last decade, the influence of Piaget's genetic epistemological theory of cognitive development has become very evident, with a visible emphasis on cognitive stimulation and active learning through concrete experiences. In addition to this, in view of the need to prepare children for school, activities for developing readiness for reading, writing, and number work are also included, particularly for children between 4 and 5 years old, who are ready to enter school.

Although Anganwadis all over the country function from early in the morning, there are regional variations in their daily duration. In the northern and eastern regions, the 3 to 6 year-olds come into the AW for one to two hours, whereas in the southern parts of the country, children stay for as long as five hours a day.

In actual practice, preschool education is transacted for no more than two hours every day, six days a week, even though children may stay longer. The daily routine of an AW begins with the AW being cleaned by the helper, who then goes out to collect and bring children in, if necessary. Once the children have been assembled, the AW worker begins the session with a cleanliness check, warming-up exercises, and prayer. This is followed by an hour or two of preschool education, after which the children are provided the nutritional supplement, along with the other beneficiaries. The worker then updates her records and registers and the afternoon time is spent either on home visits or convening community meetings. The curriculum for the preschool education component in ICDS in which the AW workers are trained is development-oriented and thematic in content, with an emphasis on play way methodology. Each week is given a theme, around which all developmental activities are to be interwoven. Stress is laid on concept formation and development of language skills through stories, rhymes, and conversation. The children in the AWs are a mixed age group of 3 to 6 year olds. Generally, they are kept together in a large group for all activities, due either to lack of space, or for the convenience of the worker. As a result, most activities are targeted at the 4 year olds.

There is a growing realization that centrally planned and produced materials and approaches may not always be relevant, given India's diverse contexts. Therefore, the national framework for the ECE component is entirely suggestive and not prescriptive. Decentralization to the state and substate levels is emphasized and encouraged, and state-level resource centers have been set up for ECE in the state education departments, in order to strengthen and support this component of the ICDS. These resource centers are primarily involved in supplementing training of field personnel in ECE, and the development of resource material in different media which would be region-specific and based on the local culture and environment. The resource material thus developed is based on local folklore, songs, rhymes, and riddles, and local culture and festivals. There is also an emphasis on the use of local material in the training of personnel.

A major deterrent to the practice of the advocated play way method in the AWs is the expectations of the parents who send their children to AWs with the intention that they should be taught to read and write. Anganwadis are either perceived as nutrition centers (possibly in centers where little else is visible), or as primary schools where children have to learn the three R's (reading, 'riting, 'rithmetic). There is a general belief or attitude that play and learning are antithetical to each other, and that children should be made to learn seriously the three R's through formal, didactic methods. In practice, therefore, more and more AWs are succumbing to parental or community pressures and beginning to teach the three R's to these young children, since these provide more tangible indicators of children's achievement. Conscious and systematic efforts are now being made to discourage this practice by providing a two-hour schedule of preschool activities planned thematically on a daily and weekly basis. Systematic efforts are also being made to use both folk and technological media in order to create the necessary sensitivity and educate the parents regarding the needs and capacities of children at this age and the significance of play for them.

TRAINING AND MONITORING IN THE ICDS CONTEXT

Once the project site is selected and approval obtained from the central government, the state government initiates the selection and training of the three levels of staff: the CDPO, the supervisor, and the Anganwadi worker. All AW workers and supervisors are women, but it has not always been possible to appoint female CDPOs.

A uniform curriculum has been developed by the National Institute of Public Cooperation and Child Development (NIPCCD) for the preservice training of all three tiers. The CDPOs are trained for two months at NIPCCD in child development, accounting, finance management, survey techniques, and community organization. The three months' training of AW workers is carried out by the nongovernmental organizations and home science colleges. The curriculum includes courses in child development, community work, identification of disabilities, record-keeping, survey techniques, family planning, preschool education, and nutrition and health education. Although a common training curriculum is given, the individual institutions have to adapt the content and methodology to match the level and background of their trainees, who, for example, are sometimes illiterate. The supervisors also undergo three months' training, the content of which is similar to the AW workers' training, with an added managerial component. Their training is done either by home science colleges or schools of social work in the universities.

The responsibility for monitoring the implementation of the ICDS program is shared by the Department of Women and Child Development, the Central Technical Committee, and the National

Institute of Public Cooperation and Child Development. The basic data originating at the AWs is supplemented by periodic surveys and special studies. The records kept by the AW workers of immunization, health checks, births, deaths, attendance at preschool learning centers, supplementary feeding, nutrition, and health education and growth charts are consolidated by CDPOs and forwarded to district and state monitoring cells, which send them on to the central government. The health component is monitored through monthly reports sent by the medical officers of the Primary Health Centers to district and state directorates of health. In addition, the Central Technical Committee also undertakes special studies and follow-up of the base line studies. The social inputs are monitored by a special cell located at NIPCCD through data collected by consultants based in university departments of home science and social work.

EVALUATION AND IMPACT STUDIES

The Planning Commission of India conducted two major evaluations of ICDS in 1978 and 1982. The positive results of these evaluations led the government of India to decide to accelerate the expansion of ICDS in 1982. UNICEF supported an independent assessment in 1983, which clearly established the cost-effectiveness of the program. It studied the outreach of the program in 16 ICDS projects spread over eight states and one union territory. The study, which was based on observations, secondary data, and interviews with beneficiaries (mothers of children under the age of 6), reported positive outcomes, such as substantial enrolment of scheduled castes and tribal children as beneficiaries (NIPCCD, 1992).

During the 1980s, several academic institutions also conducted microlevel impact studies of ICDS. A major chunk of ICDS studies has examined the health and nutrition components of the scheme. During the period of 1976–1988, about 624 baseline repeat surveys and over 250 research studies carried out by the medical personnel focusing on crucial health and nutrition indicators such as infant mortality rate, nutritional status, morbidity patterns, and immunization coverage indicated a definite improvement in the health status of the target population covered by ICDS (Tandon, 1990).

Specifically, studies reported by the Central Technical Committee indicated definite improvement in mortality rates in children from malnutrition. The rates ranged from 3.8 to 5.8 percent maximum among

ICDS beneficiaries, as compared to nearly 15 to 35 percent among the non-ICDS population. A similar picture emerged with regard to morbidity. Another large scale multicentric study conducted in 16 states demonstrated a slightly positive impact on the birth rate and infant mortality rate for ICDS versus non-ICDS populations. The birth rate was 29.5 and 27.9 for rural and urban populations respectively in the non-ICDS population, whereas in ICDS it was 26.3 and 27.4 respectively. The infant mortality rate was reported to be 85.5 for rural and 87.0 for urban non-ICDS populations, while for ICDS the comparative statistics were 67.0 and 80.0 (Tandon & Sachdeva, 1996).

Studies of the impact of preschool education have generally yielded positive results. A follow-up study of the AW children showed that the children who attended AWs were better adjusted and picked up new materials faster in the first two years of schooling (Sunderlal & Rajwati, 1981). Two other studies showed that, by comparison with non-ICDS children, children attending AWs scored higher in language and cognitive development (Khosla, 1986) and performed better in first and second grades of primary school (Sood, 1987). Another study showed a significant positive relationship between the competence of the Anganwadi worker and the cognitive scores of children, especially in the 4-plus and 5-plus group (Pandey, 1988).

In 1989–1990 an impact evaluation of the ICDS on the psychosocial development of children between 3 and 6 years of age was carried out in three states: Andhra Pradesh, Karnataka, and Tamil Nadu. Ten to fifteen villages, each with a population of about 1,000 and with a functioning AW were randomly selected at each of the seven research centers. Approximately 750 children were covered at each center, with 250 children in each age group, that is, 3 to <4, 4 to <5 and 5 to <6 years. The surveyed children were sub-grouped into: (1) a beneficiary group, that is, children who had participated regularly (three days or more in a week for a minimum period of six months) in the AW program; (2) a control group, when children did not meet the above criteria of participation. A culture-appropriate ICDS development screening test battery was used to assess psychosocial development. The battery included relevant items (milestones) in five major areas of psychosocial development. The 50th percentile was taken as the average age. Scoring was done by arranging the items in order of difficulty based on the 50th percentile age of attainment. The age at which the child failed all other items was identified in the motor and mental areas. Thus, each child had a motor score and a mental score equal to their motor and mental age. The total of motor and mental scores was termed as "development age." The results of the study indicated that the beneficiary children in all three states achieved significantly higher motor, mental, and developmental age scores than the control group.

As a part of the Project on Monitoring and Evaluation of Social Components, five in-depth studies were conducted on the preschool component in five different ICDS blocks. Of the 15 AWs included in the larger project, two AWs at the extreme polarities were identified in terms of quality of programs through participatory observation. These were termed "highest-ranking" and "lowest-ranking" AWs. A non-ICDS area in the neighborhood was selected as a control. Comparisons among these showed that: (1) the AW children scored higher in motor skills, conceptual and readiness skills, language skills, and personal social behavior when compared with non-ICDS children; (2) preschool children from the highest ranked AWs performed better on all skills except personal social behavior by comparison with children from the lowest ranking AWs; (3) primary school children who had been through AWs performed better in grades one and two as compared with non-ICDS children—moreover, the children from the highest-ranking AWs excelled in academic performance and school adjustment when compared with children who came to the primary schools from the lowest ranking AWs; (4) the mothers' level of awareness about the value of preschool education and health and nutritional needs of children was higher in the ICDS area than that in the non-ICDS area; and (5) awareness and involvement in child-care were better in the mothers of the highest-ranking AWs than in those from the lowest-ranking AWs (Sharma, 1987).

It is becoming imperative to ensure some degree of quality control, particularly if one considers the findings of the larger project indicating that children in many AWs attend only to collect food. Often AWs are devoid of play material or attractive display. In terms of activities, except for singing rhymes and counting, no other stimulating activities are carried out in the daily program.

The other type of study undertaken examined the intervention. These studies were conducted on the assumption that given adequate training, the AWs should be in a position to run fairly satisfactory preschool programs. The major findings were: (1) even in remote tribal areas with semi-literate workers, after a short training of the AW workers and a supply of minimum materials, the AW children from the experimental group performed much better in language and cognitive tasks after eight months of intervention than children in the control group whose AW workers did not receive any training (Muralidharan & Kaur, 1984); (2) there was a significant difference between pre- and postintervention scores in the knowledge and skills of AW workers and in the cognitive abilities of children (Sahni & Agarwal, 1984); and (3) intervention through radio broadcasts coupled with supplying simple manuals to AW workers resulted in children performing better in language skills (Muralidharan, 1990).

In 1990, the Department of Women and Child Development proposed comprehensively reviewing the scheme, and entrusted the NIPCCD with the task of evaluating ICDS on a national level. The study, which was carried out during 1990–1992, was conducted with the objectives of ascertaining the benefits of the ICDS scheme and the differences in implementation and utilization of services in urban, rural, and tribal areas; of identifying problems and bottlenecks; and of ascertaining the degree of community involvement in the implementation of ICDS. The sample for the study was drawn from 54 rural, 28 tribal, and 18 urban projects selected from the 25 states and one Union Territory (National Institute of Public Cooperation and Child Development, 1992). The findings of the study, with particular reference to family, school, and literacy, were as follows:

1. A majority of AWs (60 percent) were found to have clean surroundings, and in around 75 percent of AWs, drinking water was available from taps and hand pumps.

2. As compared to earlier evaluations, there was a definite improvement in the educational qualifications of AW workers. Fifty percent of AW workers had completed 10 years of schooling, and 13 percent had higher qualifications.

3. The time allocation for the AW workers was one to two hours for preschool education (60 percent), one hour for nutrition programs (79 percent), one hour for maintenance of records (80 percent), and one hour on home visits (50 percent).

4. The coverage of 3 to 6 year olds for the preschool program was around 56 percent in the urban and rural areas, but a little less in tribal areas.

5. Comparison between ICDS and non-ICDS areas indicated that much fewer children (23.5 percent) were receiving preschool education in non-ICDS areas as compared to 85 percent in ICDS areas.

6. While 50–56 percent of the children attending AWs could do rote counting and manipulate crayons with control, a very small percentage of non-ICDS children could recognize or identify colors.

7. Of all the children in the age group 4–15 years, both in ICDS and non-ICDS areas, 89 percent of the children with preschool experience were found to be continuing their education in primary school as compared to 52–60 percent without preschool experience. A lower percentage of the children with preschool experience was found to be in the "never enrolled" category in both ICDS and non-ICDS areas.

8. Of all the children currently in primary school, the number with preschool experience was 85 percent in ICDS areas, but only 15 percent in non-ICDS areas.

A combined longitudinal and cross-sectional study was conducted on 31,483 children in primary grades in eight states of the country to find out the impact of ECE experience on the rates of retention in the primary grades. The study indicated differences in percentages of retention between children with ECE experience and those with direct entry into school, the range being from 8.04 percent to as high as 20.52 percent (Kaul, Ramachandran, & Upadhyaya, 1993).

A study conducted in 1996 by the National Council of Educational Research and Training in collaboration with state agencies in 10 states on the "Status of Preschool Education Component of the ICDS and its perception and extent of utilization by the community" indicated that approximately 95 percent of Anganwadis resort to teaching the three R's as a major part of the curriculum, possibly due to persistent parental pressures. The study, however, clearly demonstrates a positive attitude of the community toward the AW program, and indicates a felt demand for the service.

CONCLUSION

The Government of India's National Policy on Education 1986 (NPE) gave due importance to Early Childhood Care and Education (ECCE). It viewed ECCE as a crucial input in the strategy of human resource development, as a feeder and support program for primary education, and as a support service for working women.

While describing the content and process of ECCE, the Program of Action 1992 advocated an approach for the total development of the child. It suggested that in addition to regular medical checks, supplementary nutrition, and growth monitoring, the program should include child-centered and process-oriented play activities aimed to foster joy and curiosity in children, promote language and cognitive skills, develop creativity and confidence, and promote muscular development. It is also stated that norms and minimum standards will be devised with a view to ensuring better quality of ECCE practices. All efforts are being made to establish linkage between ECCE centers and primary schools. At the moment, district-level primary education programs in which ECCE and convergence of services have been identified as an important core component are being planned under the Social Safety Net Scheme.

ICDS is probably the world's largest scheme for preschool children and mothers. It has been in existence for more than 20 years and has yielded dividends in terms of a decrease in infant mortality rate, better nutritional status of children, and higher enrolment and better retention in primary schools. It has reached out to poor and needy families and has made ECCE services accessible to them. The ICDS workers at the grassroots level are mostly local women of the community who easily identify themselves with the needs and problems of the families. These women are considered as honorary workers and paid a nominal honorarium of Rs. 400 per month. The intersectoral approach of ICDS as well as the involvement of voluntary organizations, social activists, and professionals are some of the major strengths of the scheme. Keeping these points in mind, it is felt that this scheme can be replicated in other sociocultural contexts to reach out to children and mothers with similar problems and needs.

However, the situation of the ICDS merits some criticism as well. The major issue in its implementation is that of quality. Rapid quantitative expansion in the last few years, leading to universalization of this facility in the country, has made the task of ensuring some degree of quality control extremely challenging.

To this end, the major areas that need to be imperatively addressed are those of resources, training, monitoring, and community participation. Research studies have clearly indicated that preschool education *per se* is not sufficient: rather, the quality of the program offered is important. Also, a high-cost program need not be a good-quality program, but a low-cost program cannot be a good quality program unless certain optimal facilities are provided. At present, the facilities and resources available to the AW workers are the barest minimum, with limited physical space, limited materials, and an extremely low honorarium for the worker, which altogether do not add up to a very motivating, facilitative, and encouraging work situation. It has been strongly recommended, therefore, that a certain minimum of facilities must be provided if the ICDS is to deliver results.

The second area that needs to be addressed is that of training. The existing provision of a three months' job training followed by a short refresher after a few years for the AW workers is just not adequate, particularly since in most cases they do not have very high academic qualifications. In a few states workers in some interior areas are even semi-literate or illiterate. In such cases the nature of training imparted is therefore far beyond their level of comprehension. Continuous training inputs based on field demonstrations and practice sessions are therefore essential, both to refresh the skills of the workers and to sustain their interest and motivation.

Even with the best of training, the AWs often do not implement the program as advised, primarily since it involves a high level of motivation and competence to be able to generate new material/activities and plan their preschool education program in an effective manner. The workers also succumb to the pressure from parents to teach the three R's. It is therefore imperative to educate the parents and community about the right kind of preschool education, so that they can effectively provide support and monitoring. The preferred mode in all social sector programs in the country today is decentralization to the level of the community, with Panchayati Raj (community governance) having been instituted across the country in a statutory form. It is envisaged that the scheme should adopt measures that will help build a sense of ownership in the community, so that the program can be closely planned and monitored by the community in order to facilitate maintenance of quality control. Advocacy and community education have therefore been identified as crucial areas to be addressed in the immediate future. The need to network with the nongovernmental sector and related organizations for effective convergence of services has also been highlighted as an area demanding attention.

The implementation of the ICDS program has demonstrated the impact of the quality of supply of service on the creation of demand for it. Wherever the center is running well, the community has come forward to support and assist with both material and human resources. Yet by and large, the program is identified as a government program, and the community expects it to be run at government expense. To run the program with an element of interest, efficiency, and accountability, there can be no alternative to community ownership of the program and its decentralized, community-based management, but there is growing realization that if this is to be achieved, the community has to be prepared and empowered to carry out this role.

REFERENCES

Department of Women and Child Development (1991). *15 years of ICDS: an Overview.* New Delhi: Author.

Kaul, V., Ramachandran, C., & Upadhyaya, G. C. (1993). *Impact of ECE on retention in primary grades.* New Delhi: National Council of Educational Research and Training.

Khosla, R. (1986). *Preschool education in the ICDS—an impact study.* New Delhi: National Institute of Public Cooperation and Child Development.

Muralidharan, R. (1990). Early childhood education: Issues, policies, programs and actions. *ICCW News Bulletin.*

Muralidharan, R., & Kaur, B. (1984). *The Impact of an intervention program on the language and cognitive development of preschool children from urban Anganwadis.* New Delhi: National Council of Education Research and Training, Mimeo.

National Council of Educational Research and Training (1996). *Status of preschool education component of ICDS and its perception and extent of utilization by the community.* Unpublished Manuscript.

National Institute of Public Cooperation and Child Development (1984). *Manual on Integrated child development service.* New Delhi: Author.

National Institute of Public Cooperation and Child Development (1992). *National Evaluation of Integrated Child Development Services.* New Delhi: Author.

Pandey, H. (1988). *Impact of the preschool education component in the ICDS program on the cognitive development of children.* Unpublished doctoral dissertation, Bharathiar University, Coimbatore, India.

Sadka, N. L. O. (1984). *Integrated child development services.* New Delhi: UNICEF.

Sahni, S., & Agarwal S. (1984). *A study of an intervention in ongoing ICDS program to promote cognitive abilities of preschoolers.* Unpublished master's thesis, Haryana Agricultural University, Hissar, India.

Sharma, A. (1987). *Monitoring of social components of ICDS: A pilot project.* New Delhi: National Institute of Public Cooperation and Child Development.

Sood, N. (1987). *An evaluation of nonformal preschool education component in Mongolpuri ICDS block.* New Delhi: National Institute of Public Cooperation and Child Development.

Sunderlal, A. & Rajwati, A. (1981). *Early childhood education—an effect to enhance school enrolment.* Rohtak, India: Medical College, Department of Preventive and Social Medicine.

Tandon, B. N. (Ed.), (1990). *ICDS—Evaluation and Research 1975–1988.* New Delhi: Department of Women and Child Development.

Tandon, B. N. & Sachdeva, Y., (Eds.), (1996). *Survey, evaluation and research system in integrated child development services, 1970–1995.* New Delhi: Department of Women and Child Development.

UNICEF (1997). *The state of the world's children.* New York: Oxford University Press.

CHAPTER FOURTEEN

Success for All: Effects of Prevention and Early Intervention on Elementary Students' Reading

Robert E. Slavin and *Nancy A. Madden*

Every September, three million 6 year-olds enter United States kindergartens. Every one of them is absolutely confident that he or she is going to do well in school. Every one of them is smart and knows it. Every one is highly motivated, eager to learn.

Just two years later, many of these bright, enthusiastic children have learned a hard lesson. Many have failed first grade; in some urban districts, as many as 20 percent of first graders are retained each year. Others barely pass, but are beginning to see that they are not making it. In particular, some students know that they are not reading as well as their classmates. As they proceed through the elementary grades, many students begin to see that they are failing at their full-time jobs. When this happens, things begin to unravel. Failing students begin to have poor motivation and poor self-expectations, which lead to continued poor achievement, in a declining spiral that ultimately leads to despair, delinquency, and dropout.

Remediating learning deficits after they are already well-established is extremely difficult. Children who have already failed to learn to read, for example, are now anxious about reading, which interferes with their ability to focus on it. Their motivation to read may be low. Clearly, the time to provide additional help to children who are at risk is early, when children are still motivated and confident and when any learning deficits are relatively small and remediable. The most important goal in educational programming for students at risk of school failure is to try to make certain that we do not squander the greatest resource we have: the enthusiasm and positive self-expectations of young children themselves.

In practical terms, what this perspective implies is that services for at-risk children must be shifted from an emphasis on remediation to an emphasis on prevention and early intervention. Prevention means providing developmentally appropriate preschool and kindergarten programs so that students will enter first grade ready to succeed, and it means providing regular classroom teachers with effective instructional programs, curricula, and staff development to enable them to see that most students are successful the first time they are taught. Early intervention means that supplementary instructional services are provided early in students' schooling and that they are intensive enough to bring at-risk students quickly to a level at which they can profit from good quality classroom instruction.

In this chapter, we describe the nature and outcomes of a program designed around this vision, a program that emphasizes prevention and early intensive intervention to see that all children in schools serving disadvantaged students are successful in basic skills the first time they are taught, and that they can build on that success throughout the elementary years.

The name of this program is Success for All. The idea behind Success for All is to use everything we know about effective instruction for students at risk to direct all aspects of school and classroom organization toward the goal of preventing academic deficits from appearing in the first place, recognizing and intensively intervening with any deficits that do appear, and providing students with a rich and full curriculum to enable them to build on their firm foundation in basic skills. The commitment of Success for All is to do whatever it takes to see that every child makes it through third grade at or near grade level in reading and other basic skills, and then goes beyond this in the later grades.

Success for All is currently being implemented in 457 schools in 120 districts in 31 U.S. states (Fall, 1996). Almost all are among the most disadvantaged and lowest-achieving schools in their respective districts; most qualify as Title I schoolwide projects, which means that at least 50 percent of students are in poverty. Many serve student bodies that are almost 100 percent African American or 100 percent Hispanic, although many are integrated. The schools are located in all parts of the United States, and are located in rural as well as urban settings. Adaptations of the program are also being implemented in Canada, Australia, Israel, Mexico, and the Netherlands.

The main elements of Success for All are described in the following section.

OVERVIEW OF SUCCESS FOR ALL COMPONENTS

Success for All has somewhat different components at different sites, depending on the school's needs and the resources available to implement the program. However, there is a common set of elements characteristic of all (adapted from Slavin, Madden, Dolan, & Wasik, 1996).

Reading Program

Success for All uses a reading curriculum based on research and effective practices in beginning reading (e.g., Adams, 1990), and on effective use of cooperative learning (Slavin, 1995; Stevens, Madden, Slavin, & Farnish, 1987).

Reading teachers at every grade level begin the reading time by reading children's literature to students and engaging them in a discussion of the story to enhance their understanding of the story, listening and speaking vocabulary, and knowledge of story structure. In kindergarten and first grade, the program emphasizes the development of oral language and prereading skills through the use of thematically-based units that incorporate areas such as language, art, and writing under a science or social studies topic. A component called Story Telling and Retelling (STaR) involves the students in listening to, retelling, and dramatizing children's literature. Big books as well as oral and written composing activities allow students to develop concepts of print as they also develop knowledge of story structure. There is also a strong emphasis on phonetic awareness activities that help to develop auditory discrimination and support the development of reading readiness strategies.

Reading Roots is typically introduced in the second semester of kindergarten or in first grade. This K–1 beginning reading program uses as its base a series of phonetically regular but meaningful and interesting minibooks and emphasizes repeated oral reading to partners as well as to the teacher. The minibooks begin with a set of "shared stories," in which part of a story is written in small type (read by the teacher) and part is written in large type (read by the students). The student portion uses a phonetically controlled vocabulary. Taken together, the teacher and student portions create interesting, worthwhile stories. Over time, the teacher portion diminishes and the student portion lengthens, until students are reading the entire book. This scaffolding allows students to read interesting literature when they only know a few letter sounds.

Letters and letter sounds are introduced in an active, engaging set of activities that begins with oral language and moves into written symbols. Individual sounds are integrated into a context of words, sentences, and stories. Instruction is provided in story structure, specific comprehension skills, metacognitive strategies for self-assessment and self-correction, and integration of reading and writing.

Spanish bilingual programs use an adaptation of *Reading Roots* called *Lee Conmigo* ("Read With Me"). *Lee Conmigo* employs the same instructional strategies as *Reading Roots*, but uses Spanish reading materials.

When students reach the primer reading level, they use a program called *Reading Wings,* an adaptation of Cooperative Integrated Reading and Composition (CIRC) (Stevens et al., 1987). *Reading Wings* uses cooperative learning activities built around story structure, prediction, summarization, vocabulary building, decoding practice, and story-related writing. Students engage in partner reading and structured discussion of stories or novels, and work toward mastery of the vocabulary and content of the story in teams. Story-related writing is also shared within teams. Cooperative learning both increases students' motivation and engages students in cognitive activities known to contribute to reading comprehension, such as elaboration, summarization, and rephrasing (see Slavin, 1995). Research on CIRC has found it to increase significantly students' reading comprehension and language skills (Stevens et al., 1987).

In addition to these story-related activities, teachers provide direct instruction in reading comprehension skills, and students practice these skills in their teams. Classroom libraries of trade books at students' reading levels are provided for each teacher, and students read books of their choice for homework for 20 minutes each night. Home readings are shared via presentations, summaries, puppet shows, and other formats twice a week during "book club" sessions.

Materials to support *Reading Wings* through the sixth grade (or beyond) exist in English and Spanish. The English materials are built around children's literature and around the most widely used basal series and anthologies. Supportive materials have been developed for more than 100 children's novels and for most current basal series. Spanish materials are similarly built around Spanish-language novels or basals.

Beginning in the second semester of program implementation, Success for All schools usually implement a writing/language arts program based primarily on cooperative learning principles (see Slavin, Madden, & Stevens, 1989/90).

Students in grades one to three (and sometimes four to five or four to six) are regrouped for reading. The students are assigned to heterogeneous, age-grouped classes most of the day, but during a regular 90-minute reading period they are regrouped by reading performance levels into reading classes of students all at the same level. For example, a 2–1 reading class might contain first-, second-, and third-grade students all reading at the same level. The reading classes are smaller than homerooms because tutors and other certified staff (such as librarians or art teachers) teach reading during this common reading period. Regrouping allows teachers to teach the whole reading class without having to break the class into reading groups. This greatly reduces the time spent in seatwork and increases direct instruction time, eliminating workbooks, dittos, or other follow-up activities that are needed in classes that have multiple reading groups. The regrouping is a form of the Joplin Plan, which has been found to increase reading achievement in the elementary grades (Slavin, 1987).

Eight-Week Reading Assessments

At eight-week intervals, reading teachers assess student progress through the reading program. The results of the assessments are used to determine who is to receive tutoring, to change students' reading groups, to suggest other adaptations in students' programs, and to identify students who need other types of assistance, such as family interventions or screening for vision and hearing problems. The assessments are curriculum-based measures that include teacher observations and judgments as well as more formal measures of reading comprehension.

Reading Tutors

One of the most important elements of the Success for All model is the use of tutors to promote students' success in reading. One-to-one tutoring is the most effective form of instruction known (see Wasik & Slavin, 1993). The tutors are certified teachers with experience teaching Title I, special education, and/or primary reading. Often, well-qualified paraprofessionals also tutor children with less severe reading problems. In this case, a certified tutor monitors their work and assists with the diagnostic assessment and intervention strategies. Tutors work one-on-one with students who are having difficulties keeping up with their reading groups. The tutoring occurs in 20-minute sessions during times other than reading or math periods.

In general, tutors support students' success in the regular reading curriculum, rather than teaching different objectives. For example, the tutor will work with a student on the same story and concepts being read and taught in the regular reading class. However, tutors seek to identify learning problems and use different strategies to teach the same skills. They also teach metacognitive skills beyond those taught in the classroom program. Schools may have as many as six or more teachers serving as tutors depending on school size, need for tutoring, and other factors.

During daily 90-minute reading periods, certified tutors serve as additional reading teachers to reduce class size for reading. Reading teachers and tutors use brief forms to communicate about students' specific problems and needs and meet at regular times to coordinate their approaches with individual children.

Initial decisions about reading group placement and the need for tutoring are based on informal reading inventories that the tutors give to each child. Subsequent reading group placements and tutoring assignments are made using the curriculum-based assessments described above. First graders receive priority for tutoring, on the assumption that the primary function of the tutors is to help all students be successful in reading the first time, before they fail and become remedial readers.

Preschool and Kindergarten

Most Success for All schools provide a half-day preschool and/or a full-day kindergarten for eligible students. The preschool and kindergarten programs focus on providing a balanced and developmentally appropriate learning experience for young children. The curriculum emphasizes the development and use of language. It provides a balance of academic readiness and nonacademic music, art, and movement activities in a series of thematic units. Readiness activities include use of the Peabody Language Development Kits and STaR in which students retell stories read by the teachers. Prereading activities begin during the second semester of kindergarten.

Family Support Team

Parents are an essential part of the formula for success in Success for All. A Family Support Team works in each school, serving to make families feel comfortable in the school and become active supporters of their child's education as well as providing specific services. The Family Support Team consists of the school's parent liaison, vice-principal (if any), counselor (if any), facilitator, and any other appropriate staff either already present in the school or added to the school staff.

The Family Support Team first works toward good relations with parents and toward increasing involvement in the schools. Family Support Team members may complete "welcome" visits for new families. They organize many attractive programs in the school, such as parenting skills workshops. Many schools use a program called "Raising Readers," in which parents are given strategies to use in reading with their own children.

The Family Support Team also intervenes to solve problems. For example, they may contact parents whose children are frequently absent to see what resources can be provided to assist the family in getting their child to school. Family support staff, teachers, and parents work together to solve school behavior problems. Also, family support staff is called on to provide assistance when students seem to be working at less than their full potential because of problems at home. Families of students who are not receiving adequate sleep or nutrition, who need glasses, who are not attending school regularly, or who are exhibiting serious behavior problems may receive family support assistance.

The Family Support Team is strongly integrated into the academic program of the school. It receives referrals from teachers and tutors regarding children who are not making adequate academic progress, and thereby constitutes an additional stage of intervention for students in need above and beyond that provided by the classroom teacher or tutor. The Family Support Team also encourages and trains the parents to fulfill numerous volunteer roles within the school, ranging from providing a listening ear to emerging readers to helping in the school cafeteria.

Program Facilitator

A program facilitator works at each school to oversee (with the principal) the operation of the Success for All model. The facilitator helps plan the Success for All program, helps the principal with scheduling, and visits classes and tutoring sessions frequently to help teachers and tutors with individual problems. He or she works directly with the teachers on implementation of the curriculum, classroom management, and other issues; helps teachers and tutors deal with any behavior problems or other special problems; and coordinates the activities of the Family Support Team with those of the instructional staff.

Teachers and Teacher Training

The teachers and tutors are regular certified teachers. They receive detailed teachers' manuals supplemented by three days of in-service training at the beginning of the school year. For classroom teachers of grades 1–5 and for reading tutors, these training sessions focus on implementation of the reading program, and their detailed teachers' manuals cover general teaching strategies as well as specific lessons. Preschool and kindergarten teachers and aides are trained in the use of the STaR and Peabody programs, thematic units, and other aspects of the preschool and kindergarten models. Tutors later receive two additional days of training on tutoring strategies and reading assessment.

Throughout the year, additional in-service presentations are made by the facilitators and other project staff on such topics as classroom management, instructional pace, and cooperative learning. Facilitators also organize many informal sessions to allow teachers to share problems and problem solutions, suggest changes, and discuss individual children. The staff development model used in Success for All emphasizes relatively brief initial training with extensive classroom follow-up, coaching, and group discussion.

Advisory Committee

An advisory committee composed of the building principal, program facilitator, teacher representatives, parent representatives, and family support staff meets regularly to review the progress of the program and to identify and solve any problems that arise. In most schools, existing site-based management teams are adapted to fulfill this function. In addition, grade-level teams and the Family Support Team meet regularly to discuss common problems and solutions and to make decisions in their areas of responsibility.

Special Education

Every effort is made to deal with students' learning problems within the context of the regular classroom, as supplemented by tutors. Tutors evaluate students' strengths and weaknesses and develop strategies to teach in the most effective way. In some schools, special education teachers work as tutors and reading teachers with students identified as learning disabled as well as other students experiencing learning problems who are at risk for special education placement. One major goal of Success for All is to keep students with learning problems out of special education if at all possible, and to serve any students who do qualify for special education in a way that does not disrupt their regular classroom experience (see Slavin, 1996).

Funding

Most funds to support implementation of Success for All are reallocations of funds high-poverty schools would typically receive whether or not they are implementing the program. In particular, high-poverty schools in the United States receive federal Title I funds. These can only be used for purposes directly related to improving the performance of low achievers. This means that schools with low per-pupil expenditures (such as those in most inner-city districts) may nevertheless have a substantial amount of funding to use for purposes beyond such basic costs as teachers' salaries, buildings, and textbooks. Traditionally, Title I money has overwhelmingly supported remedial teachers and classroom aides. Success for All typically uses these positions in different ways (as teachers and facilitators), rather than adding resources to the school. In addition to Title I, many schools incorporate special funding from special education, bilingual education, state funds for high-poverty schools, and so on.

Relentlessness

While the particular elements of Success for All may vary from school to school, there is one feature we try to make consistent in all: a relentless focus on the success of every child. It would be entirely possible to have tutoring and curriculum change and family support and other services yet still not ensure the success of at-risk children. Success does not come from piling on additional services, but rather from coordinating human resources around a well-defined goal, constantly assessing progress toward that goal, and never giving up until success is achieved.

None of the elements of Success for All are completely new or unique to this program. What is most distinctive about the program is its schoolwide, coordinated, and proactive plan for translating positive expectations into concrete success for all children. Every child can complete elementary school reading confidently, strategically, and joyfully and can maintain the enthusiasm and positive self-expectations with which they came to first grade. The purpose of Success for All is to see that this vision can become a practical reality in every school.

RESEARCH ON SUCCESS FOR ALL

From the very beginning, there has been a strong focus in Success for All on research and evaluation. Evaluations have compared Success for All schools to matched comparison schools on measures of reading performance, starting with cohorts in kindergarten or in first grade, and continuing to follow these students as long as possible (details of the evaluation design appear below). Vagaries of funding and other local problems have ended some evaluations prematurely, but most have been able to follow Success for All schools for many years. As of this writing, there are seven years of continuous data from the six original schools in Baltimore and Philadelphia, and varying numbers of years of data from seven other districts, making a total of 23 schools (plus their matched control schools). Table 14-1 lists the districts and characteristics of the schools.

In order to summarize the outcomes from all schools and all years involved in experimental control comparisons, this chapter uses a method of analysis called a multi-site replicated experiment (Slavin &

Madden, 1993), in which each grade-level *cohort* (students in all classes in that grade in a given year) in each school is considered a replication. In other words, if three first grades have proceeded through school X, each first-grade cohort (compared to its control group) produces an effect size representing the experimental-control difference in student achievement that year. An effect size is the difference between experimental and control means divided by the control group's standard deviation. For example, across 23 schools ever involved in Success for All evaluations, there are a total of 55 first-grade cohorts (about 4,000 students in experimental schools and a similar number in control schools) from which experimental and control achievement data have been collected (see Slavin et al., 1996).

In addition to applying the multi-site replicated experiment design to reading data from Success for All schools, this chapter also summarizes results of several studies in particular subsets of schools. These include studies of outcomes of the Spanish version of Success for All, *Lee Conmigo;* studies of Success for All with students in English as a Second Language (ESL) programs; studies of special education outcomes of the model; and studies comparing Success for All and Reading Recovery. This chapter summarizes the state of research on Success for All in all study sites as of the seventh year of program implementation.

EVALUATION DESIGN

A common evaluation design, with variations due to local circumstances, has been used in all Success for All evaluations (see Madden, Slavin, Karweit, Dolan, & Wasik, 1993; Slavin et al., 1996). Every Success for All school involved in a formal evaluation is matched with a control school that is similar in poverty level (percent of students qualifying for free lunch), historical achievement level, ethnicity, and other factors. Across the 23 control schools in nine districts teaching practices and school organization varied widely, but most control schools used traditional basal readers and reading groups (the exception was the two California districts, in which control teachers generally used some form of whole language approach, children's literature, and flexible grouping). Title I funds in control schools were primarily used for remedial pull-outs for children having reading problems and/or for classroom aides; one control school in

Table 14-1. Characteristics of Success for All Schools in the Longitudinal Study

District/School	Enrollment	% Free Lunch	Ethnicity	Date Began SFA	Data Collected	Pre-School ?	Full day K?	Comments
Baltimore								
B1	500	83	B-96% W-4%	1987	88-94	yes	yes	First SFA school; had additional funds first 2 years.
B2	500	96	B-100%	1988	89-94	some	yes	Had add'l funds first 4 years.
B3	400	96	B-100%	1988	89-94	some	yes	
B4	500	85	B-100%	1988	89-94	some	yes	
B5	650	96	B-100%	1988	89-94	some	yes	
Philadelphia								
P1	620	96	A-60% W-20%					Large ESL program for Cambodian children.
			B-20%	1988	89-94	no	yes	
P2	600	97	B-100%	1991	92-93	some	yes	
P3	570	96	B-100%	1991	92-93	no	yes	
P4	840	98	B-100%	1991	93	no	yes	
P5	700	98	L-100%	1992	93-94	no	yes	Study only involves students in Spanish bilingual program.
Charleston, SC								
CS1	500	40	B-60% W-40%	1990	91-92	no	no	

Table 14-1 (continued)

District/School	Enrollment	% Free Lunch	Ethnicity	Date Began SFA	Data Collected	Pre-School?	Full day K?	Comments
Memphis, TN								
MT1	350	90	B-95% W-5%	1990	91-94	yes	no	Program implemented only in grades K-2.
MT2	530	90	B-100%	1993	94	yes	yes	
MT3	290	86	B-100%	1993	94	yes	yes	
MT4	370	90	B-100%	1993	94	yes	yes	
Ft. Wayne, IN								
F1	330	65	B-56% W-44%	1991	92-94	no	yes	SFA schools (& controls) are part of desegregatiom plan.
F2	250	55	B-55% W-45%	1991	92-94	no	yes	SFA schools (& controls) are part of desegregatiom plan.
Mongomery, AL								
MA1	450	95	B-100%	1991	93-94	no	yes	
MA2	460	97	B-100%	1991	93-94	no	yes	
Caldwell, ID								
CI1	400	20	W-80% L-20%	1991	93-94	no	no	Study compares two SFA schools to Reading Recovery school.

Table 14-1 (continued)

District/School	Enrollment	% Free Lunch	Ethnicity	Date Began SFA	Data Collected	Pre-School ?	Full day K?	Comments
Modesto, CA								
MC1	640	70	W-54% L-25% A-17% B-4%	1992	94	yes	no	Large ESL program for students speaking 17 languages.
MC2	560	98	L-66% W-24% A-10%	1992	94	yes	no	Large Spanish bilingual program.
Riverside, CA								
R1	930	73	L-54% W-33% B-10% A-3%	1992	94	yes	no	Large Spanish bilingual and ESL programs. Year-round school.

Key

B—African American   L—Latino
A—Asian American   W—White

Source: Adapted from R. E. Slavin, N. A. Madden, L. Dolan, B. A. Wasik, S.M. Ross, L.J. Smith, & M.R. Dianda (1996), Success for All: A summary of Research, *Journal of Education of Students Placed at Risk, 1,* 41–76. Copyright 1996 Lawrence Erlbaum Associates. By permission of the publisher.

Caldwell, Idaho, had a Reading Recovery program. Most control schools had Title I-funded parent liaisons or home-school coordinators, and other support staff such as counselors, social workers, and ESL or bilingual teachers. (For more information on the particular conditions of each experimental-control comparison each year, including data establishing the initial equivalence of experimental and control schools, see the individual site reports listed in the references).

Children in the Success for All schools are matched on district-administered standardized test scores given in kindergarten, or (starting in 1991 in six districts) on Peabody Picture Vocabulary Test (PPVT) scores given by the project in the fall of kindergarten or first grade. In some cases, analyses of covariance rather than individual child matches were used, and at Key School in Philadelphia, schools were matched but individual children could not be (because the school serves many limited-English-proficient students who were not tested by the district in kindergarten).

The measures used in the evaluations were as follows:

1. *Woodcock Reading Mastery Test.* Three Woodcock scales, Word Identification, Word Attack, and Passage Comprehension, were individually administered to students by trained testers. Word Identification assesses recognition of common sight words, Word Attack assesses phonetic synthesis skills, and Passage Comprehension assesses comprehension in context. Students in Spanish bilingual programs were given the Spanish versions of these scales.

2. *Durrell Analysis of Reading Difficulty.* The Durrell Oral Reading scale was also individually administered to students in grades 1–3. It presents a series of graded reading passages which students read aloud, followed by comprehension questions.

3. *Gray Oral Reading Test.* Comprehension and passage scores from the Gray Oral Reading Test were obtained from students in grades 4–5.

In all cases, tests were administered by testers who were unaffiliated with the project. Every attempt was made to keep testers unaware of whether a school was a Success for All school or a control school. Testers were trained to a high degree of reliability, and then observed on a sampling basis to be sure they were administering the tests properly.

Except at Key School, analyses of covariance with pretests as covariates were used to compare raw scores in all evaluations, and separate analyses were conducted for students in general and for students in the lowest 25 percent of their grades. At Key School, analyses of variance were used and results were reported separately for Asian (mostly Cambodian) students and for non-Asian students.

The tables and figures presented in this chapter summarize student performance in grade equivalents (adjusted for covariates) and effect size (proportion of a standard deviation separating the experimental and control groups), averaging across individual measures. Neither grade equivalents nor averaged scores were used in the analyses, but they are presented here as a useful summary. Outcomes are presented for all students in the relevant grades in Success for All and control schools, and also those for the students in the lowest 25 percent of their grades, who are most at risk. In most cases, the low 25 percent was determined based on Peabody Picture Vocabulary Test scores given as pretests. In Baltimore and Charleston, South Carolina, however, Peabody pretests were not given and low 25 percent analyses involve the lowest-performing students at posttest. At Philadelphia's Key School, outcomes are shown separately for Asian and non-Asian students.

Each of the evaluations summarized in this chapter follows children who began in Success for All in first grade or earlier, in comparison to children who had attended the control school over the same period. Because Success for All is a prevention and early intervention program, students who start in it after first grade are not considered to have received the full treatment (although they are of course served within the schools). For more details on methods and findings, see Slavin et al. (1996) and the full site reports.

READING OUTCOMES

The results of the multi-site replicated experiment evaluating Success for All are summarized in Figure 14-1. Statistically significant ($p = .05$ or better) positive effects of Success for All (compared to controls) were found on every measure at every grade level, 1–5. For students in general, effect sizes (*ES*) averaged around a half standard deviation at all grade levels. Effects were somewhat higher than this for the

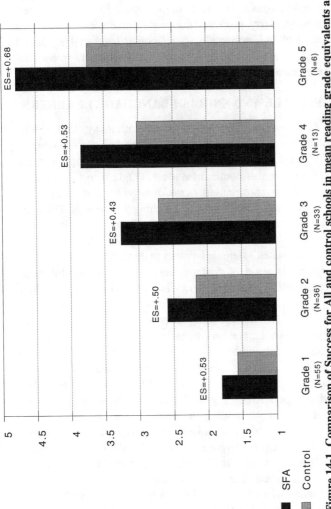

Figure 14-1. Comparison of Success for All and control schools in mean reading grade equivalents and effect sizes 1988–1994. (Adapted from R. E. Slavin, N. A. Madden, L. Dolan, B. A. Wasik, Ross, Smith, Diarda (1996), Success for All: A summary of Research, *Journal of Education of Students Placed at Risk, 1,* 41–76. Copyright 1996 Lawrence Erlbaum Associates. By permission of the publisher.)

Woodcock Word Attack scale in first and second grades, but in grades 3–5 effect sizes were more or less equivalent on all aspects of reading. Consistently, effect sizes for students in the lowest 25 percent of their grades were particularly positive, ranging from $ES = +1.03$ in first grade to $ES = +1.68$ in fourth grade. Again, cohort-level analyses found statistically significant differences favoring low achievers in Success for All on every measure at every grade level.

SUCCESS FOR ALL AND ENGLISH-LANGUAGE LEARNERS

Success for All is increasingly used in schools with many children who enter school speaking little or no English. Of the 457 current schools, more than 150 have substantial numbers of English-language learners. Most of these are Spanish-dominant students taught using the Spanish adaptation of the program called *Lee Conmigo* ("Read With Me"). Others use a program adaptation for teaching English as a Second Language (ESL). The language of instruction and age of transition from Spanish to English reading follow district policies, which vary considerably from state to state and district to district.

The first application of Success for All to English language learners began in Philadelphia's Francis Scott Key School, which serves a high-poverty neighborhood in which more than 60 percent of students enter the schools speaking Cambodian or other Southeast Asian languages. An adaptation of Success for All was designed to meet the needs of these children. This adaptation focused on integrating the work of ESL teachers and reading teachers, so that ESL teachers taught a reading class and then helped limited-English-proficient (LEP) students with the specific language and reading skills needed to succeed in the school's (English) reading program. In addition, a cross-age tutoring program enabled fifth graders, now fully bilingual in English and Cambodian, to help kindergartners succeed in the English program. The performance of students at Key School has been compared to that of students in a matched comparison school each year, and the results have consistently favored Success for All for Asian as well as non-Asian students through the fifth grade (Slavin & Yampolsky, 1991; Slavin & Madden, 1995).

In 1992, a Spanish adaptation of the Success for All reading program called *Lee Conmigo* was developed for use in Spanish bilingual programs. During the 1992–1993 school year, the entire Success for All program (including *Lee Conmigo* for LEP students) was implemented in one Philadelphia school serving a predominately Latino (mostly Puerto Rican) student body. The first- and second-year results showed the Spanish bilingual students to be performing substantially better than controls on individually administered tests of Spanish (Slavin & Madden, 1994; Slavin & Madden, 1995).

A third evaluation of Success for All with English-language learners was carried out by Dianda and Flaherty (1995) at the Southwest Regional Laboratory in southern California. This study involved three schools. Two schools had substantial Spanish bilingual programs. The third, using an ESL approach, served a highly diverse student body speaking 17 languages. Students in all three schools were compared to matched students in matched schools. In each case, students were assessed in the language of instruction (English or Spanish). Students in the Success for All schools scored substantially higher than controls whether they were instructed and tested in Spanish ($ES = +1.03$) or in English ($ES = +1.02$).

COMPARING SUCCESS FOR ALL AND READING RECOVERY

Reading Recovery is one of the most extensively researched and widely used innovations in elementary education. Like Success for All, Reading Recovery provides one-to-one tutoring to first graders who are struggling in reading. Research on Reading Recovery has found substantial positive effects of the program as of the end of first grade, and longitudinal studies have found that some portion of these effects maintain at least through third grade (DeFord, Pinnell, Lyons, & Young, 1988; Pinnell, Lyons, DeFord, Bryk, & Seltzer, 1994).

Schools and districts attracted to Success for All are also often attracted to Reading Recovery, as the two programs share an emphasis on early intervention and a strong research base. Increasing numbers of districts have both programs in operation in different schools. One of the districts in the Success for All evaluation, Caldwell, Idaho, happened to be one of these. Ross, Smith, Casey and Slavin (1995) used this opportunity to compare the two programs. First graders in the Success for All schools performed better than students in the Reading Recovery school overall ($ES = +.17$). Differences for special education students were substantial, averaging an effect size of +.77. Excluding the special education students, there were no differences in reading performance between tutored students in the Success for All and

Reading Recovery schools ($ES = .00$). In light of earlier research, these outcomes suggest that both tutoring programs are highly effective for at-risk first graders.

Another study, by Ross, Smith, Lewis and Nunnery (1996) in Tucson, Arizona, also compared Success for All and Reading Recovery. In this study tutored children as well as nontutored first graders scored substantially higher in Success for All than in Reading Recovery schools.

SUCCESS FOR ALL AND SPECIAL EDUCATION

Perhaps the most important goal of Success for All is to place a floor under the reading achievement of all children, to ensure that every child performs adequately in this critical skill. This goal has major implications for special education.

The philosophy behind the treatment of special education issues in Success for All is called "neverstreaming" (Slavin, 1996; Slavin et al., 1991). That is, rather than waiting until at-risk students fall far behind, are assigned to special education, and then perhaps integrated into regular classes, Success for All schools intervene early and intensively with students who are at risk to try to keep them out of the special education system.

Several studies have focused on questions related to special education. One of the most important outcomes in this area is the consistent finding of particularly large effects of Success for All for students in the lowest 25 percent of their classes. While effect sizes for students in general have averaged around +0.50 on individually administered reading measures, effect sizes for the lowest achievers have averaged in the range of +1.00 to +1.50 across the grades. Across five Baltimore schools, less than 4 percent of third graders averaged two years behind grade level, a usual criterion for special education placement. In contrast, 12 percent of control third graders scored this poorly. Baltimore data has also shown a reduction in special education placements for learning disabilities of about half (Slavin, Madden, Karweit, Dolan, & Wasik, 1992). A study of two Success for All schools in Ft. Wayne, Indiana, found that over a two-year period, 3.2 percent of Success for All students in grades K–1 and 1–2 were referred to special education for learning disabilities or mild mental handicaps. In contrast, 14.3 percent of control students were referred in these categories (Smith, Ross, & Casey, 1994).

Taken together, these findings support the conclusion that Success for All both reduces the need for special education services (by raising the reading achievement of very low achievers) and reduces special education referrals and placements.

Another important question concerns the effects of the program on students who have already been assigned to special education. Here again, there is evidence from several different sources. In the study comparing Reading Recovery and Success for All described above, it so happened that first graders in special education in the Reading Recovery group were not tutored, but instead received traditional special education services in resource rooms. In the Success for All schools, first graders who had been assigned to special education were tutored one-to-one (by their special education teachers) and otherwise participated in the program in the same way as all other students. As noted earlier, special education students in Success for All were reading substantially better ($ES = +.77$) than special education students in the comparison school (Ross et al., 1995). In addition, Smith et al. (1994) combined first-grade reading data from special education students in Success for All and control schools in four districts: Memphis (Tennessee), Ft. Wayne (Indiana), Montgomery (Alabama), and Caldwell (Idaho). Success for All special education students scored substantially better than controls (mean $ES = +.59$).

PRACTICAL IMPLICATIONS

The results of evaluations of 23 Success for All schools in nine districts in eight U.S. states clearly show that the program increases student reading performance. In every district, Success for All students learned significantly more than matched control students. Significant effects were not seen on every measure at every grade level, but the consistent direction and magnitude of the effects show unequivocal benefits for Success for All students. Evidence showed particularly large impacts on the achievement of limited-English-proficient students in both bilingual and ESL programs, and on both reducing special education referrals and improving the achievement of students who have been assigned to special education. It compares the outcomes of Success for All with those of another early intervention program, Reading Recovery.

The Success for All evaluations have used reliable and valid measures, individually administered tests that are sensitive to all aspects of reading: comprehension, fluency, word attack, and word identification. Performance of Success for All students has been compared to that of matched students in matched control schools, who provide the best indication of what students without the program would have achieved. Replication of high-quality experiments in such a wide variety of schools and districts is extremely unusual.

An important indicator of the robustness of Success for All is the fact that of the more than 300 schools that have used the program for periods of one to eight years, only 10 have dropped out (in all cases because of changes of principals). Many other Success for All schools have survived changes of superintendents, principals, facilitators, and other key staff; plus major cuts in funding, and other serious threats to program maintenance.

The research summarized here demonstrates that comprehensive, systemic school-by-school change can take place on a broad scale in a way that maintains the integrity and effectiveness of the model. The 23 schools in nine districts that we are studying in depth are typical of the larger set of schools currently using Success for All in terms of quality of implementation, resources, demographic characteristics, and other factors. Program outcomes are not limited to the original home of the program; in fact, outcomes tend to be somewhat better outside of Baltimore. The widely-held idea based on the Rand study of innovation (Berman & McLaughlin, 1978; McLaughlin, 1990) that comprehensive school reform must be invented by school staffs themselves is certainly not supported in research on Success for All. While the program is adapted to meet the needs of each school, and while school staffs must agree to implement the program by a vote of 80 percent or more, Success for All is an externally developed program with specific materials, manuals, and structures. The observation that this program can be implemented and maintained over considerable time periods and can be effective in each of its replication sites certainly supports the idea that every school staff need not reinvent the wheel.

The demonstration that an effective program can be replicated and can be effective in its replication sites removes one more excuse for the continuing low achievement of disadvantaged children. In order to ensure the success of disadvantaged students, we must have the political commitment to do so, with the funds and policies to back up this commitment. Success for All does require a serious commitment to restructure elementary schools and to reconfigure use of funds to emphasize prevention and early intervention rather than remediation.

These and other systemic changes in assessments, accountability, standards, and legislation can facilitate the implementation of Success for All and other school reform programs. However, we must also have methods known not only to be effective in their original sites, but also to be replicable and effective in other sites. The evaluations presented in this chapter provide a practical demonstration of the effectiveness and replicability of one such program.

THE IMPORTANCE OF EARLY INTERVENTION

The findings of the Success for All evaluations indicate that focusing on prevention and early intervention can significantly increase the reading performance of disadvantaged and at-risk students, as well as reduce retentions and special education placements. In particular, the program substantially increases the achievement of those students who are most at-risk. Not every Success for All third grader who has been in the program since first grade is reading at grade level, but virtually every one is reading close enough to grade level to profit from good classroom instruction without a continuing need for remedial or special education.

One interesting finding in research on Success for All is that the program's effects are much less pronounced for students who begin in the program after the first grade than for those who begin in preschool, kindergarten, or first grade. Success for All always begins in grades K–3 or preK–3. A typical pattern is for the program to be highly successful in first grade the first year, in first and second grades the second year, and in first, second, and third grades the third year of implementation (see Madden, Slavin, Karweit, Dolan, & Wasik, 1991). This finding points out the importance of prevention and early intervention. A second or third grader who is already far behind in basic skills may not profit as much from improvements in regular classroom instruction or even from remedial tutoring. In contrast, students who end first grade with a solid foundation of success in reading can profit from enhanced classroom instruction and continue to build on this foundation. What this implies is that *both* early intervention *and* improvement in classroom practice are needed. Early intervention alone is not enough. For example, Reading Recovery (Pinnell, 1989) provides one-to-one tutoring to first graders but does not change regular classroom instruction. Longitudinal studies of this approach have found that gains made in first grade are maintained but do not grow over time.

At the same time, improvement in classroom practice may not be enough in itself for students who are already experiencing difficulties, as we are finding in our Success for All research. What is needed is a strategy of preventing learning problems from appearing in the first place and then improving classroom instruction throughout the grades to fan the flame of learning ignited in preschool, kindergarten, and first grade (see Slavin, Karweit, & Wasik, 1992/93, 1994).

IMPROVING OUTCOMES OVER TIME

An analysis of reading data from successive cohorts of students over time shows that the effects of Success for All are improving each year. For example, first graders in the first year of program implementation exceed matched control students by 34 percent of a standard deviation. First graders in the second year of implementation exceed their controls by 57 percent of a standard deviation. This pattern continues for first graders and is equally apparent for second and third graders.

There are two likely interpretations of this trend. First, teachers and schools are getting better at program implementation each year. Fullan (1982) has noted that major change in schools takes years to be fully operational, and this data supports his view. However, the data also may support the effects of early intervention. First-year first graders began in Success for All in first grade. Second-year first graders began in kindergarten, and third-year first graders began in prekindergarten. Cumulative effects of these early experiences are also likely explanations for the growing effects at each grade level.

The Success for All evaluations took place in some of the most disadvantaged schools in the country, including the very highest-poverty schools in Baltimore, Philadelphia, and Memphis. These schools suffer from all the problems of high-poverty schools, from underfunding to low staff morale (in many cases) to bureaucratic problems of large urban systems to unsafe neighborhoods to limited ability on the part of many parents to support their children's success in school. Yet these schools have many resources that have traditionally been underutilized: many dedicated teachers and administrators who care deeply about children; many parents who are able to support the school if they are invited to do so; and most of all, young children who have not yet experienced anything that would contradict their very positive self-images as learners. What Success for All shows is that even in the most disadvantaged of schools with all of the problems so often associated with these schools, the staff, parental support, and student strengths that have always been there can be activated to significantly enhance the educational outcomes for children.

Success for All provides one practical demonstration of what a comprehensive program of prevention and early intervention might look like. The results of the Success for All evaluations show that a schoolwide focus on prevention and early intervention, improvement of classroom practice, and constant, curriculum-based assessment of students and of the program itself can have major payoffs for children. We would not suggest that the particular constellation of elements implemented in Success for All is ideal or optimal. In fact, the program itself varies in important ways from site to site depending on the nature, needs, and resources of each. What is common to all Success for All sites and must become common to high-poverty schools as a whole is a relentless focus on the success of all children, and a commitment to see that learning problems are prevented as much as possible and are recognized and intensively remediated early on if they do appear. The first line of defense is preschool, kindergarten, and improved classroom practice. If this is not enough, tutoring or family support services are brought in, or changes are made in classroom instruction to meet individual needs. If these are not enough, the school staff experiments with other solutions. The commitment is never to give up until a child is succeeding.

Next September, another three million confident, eager, and motivated 5-year-olds will enter United States kindergartens. The essential goal of policy for at-risk children must be to see that every one of these children leaves the primary grades as confident, as eager, and as motivated as they came in, with the skills they need to make it in the later grades and a well-founded expectation that the rest of their schooling will be as rich and as successful as that which they have experienced so far.

NOTES

1. The research discussed in this chapter was primarily supported by grants from the Office of Educational Research and Improvement, United States Department of Education (Nos. OERI-R–117-R90002 and R–117-D40005), and the Carnegie Corporation of New York, the Pew Charitable Trusts, and the Abell Foundation. However, any opinions expressed are our own, and do not represent the positions or policies of our funders.

REFERENCES

Adams, M. J. (1990). *Beginning to read: Thinking and learning about print.* Cambridge, MA: MIT Press.

Berman, P., & McLaughlin, M. (1978). *Federal programs supporting educational change: A model of education change, Vol. VIII: Implementing and sustaining innovations.* Santa Monica, CA: Rand.

DeFord, D. E., Pinnell, G. S., Lyons, C. A., & Young, P. (1988). *Ohio's Reading Recovery program: Vol. VII, Report of the follow-up studies.* Columbus: Ohio State University.

Dianda, M. R., & Flaherty, J. F. (1995, April). *Effects of Success for All on the reading achievement of first graders in California bilingual programs.* Paper presented at the annual meeting of the American Educational Research Association, San Francisco, CA.

Fullan, M. (1982). *The meaning of educational change.* New York: Teachers College Press.

Madden, N. A., Slavin, R. E., Karweit, N. L., Dolan, L., & Wasik, B. A. (1991). Success for All. *Phi Delta Kappa, 72,* 593–599.

Madden, N. A., Slavin, R. E., Karweit, N. L., Dolan, L. J., & Wasik, B. A. (1993). Success for All: Longitudinal effects of a restructuring program for inner-city elementary schools. *American Educational Research Journal, 30,* 123–148.

McLaughlin, M. W. (1990). The Rand change agent study revisited: Macro perspectives and micro realities. *Educational Researcher, 19*(9), 11–16.

Pinnell, G. S. (1989). Reading Recovery: Helping at-risk children learn to read. *Elementary School Journal, 90,* 161–182.

Pinnell, G. S., Lyons, C. A., DeFord, D. E., Bryk, A. S., & Seltzer, M. (1994). Comparing instructional models for the literacy education of high risk first graders. *Reading Research Quarterly, 29,* 8–38.

Ross, S. M., Smith, L. J., Casey, J., & Slavin, R. E. (1995). Increasing the academic success of disadvantaged children: An examination of alternative early intervention programs. *American Educational Research Journal, 32,* 773–800.

Ross, S. M., Smith, L. J., Lewis, T., & Nunnery, J. (1996). *1995–96 Evaluation of Roots and Wings in Memphis city schools.* Memphis: University of Memphis, Center for Research in Educational Policy.

Slavin, R. E. (1987). Ability grouping and student achievement in elementary schools: A best-evidence synthesis. *Review of Educational Research, 57,* 347–350.

Slavin, R. E. (1995). *Cooperative learning: Theory, research, and practice* (2nd ed.). Boston: Allyn & Bacon.

Slavin, R. E. (1996). Neverstreaming: Preventing learning disabilities. *Educational Leadership 53*(5), 4–7.

Slavin, R. E., & Madden, N. A. (1993, April). *Multi-site replicated experiments: An application to Success for All.* Paper presented at the annual meeting of the American Educational Research Association, Atlanta, GA.

Slavin, R. E., & Madden, N. A. (1994). *Implementing Success for All in the Philadelphia public schools* (Final report to the Pew Charitable Trusts). Baltimore, MD: Johns Hopkins University, Center for Research on Effective Schooling for Disadvantaged Students.

Slavin, R. E., & Madden, N. A. (1995, April). *Effects of Success for All on the achievement of English language learners.* Paper presented at the annual meeting of the American Educational Research Association, San Francisco, CA.

Slavin, R. E., & Yampolsky, R. (1991). *Effects of Success for All on students with limited English proficiency: A three-year evaluation.* Baltimore, MD: Johns Hopkins University, Center for Research on Effective Schooling for Disadvantaged Students.

Slavin, R. E., Karweit, N. L., & Wasik, B. A. (1992/93). Preventing early school failure: What works? *Educational Leadership, 50*(4), 10–18.

Slavin, R. E., Karweit, N. L., & Wasik, B. A. (1994). *Preventing early school failure: Research on effective strategies.* Boston: Allyn & Bacon.

Slavin, R. E., Madden, N. A., Dolan, L. J., & Wasik, B. A. (1996). *Every child, every school: Success for All.* Newbury Park, CA: Corwin.

Slavin, R. E., Madden, N. A., Karweit, N. L., Dolan, L., & Wasik, B. A. (1992). *Success for All: A relentless approach to prevention and early intervention in elementary schools.* Arlington, VA: Educational Research Service.

Slavin, R. E., Madden, N. A., Karweit, N. L., Dolan, L., Wasik, B. A., Shaw, A., Mainzer, K. L., & Haxby, B. (1991). Neverstreaming: Prevention and early intervention as alternatives to special education. *Journal of Learning Disabilities, 24,* 373–378.

Slavin, R. E., Madden, N. A., & Stevens, R. J. (1989/90). Cooperative learning models for the 3 R's. *Educational Leadership, 47* (4), 22–28.

Smith, L. J., Ross, S. M., & Casey, J. P. (1994). *Special education analyses for Success for All in four cities.* Memphis: University of Memphis, Center for Research in Educational Policy.

Stevens, R. J., Madden, N. A., Slavin, R. E., & Farnish, A. M. (1987). Cooperative Integrated reading and composition: Two field experiments. *Reading Research Quarterly, 22*, 433–454.

Wasik, B. A., & Slavin, R. E. (1993). Preventing early reading failure with one-to-one tutoring: A review of five programs. *Reading Research Quarterly, 28*, 178–200.

Index